From Leaning to Leaders

Life after Lean on Me

Dr. Joe Clark's Legacy & The REAL Students
from the movie *Lean on Me*

By Dr. Pinky Miller

Know Our Story, LLC

www.Drpinkymiller.com

www.leanonme-drjoeclarkscholarship.com

FROM LEANING TO LEADERS: LIFE AFTER LEAN ON ME

DR. JOE CLARK'S LEGACY & THE REAL STUDENTS FROM THE MOVIE LEAN ON ME

Published by Know Our Story, LLC

3035 Stone Mountain Street # 2233
Lithonia, GA 30058

Printed in the United States of America

ISBN: 10: 0-578-46093-9
ISBN-13: 978-0-578-46093-2

Eastside High School logo and photos are used with permission from Paterson, New Public Schools.

Library of Congress Control Number: 2019916778

Books in the *Life after Lean on Me* Biographical Series

Life after Lean on Me: The Dr. Pinky Miller Story

Life after Lean on Me: Dissertation Research: What happened to the REAL students after the movie Lean on Me?

From Leaning to Leaders: Life after Lean on Me
Dr. Joe Clark's Legacy & The REAL Students

Life after Lean on Me: The Diana Moore Story (coming soon)

Life after Lean on Me: The Jason Booker Story (coming soon)

*Life after Lean on Me: The Dr. Pinky Miller Story II (*coming soon)

www.Drpinkymiller.com
www.leanonme-drjoeclarkscholarship.com

JOE CLARK

Table of Contents

ACKNOWLEDGEMENTS 11

In Loving Memory – Dr. Thomas L. Page 13

Book Dedication – Dr. Gloria Irene Clark 19

Dr. Joseph Louis Clark Legacy Scholarship Mission.....................24

Ready for the FREE showing of the Lean on Me movie 58

Jermaine "SAMS" Hopkins is Here!...................................62

Meet and Greet Event at the Alpha Performing Arts Center............64

The Lean on Me 30th Anniversary – Dr. Joe Clark Legacy Scholarship Luncheon 69

Dr. Joseph Louis Clark Biography...................................98

The Red-Carpet Event at the Alpha Performing Arts Center 126

Sunday Morning Worship with Alumni Pastor William and First Lady Kim Cash...129

Dr. Clark has a Facebook Page..151

Eastside High School Senior Awards Day – June 5, 2019.................153

Eastside High School 2019 170

School of Information Technology 202

School of Government and Public Administration.........................213

Culinary Arts, Hospitality and Tourism.............................222

CHAPTER 1 232

The Problem...232

The Rationale of the Book 233

Introduction 234

Paterson, New Jersey 235

Eastside High School..238

The Average EHS Student Background 244

The Environment 245

CHAPTER 2 248

Dr. Frank Napier, Jr. 248

Dr. Joe Louis Clark 250

Mr. Joe Clark's Experiences at Eastside 260

CHAPTER 3 262

Leadership 262

Leadership and Power 263

CHAPTER 4 264

Principal Leadership and Effective Schools 264

Impact of African American Principals 265

CHAPTER 5 266

Researcher Role and Biases 266

Participant Criteria 267

Participant Characteristics 268

CHAPTER 6 269

Table 1 - Teacher and Administrator Profiles 269

Demographic Information of Teachers and Administrators 270

Teacher and Administrator Participant Profiles 271

Famous People Who Visited EHS 295

CHAPTER 7 317

Student Profiles 317

Demographic Information of Students 317

Table 2 - Student Profiles 318

Student Participant Profiles 319

CHAPTER 8 366

Dr. Clark's Leadership in His Own Words............................366

Dr. Clark's Advice to Parents..377

Dr. Clark's Recent Thoughts on Education...........................378

Joe Clark's Leadership..380

CHAPTER 9 385

Strategies Dr. Clark Used to Transform Eastside High School........385

Cleaning EHS: Guiding Students in Positive Ways..............385

Supporting and Encouraging the Five Percenter Students to Learn
More than the Lessons..391

Lessons/Accountability/Intimidation of Teachers...........392

Walk to the Right! Creating Order Out of Chaos 398

Weeding Out the Miscreants and Thugs: How Dr. Clark Kept the
Drug Dealers Out of the School 400

Creating Community: Garnering Support for Reform 405

The Bullhorn - He's Everywhere!.......................................408

Utilizing and Enforcing Strong Discipline........................410

Being a Father Figure and Role Model 413

Creating a Strong School Spirit by Utilizing the Alma Mater 415

CHAPTER 10 419

Emerging Themes from Teachers and Administrators 419

Impact and Contributions...419

Not so Positive Memories of Eastside High School 420

Relationship with Dr. Clark..421

Controversies at Eastside High School................................422

Dr. Clark's Leadership Style...423

Student Interactions..425

Administrator and Teacher Interactions...426

Perceptions of Dr. Clark...427

Support and Availability..428

Expressions of Gratitude and Appreciation 429

CHAPTER 11 431

Unsung Heroes...431

Reverend Michael D. McDuffie – Class of 1981 431

Mr. Alonzo Moody...442

Mr. William Peter Nelson, Jr. 449

CHAPTER 12 460

Lean on Me Movie..460

Some Embellishments in the Lean on Me Movie 462

The Impact of the Lean on Me Movie 464

The Eastside "Song Birds"...468

The 1989 Lean on Me Gala and Premier..468

Additional Information Regarding the Lean on Me Movie.............473

Lean on Me 25th Anniversary - 2014 473

CHAPTER 13 476

Emerging Themes..476

Dr. Clark's Administrator and Teacher Interactions.......................479

Impact and Contribution to Students' Lives.................................480

Expressions of Gratitude and Appreciation 483

CHAPTER 14 485

Discussion 485

How do Dr. Clark's Former Students, Teachers, and Administrators Perceive his Leadership Style as Principal? 485

What Impact, if any, did Former Students, Teachers, and Administrators Perceive that Dr. Clark's Leadership Style as Principal of EHS has on their Lives? 489

CHAPTER 15 491

Conclusions 491

The study's first major conclusion addresses the question, how do the informants perceive Dr. Clark's leadership style?........................491

The second major conclusion addressed the question, what impact, if any, did the informants perceive that Dr. Clark's had on their lives?491

The third major conclusion of this case study is Dr. Clark's ability to establish and enforce strong discipline at Eastside........................492

CHAPTER 16 494

Concluding Comments 494

CHAPTER 17 497

What Happened to Dr. Clark once he Left EHS? 497

Where is Dr. Clark Now?........................498

Alumni Profiles........................499

What Happened to the REAL Students from Eastside High School? 499

1 – Mr. Gerard Booker – Class of 1985........................499

2 – Ms. Tomacinia Carter – Class of 1985........................500

3 - Reverend William H. Cash – Class of 1986 502

4 - Ms. Tammy Cockfield - Class of 1985........................503

5 - Ms. Ashon Curvy Moreno - Class of 1988 504

6 – Ms. Maritza Davila – Class of 1989 505

7 – Ms. Deanna Michele De Vore – Class of 1987 507

8 – Mr. Rodney De Vore – Class of 1987..........................508

9 – Ms. Denise Durnell – Trigg – Class of 1986..............510

10 - Mr. Kenneth Eatman - Class of 1985.....................511

11 - Ms. Leslie Etheridge – Class of 1986....................512

12 - Mr. Eric Gass – Class of 1986...............................513

13 - Mr. Troy D. Gillispie – Class of 1986....................515

14– Mr. Winston Goode – Class of 1985 516

15 - Ms. Coretta Goodwin-Smith – Class of 1986 517

16 - Tonya Ingram – Class of 1986 518

17 - Ms. Shanell Irving – Class of 1985 519

18 - Mr. Ainsworth Jackson – Class of 1986................521

19 – Dr. Michael V. Jackson - Class of 1985 522

20 – Rev. Dr. Janeide A. Matthews-Chillis – Class of 1984.............524

21 - Minister Lady Jamie McDuffie – Class of 1984 526

22 – Mr. Eric McKenzie - Class of 1986 528

23 - Mr. Vaughn McKoy, JD, MBA – Class of 1986 529

24 - Daryl L. Miller – Class of 1986.............................532

25 – Dr. Olandha Pinky (Seldon) Miller – Class of 1986 533

26 – Dr. Lilisa Mimms – Class of 1987 534

27 - Mr. Zatiti K. Moody – Class of 1993.....................536

28 - Diana "Dottie" Moore – Class of 1988 540

29 - Terrie Moore – Class of 1986...............................542

30 - Mr. Laron Lateef Moses – Class of 1984...............545

31 - Mr. Darren Napier – Class of 1986 545

32 - Dr. Alfreda (Lawrence) Paige – Class of 1987 547

33 - Ms. Elena Payamps – Class of 1985 550

34 - Reverend Helena Pierce – Class of 1986 555

35 - Jennifer (Carrion) Reed – Class of 1986 557

36 – Riff – Class of 1988...558

37 – Ms. Janice Robinson – Class of 1985.....................................560

38 – Mr. Andre Ruff – Class of 1986 564

39 – Ms. Shwana Ruth-Bridges, ESQ – Class of 1986 566

40 - Mr. Wilson Santos – Class of 1989...568

41 – Mr. Gregory C. Scott – Class of 1986 570

42 - Mr. Antoney Smith - Class of 1987 574

43 – Ms. Paulette Steeves - Class of 1988 577

44 - Mr. Marc Stevens – Class of 1988 578

45 - Mr. Marvin Sykes – Class of 1987 579

46 - Ms. Juanita Thomas-Boyd – Class of 1986 582

47 – Ms. Vivian Thorpe – Class of 1986 584

48 - Reverend Janel D. Tinsley-York - Class of 1987......................585

49 - Mr. Timothy M. Tobias, MSW – Class of 1986 587

50 - Darnell Van Rensalier – Class of 1987 588

51 – Mr. Nathaniel Waithe – Class of 1986 591

52 – Ms. Lisa Webb-Carrington – Class of 1987 593

53 - Mr. Keith Williams – Class of 1984...595

54 – Mr. Mike Williams – Class of 1987 596

55 - Mr. Bernard Wilson – Class of 1984..598

REFERENCES..600

INDEX 603

Acknowledgments

To my supportive, caring, and loving daughters Janay Boucan, Evonne Bazemore, Darylynn Miller, & Olandha Miller, you all are the source of my unconditional love, determination, and joy. This book is dedicated to you because you were there with me, supported me through thick and thin. I love you tremendously!

I pray that I have been an excellent example of not allowing your circumstances to dictate where you can go in life. Don't ever give up! Trust God! Get your EDUCATION! Find your Raison d'être! Your Reason for being.

To my mother, Evonne Seldon-Burroughs, you are my rock and my inspiration. You are my example of a mother who will take care of her family regardless of what challenges may come her way. You are my Shero!

To my Eastside High School and New Jersey Family, Daryl Miller, Dominique Miller, Chanie (Thomas) Peterson, Theresa Golz, Mike Osofsky, Karen Johnson, Zatiti Moody, Marylyn DiMartino, William Zisa, Barry Rosser, Vivian Gaines, Julian Jenkins, Troy Gillispie, Shwana Ruth-Bridges, Andrew Cameron, Roger Cameron, Cleve Josephs, Angela Cusack, Sonji Barbour, Keith Williams, Aprilynn Harrison, Laron Moses, Kawan Moore, Keisha Moore, Rev. Michael D. McDuffie, Alonzo Moody, William Peter Nelson, Jr. Denise Durnell, Annette Depass, Nadine Depass, Leslie Gist-Etheridge, Cassandra Davis, Gerard Booker, Tomacinia Carter, Kymberley Ruffin-Staples, Marcie Traylor, Marc Meadley, Tammy Cockfield, Vaughn McKoy, Trene Cornish, Kim Rouse, Kevin Atkinson, Antonia Atkinson, John Welsh, Mariat Kozrosh, Daniel Del Valle, Randy Simon, John

Goodman, Bobby Wise, George Featherson, Rev. William H. Cash, Ashon Curvy-Moreno, Rev. Marcus Debnam, Kenneth Eatman, Eric Gass, Coretta Goodwin-Smith, Shanell "Red" Irving, Ainsworth Jackson, Michael V. Jackson, Alfreda (Lawrence) Paige, Deanna Michele De Vore, Rodney De Vore, Minister Lady Jamie McDuffie, Little Pie McElveen, Eric McKenzie, Darren Napier, Elena Payamps, Riff, Andre Ruff, Wilson Santos, Antoney Smith, Marc Stevens, Juanita Thomas-Boyd, Vivian Thorpe, Reverend Janel D. Tinsley (York), Timothy M. Tobias, Kenneth Eatman, Winston Goode, Tonya Ingram, Evangelist Helena Jones, Diana "Dottie" Moore, Terrie Moore, Laron "Lateef" Moses, Janice Robinson, Gregory C. Scott, Paulette Steeves, Marvin Sykes, Darnell Van Rensalier, Mike A. Williams, Nathaniel Waithe, Lisa Webb Carrington, Bernard Wilson, Sybil Wilson and Alexander "Butchy" Peels. May God's grace forever fall upon you! I will always appreciate all that you have given to support this enlightening endeavor.

To my Principal, Dr. Joe Louis Clark, I thank you from the bottom of my heart! Without your strict discipline, guidance, love, and concern for my well-being and my education, I am not sure where I would be today. Please know that whenever I encountered a challenge that appeared too harsh for me to handle, I heard your loud voice in my ear telling me, "*Pinky*! You can do it!" and I believed in you just as you believed in me! I trust that I can safely speak for the majority of my classmates – YOU SAVED US!

To my Lord and Savior Jesus Christ, I thank you for all the blessings, lessons, trials, tribulations, and triumphs throughout this journey. I know that none of this would be possible without your mercy, grace, and, most of all, your love, Amen!

12

In Loving Memory – Dr. Thomas L. Page

Dr. Page was my friend, who encouraged me to be me. He blessed our *Lean on Me* - Dr. Joseph L. Clark Legacy Scholarship Fundraiser events by allowing us to utilize his Alpha Performing Arts & Restoration Center (Founder & Director) as an in-kind gift to help us raise scholarships for the students at Eastside High School. He is an alum of Eastside High School– Class of 1975.

He was a blessing to the students at Eastside and was very instrumental while working alongside Mr. Peter Nelson with the Marching 100 Band for many years. He graduated from Thomas Edison State University with a Bachelor of Arts degree in Psychology, an MSM in Science Management, and earned a Ph.D. in human services from Capella University. He is a life coach, lecturer, instructional designer, and professor. He is the author of *When Love Is Not Enough: Bringing Spirituality and Coping Back to Families and Homes* and *The Seven Deadliest Words: The Power of Words: The Power to Heal.* Dr. Page, you are truly missed. Rest in Peace, my friend.

(Eastside High Schools Jazz Band – Dr. page 3rd row on the right)

(Dr. Page was a member of Alpha Phi Alpha Fraternity Incorporated)

There are many words that could hold you back and prevent you from being the best person you can be. But those words that hold you back can be the same words that can change your life for the better. In the Seven Deadliest Words, author Dr. Thomas L. Page discusses the seven words in his personal life that transformed him. Page guides you through a series of discussions and exercises narrating how various viewpoints and experiences changed his life, and he shows what steps you can take to improve your own life.

The Seven Deadliest Words help you acknowledge some of the weaknesses that may be holding you back and preventing you from growing physically, mentally, spiritually, and emotionally. It creates strategies to enhance and build on your strengths in order to be the best you can be. Based on real-life situations and supported by passages from the Bible, Page offers a guide for Christians (and non-Christians alike) who want to conquer their past and present personal challenges and move forward in a positive way.

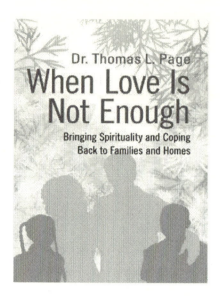

America is losing touch with her young African American male population. Parents are losing touch with their sons, and sisters are losing touch with brothers. Why is this? Why are adolescent black males becoming lost to their own self-destructive behaviors? Most parents aren't going to like to hear it, but its due to a lack of spirituality in upbringing. If a young man does not build his foundation on spirituality, he is left to build it on society.

Dr. Thomas Page has spent much of his career studying and counseling the African American males of America. He has seen the devastation caused by life without spirituality, and it is partially the fault of the parents. Parents force their children to get up and go to school every morning, and yet on Sunday, they allow the children to choose whether they will go to be spiritually fed. This choice could lead to children's downfall.

When Love Is Not Enough calls for a return to the notion of spirituality as the center of the household, by identifying with spirituality, young men can avoid identifying with drugs, alcohol, and illegal activities. Children must be spiritually fed in order to become spiritually satiated adults. It's not too late. Turn back to the strong foundation of spirituality; your children will thank you for it.

Book Dedication – Dr. Gloria Irene Clark

My third book is dedicated to the late Dr. Gloria Irene Clark, my beloved friend, sorority sister, educator, confidant, and the wife of Dr. Joseph L Clark. Gloria passed away peacefully from this life on April 3rd, 2019. Gloria was born in Dune, North Carolina, on September 11th, 1944. She attended and graduated from Harriet Harnett High School in 1962. Gloria's higher education achievements sent it on education and administration, earning a Bachelor of Science from Montclair State University; A Master of Business Administration from Jersey City State College, and a doctorate from The University of California Davis. During her collegiate career, she was initiated into Phi Delta Kappa, Delta Phi Epsilon, and the illustrious Alpha Kappa Alpha Sorority Incorporated. Gloria taught in private schools and public schools in New Jersey, specifically Eastside High School, and her last role as a high school administrator before retiring to Gainesville, Florida.

Dr. Gloria Clark bought her bright smile and clean humor, her most reliable sense of commitment, her lioness-like courage, her innovative creativity, and her unwavering perfectionism to all she did, as a homemaker, caretaker, garden creator, community server, patron of the arts, mother, mentor, compassionate friend, and prime supporter of the *Lean on Me* – Dr. Joseph L. Clark Legacy Scholarship Fund. Dr. Gloria Clark was an active cheerleader in the lives of the children, nieces, nephews, grandchildren, and the Gainesville community. She was a member of the Grand Female Protective SOC Lodge Number 10 and the Greater Fort Clark Missionary Baptist Church in Gainesville, Florida.

Dr. Gloria Clark was my friend! She was someone who allowed me the opportunity to share my love and concern for her and her husband, whom I consider as a father figure in my life. I thanked her and gave her flowers while she lived! Thank you, Soror Dr. Gloria Clark, I will always love you! Skeeee Weeee Soror!

GLORIA CLARK Obituary - Newberry, FL | Gainesville Sun.

(2018)

(1988)

(Elaine Dorsey, Gloria Clark & Pinky Miller attending church)

Dr. Joseph Louis Clark Legacy Scholarship Mission

The Alumnus of Paterson, New Jersey's Eastside High School, would like to invite you to support and sponsor scholarships for deserving graduating students of Eastside High School. The Lean on Me - Dr. Joseph L. Clark Legacy Scholarship Fund was founded by Dr. Pinky Miller and birthed from Dr. Joseph L. Clarks' life and commitment to educating children. The movie *Lean on Me* depicts Dr. Clark's career as an educator, along with his mission and passion for teaching and offering guidance to urban families.

Dr. Clark's hope is that our offspring become productive and accomplished citizens of society. The mission of the Bat and Bullhorn carrying principal is still our mission today, to keep our children safe from harm and to GIVE them an environment that fosters learning, academic achievement to the fullest, and to curtail disadvantage.

Our fundraising mission is to GIVE fifty (50) scholarships to students in every graduating class of Eastside High School pursuing higher learning. We invite you, your organization/company to support, and to contribute to the financial need of Eastside High Schools graduating students. Your financial assistance will help to foster lifetime achievement and to encourage the spirit of excellence to graduates. Let's GIVE them *"Someone to Lean On."*

The following pages will provide you the opportunity to gain some insight into the planning, preparation, and execution of the Lean on Me 30th Anniversary - Dr. Joseph Louis Clark Legacy Scholarship 2018-2019 events.

24

(V. Freeman, V. Gaines, L. Mimms, T. Campbell, J Dixon, T. Best, R. Cotton, H. Clark, J Hopkins, M. Davila, V. McKoy, P. Miller, M. Williams, L. Burns, R. Chapman, A. Lawrence, R. McKenny, C. Lawrence)

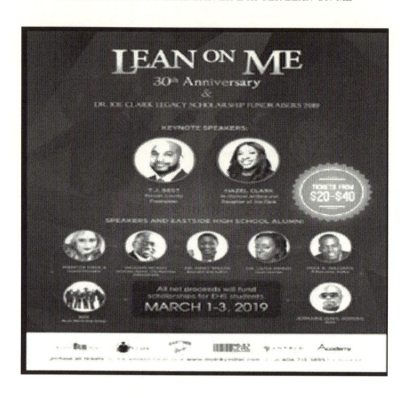

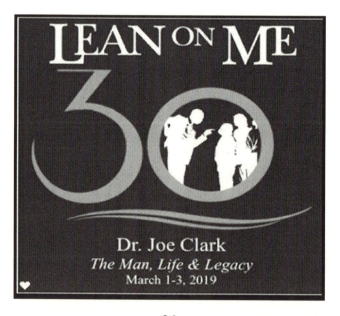

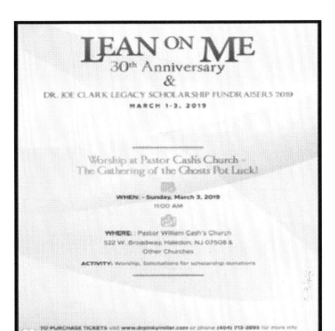

On Thursday, February 28, 2019, Dr. Pinky Miller (EHS - Class of 1986) and Ms. Maritza Davila, (EHS - Class of 1989, Council President for City of Paterson,) presented the Lean on Me-Dr. Joseph L. Clark Legacy Scholarship events to the Paterson Board of Education. The Events were unanimously approved.

The core team of the Lean on Me 30th Anniversary & Dr. Joe Clark Legacy Scholarship events were excited and ready to get to work!

(L. Burns, P. Miller, M Davila, M Traylor, R Chapman, and E. Dorsey)

Preparation for the Lean on Me 30th Anniversary – Dr. Joe Clark Legacy Scholarship Events 2019

We prepared table settings and recreated seven Eastside High School yearbooks to be utilized as wall decorations, copied, printed, cut, laminated, and glued yearbook pictures to over 200 poster boards. The boards were used to display on the walls in the gymnasium. Alumni were able to view pictures of themselves from over thirty years ago.

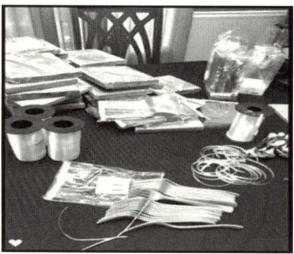

(Melissa Rayfield, Pinky Miller and Elaine Dorsey)

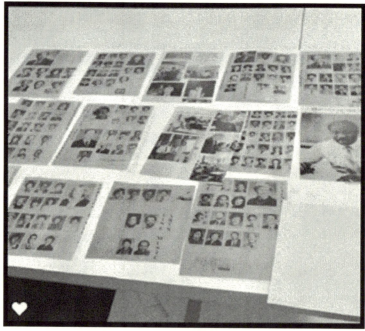

Team Work Makes the Dream Work

Alumni and current Eastside High School students, staff and administrators volunteered to assist with preparations for the big weekend's events. Supporters blew up balloons, created displays, taped balloons to the chairs and tables in the auditorium and gymnasium, cut, glued and laminated yearbook pictures to poster boards, put poster boards up in the gymnasium, decorated tables, chairs and assembled the table settings.

(Alfreda Lawrence-Paige, Pinky Miller, Keisha Moore, and students)

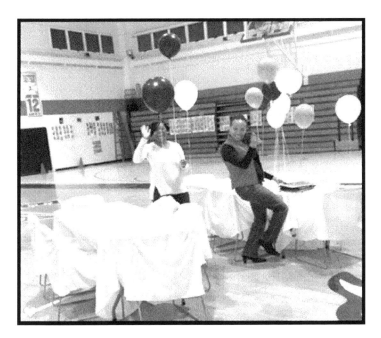

(Robbyn Chapman and Principal, Dr. Gerald Glisson helped with
decorations)

(Robbyn Chapman & Pinky Miller)

Ready for the FREE showing of the Lean on Me movie

(Alumni Embrace one another. For some, it has been thirty years since they've seen each other)

Jermaine "SAMS" Hopkins is Here!

(Pinky Miller & Jermaine "SAMS" Hopkins)

Meet and Greet Event at the Alpha Performing Arts Center

(Keisha Moore & Thomas Page, Owner of the Alpha Performing Arts Center) (Pinky Miller & L. Burns)

(Robbyn Chapman & Elaine Dorsey)

(Pinky Miller & Alfreda Lawrence-Paige)

(Keisha Moore & Pinky Miller)

(Pinky Miller & Coretta Lawrence)

(Juanita Dixon, Keisha Moore & Pinky Miller)

(Pinky Miller, Robbyn Chapman & Elaine Dorsey)

(The Alpha Performing Arts Center – Thank You, Dr. Thomas page!)

(Standing L-R - Coretta Lawrence, Alfreda Lawrence-Paige, Elaine
Dorsey, L. Burns, Siting L-R – Juanita Dixon, Robbyn Chapman,
Pinky Miller, Keisha Moore)

The Lean on Me 30ᵗʰ Anniversary – Dr. Joe Clark Legacy

Scholarship Luncheon

Hazel Clark and Jermaine "SAMS" Hopkins

(Eastside High School Drum Line, 2019)

(Pinky Miller & Monique Latise, Host & Comedian)

(Mike A. Williams)

(TJ Best, Passaic County Freeholder)

(Hazel Clark and Jermaine "SAMS" Hopkins)

(Maritza Davila)

(Vaughn McKoy)

(Eastside High School Dance Team, 2019)

(Council President, Maritza Davila presents the Proclamation of Lean on Me – Dr. Joe Clark Day)

(Paterson City Council members present the proclamations to Dr. Pinky Miller and Hazel Clark)

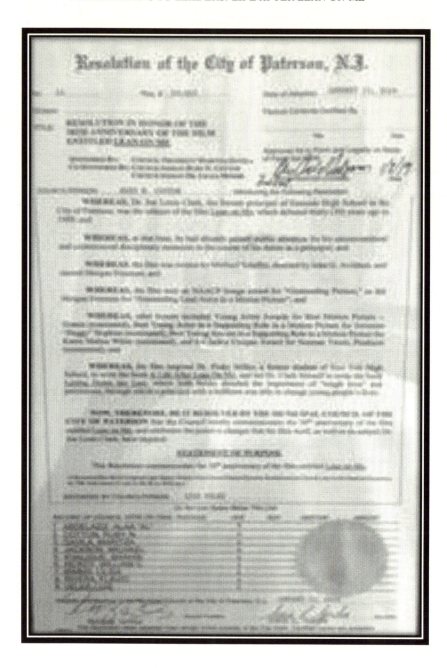

RESOLUTIONS OF THE CITY OF PATERSON NEW JERSEY

RESOLUTION IN THE HONOR OF THE 30TH ANNIVERSARY OF THE FILM ENTITLED <u>LEAN ON ME</u>

SPONSORED BY: Council President Maritza Davila
CO-SPONSORED BY: Councilwoman Ruby Cotton and Councilwoman Dr. Lilisa Mimms

January 8, 2019

WHEREAS, Dr. Joe Louis Clark, the former principal of Eastside High School in the City of Paterson, was the subject of the film <u>Lean on Me</u>, which debuted thirty (30) years ago in 1989; and

WHEREAS, at that time, he had already gained public attention for his unconventional and controversial disciplinary measures in the course of his duties as a principal; and

WHEREAS, the film was written by Michael Schiffer, directed by John G. Avildsen, and starred Morgan Freeman; and

WHEREAS, the film won an NAACP Image Award for "Outstanding Picture," as did Morgan Freeman for "Outstanding Lead Actor in a Motion Picture"; and

WHEREAS, other honors include Young Artist Awards for Best Motion Picture Drama (nominated), Best Young Actor in a Supporting Role in a motion picture for Jermaine "Huggy" Hopkins (nominated), Best Young Actress in a Supporting Role in a Motion picture for Karen Malina White (nominated) and the Jackie Coogan Award for Norman Twain, Producer (nominated); and

WHEREAS, the film inspired Dr. Pinky Miller, a former student of Eastside High School, to write the book <u>Life after Lean on Me</u> , and led Dr. Clark himself to write the book <u>Laying Down the Law</u>, where both books detailed the importance of "tough love" and persistence, through which a principal with a bullhorn was able to change young people's lives.

NOW THEREFORE, IT BE RESOLVED BY THE MUNICIPAL COUNCIL OF THE CITY OF PATERSON that the Council hereby commemorates the 30th anniversary of the film entitled <u>Lean on Me</u>, and celebrates the positive changes that the film itself, as well as it is subject Dr. Joe Louis Clark, have inspired.

STATEMENT OF PURPOSE

This Resolution commemorates the 30th anniversary of the film entitled <u>Lean on Me</u>.

SECONDED BY COUNCILPERSON Luis Velez

RECORD OF COUNCIL VOTE ON FINAL PASSAGE - AYE – Abdeaziz Alaa "AL" Cotton, Ruby, Davila, Maritza, Michael Jackson, Khalique Shahin, McCoy, William, Mimms, Lilisa, Rivera Flavio, Velez Luis

This resolution was adopted at a Municipal Council meeting in the city of Paterson, NJ on January 15, 2019. This resolution must remain in the custody of the City Clerk. No 14 – Res. # 19; 005

Resolution of the City of Paterson, N.J.

RESOLUTION HONORING DR. PINKY MILLER AS PART OF THE CITY OF PATERSON'S OBSERVANCE OF THE 30TH ANNIVERSARY OF THE FILM "LEAN ON ME"

SPONSORED BY: Council President Maritza Davila
CO-SPONSORED BY: Councilwoman Ruby Cotton and
Councilwoman Dr. Lilisa Mimms   Signed by
Corporation Counsel January 8, 2019

WHEREAS, Dr. Pinky Miller is being honored for authoring *Life after Lean on Me* as part of the city of Paterson's Observance of the 30th Anniversary of the film "Lean on Me" and

WHEREAS, Dr. Miller is a native of Paterson, New Jersey and was educated through the public school system, attending public school #24 and the famed Paterson Eastside High School; and

WHEREAS, Dr. Miller received her Bachelor of Arts in Communication Studies; her Master of Arts degree in Counseling and School Guidance, from Montclair State University; and her Doctor of Philosophy degree from Georgia State University; and

WHEREAS, Dr. Pinky Miller is an author and motivational speaker and in her authentic and enlightening book series *Life after Lean on Me* she shares her life experiences and research by articulating the impact open parentheses good, bad and indifferent that Dr. Joe Clark made upon the students, teachers, and administration during his tenure at Eastside High School; and

WHEREAS, Dr. Miller is also the Executive Producer of the forthcoming documentary Know Our Story which chronicles the successes and failures of Dr. Joe Clarks kids, the real-life legacy of the bullhorn and the baseball bat; and

WHEREAS, Dr. Miller has over 18 years of experience working in higher education and has held positions as Hall Director/Academic Advisor, Area Coordinator, Assistant/Director of Residence Life, Assistant Dean of Students and Vice President of Student Affairs; and

WHEREAS, Dr. Miller is a proud member of Alpha Kappa Alpha Sorority Incorporated; and

NOW THEREFORE, IT BE RESOLVED BY THE MUNICIPAL COUNCIL OF THE CITY OF PATERSON that Municipal Council wishes to recognize and honor Dr. Pinky Miller authoring *Life after Lean on Me* as part of the city of Paterson's Observance of the 30th Anniversary of the film, "Lean on Me."

STATEMENT OF PURPOSE

The purpose of this Resolution is to honor ***Dr. Pinky Miller*** as part of the city of Paterson's 2018 observance of the 30th Anniversary of the film, Lean on Me

SECONDED BY COUNCILPERSON Luis Velez

RECORD OF COUNCIL VOTE ON FINAL PASSAGE - AYE – Abdeaziz Alaa "AL" Cotton, Ruby, Davila, Maritza, Michael Jackson, Khalique Shahin, McCoy, William, Mimms, Lilisa, Rivera Flavio, Velez Luis

This resolution was adopted at a Municipal Council meeting in the city of Paterson, NJ on January 15, 2019. This resolution must remain in the custody of the City Clerk. No 16 – Res. # 19; 007

(Coretta Lawrence)

(Marcie Traylor)

(Jermaine "SAMS" Hopkins)

(Juanita Dixon and Lil' Pie McElveen enjoying lunch and conversation)

(Sisters - Coretta Lawrence & Alfreda Lawrence Paige – Showing they still look good thirty years later)

(Monique Latise shared her experiences at Eastside and kept the
audience laughing)

(Hazel Clark, daughter of Dr. Joe Clark, shares her experiences and the
gratitude from her father)

(Pinky Miller shares her appreciation for donations and dynamic support from the Paterson community)

(Hazel Clark, Ruby Cotton, Maritza Davila, Pinky Miller Lillisa Mimms)

(The dynamic Eastside HS Drumline and former members of the Marching 100 "Dirty Dozen")

(Jermaine "SAMS" Hopkins shared his experiences as a young actor, and the amazing impact the *Lean on Me* movie had on his life. He spoke about the importance of paying it forward to the education of students. Thank You, Jermaine!!!)

89

Paterson City Council President Maritza Davila presents Pinky Miller with a $15,000 donation from Mr. Charles Florio. Thank you, Mr. Florio, for believing in the higher education for students in Paterson, New Jersey.

(Robbyn Chapman, Jermaine "SAMS" Hopkins, Marcie Traylor)

(Maritza Davila's family and supporters Thank you, Maritza, for all your hard work and support!!!

(Dr. Lilisa Mimms presented Pinky Miller with a "Woman who Rocks" Award, 2019)

(Alumni Alfreda Lawrence- Paige, Lilisa Mimms, Pinky Miller & Coretta Lawrence "Hit those 90 degrees!")

(Little "Pie" McElveen, Shyheem Burris, Paterson Mayor Andre Sayegh)

Paterson New Jersey Mayor Andre Sayegh, & Dr. Pinky Miller discuss the program booklet that was designed by Michael Smith and Pinky Miller.

Lean on Me 30th Anniversary – Dr. Joe Clark Legacy Scholarship Luncheon 2019 – Recreated Program Booklet March 1-3, 2019

Lean on Me

Directed by: John G. Avildsen

Produced by: Norman Twain

Written by: Michael Schiffer

Starring: Morgan Freeman, Beverly Todd, Robert Guillaume, Jermaine "Sams" Hopkins, Karen Malina "Kaneesha" White

Music by: Bill Conti

Cinematography: Victor Hammer

Edited by: John G. Avildsen & John Carter

Distributed by: Warner Bros.

Release date: March 3, 1989

Running time: 124 minutes;

Language: English;

Budget: $10 million

Box office $31 million

Country: USA

Filming Location: Paterson, New Jersey

Dr. Joseph Louis Clark Biography

Dr. Joseph Louis Clark (born May 8, 1938, in Rochelle, Georgia) is the former principal of Eastside High School in Paterson, one of New Jersey's toughest inner-city schools. He is also the subject of the 1989 film Lean on Me, starring Morgan Freeman. Clark gained public attention in the 1980s for his unconventional and controversial disciplinary measures as the principal of Eastside High School.

Clark was seen as an educator who was not afraid to get tough on challenging students, one who would often carry a bullhorn or a baseball bat at school. During his time as principal, Clark expelled over 300 students who were frequently tardy or absent from school, sold or used drugs in school, or caused trouble in school. Clark's practices did result in slightly higher average test scores for Eastside High during the 1980s. After his tenure as principal of Eastside High, Clark later served as director of the Essex County Detention House in Newark, New Jersey, a juvenile detention facility. He currently resides in Newberry, Florida.

Personal Life

Clark grew up in Newark, New Jersey, and attended Central High School. Clark and Hazel are the parents of Olympic track athletes Joetta Clark Diggs, Olympian, Author and entrepreneur, and Hazel Clark, Olympian, Entrepreneur, and the Director of Sports for Bermuda. And the father-in-law of Olympic track athlete Jearl Miles Clark. His son, JJ Clark, Clark head coach at the University of Connecticut, was their coach. He also has 3 grandchildren Talitha, Jorell, and Little Hazel.

Clark continued to speak at Universities, organizations, and events worldwide, and his book "Laying Down the Law" has served as a motivator and resource for aspiring educators. He has also mentored hundreds of young educators and students throughout his retirement. Recently he appeared on the AARP magazine as a featured senior and continues to inspire a myriad of projects, including a television series entitled Lean on Me, produced by John Legend and Lebron James. Time magazine's cover article notes that Clark's style as principal was primarily disciplinarian in nature, focused on encouraging school pride and good behavior, although Clark was also portrayed as a former social activist in the film Lean on Me. Mr. Clark is married to Gloria Clark

Lean on Me movie Facts

Lean on Me is a 1989 American biographical drama film written by Michael Schiffer, directed by John G. Avildsen and starring Morgan Freeman. Lean on Me is loosely based on the story of Joe Louis Clark, a real-life inner-city high school principal in Paterson, New Jersey, whose school is at risk of being taken over by the New Jersey state government unless students improve their test scores on the New Jersey Minimum Basic Skills Test. This film's title refers to the 1972 Bill Withers song of the same name. Parts of the film, including the elementary school scenes, were filmed in Franklin Lakes, New Jersey.

Plot

By 1987, the once successful Eastside High School in Paterson, New Jersey, has deteriorated due to drugs and crime. The majority of students cannot pass basic skills testing, and even the teachers are not safe from gang violence. Mayor Bottman (Alan North) learns that the school will be turned over to state administration unless 75% of the students can pass the minimum basic skills test. He consults with school superintendent Dr. Frank Napier (Robert Guillaume), who suggests the school hire elementary school Principal Joe Clark, aka "Crazy Joe" (Morgan Freeman), a former teacher at Eastside High, as the new principal. Reluctantly, the mayor hires Clark.

Clark's immediate radical changes include expelling 300 students identified as drug dealers or abusers and troublemakers, instituting programs to improve school spirit including painting over graffiti-covered walls, and requiring students to learn the school song, and be punished if they cannot sing it on demand. When one of the expelled students is found beating up another student, Clark orders the doors of the school chained shut during school hours since alarmed security doors cannot be purchased.

Some parents react strongly to these measures, including Leonna Barrett (Lynne Thigpen), mother of one of the expelled students, who pressed the mayor to oust Clark. Clark's radicalism causes him to come into conflict with members of the faculty, particularly English teacher Mr. Darnell, whom Clark suspends for picking up a piece of trash during a recital of the school song, and choir teacher Mrs. Elliot, whom Clark fires for being insubordinate after he cancels a pre-planned choral event, the school's upcoming annual Lincoln Center concert. Napier sets Clark straight over these incidents and lectures him to start being a team player. Clark reinstates Mr. Darnell, though he is too late to re-hire Mrs. Elliot.

His actions begin to have a positive effect on his students. Thomas Sams, a student expelled for crack use, pleads to be allowed to return to school and gradually reforms. Clark also reunites one of his old elementary students, Kaneesha Carter, with her estranged mother. Unfortunately, a practice basic skills test fails to garner enough passing students. Clark confronts his staff for their failure to educate their students and to prepare them for the world. He institutes a tutorial program to strengthen academic skills and encourages remedial reading courses on Saturdays, which parents may attend alongside their children.

When the minimum basic skills test is finally assessed, the students are much better prepared and filled with a sense of self-worth. Before the results can arrive, the fire chief raids the school and discovers the chained doors. Clark is arrested for violating fire safety codes. That evening, the students gather at the meeting of the Paterson Board of Education, where school board member Leona Barrett is leading for Clark's removal. The students demand that Clark be released from jail and retained as principal.

The mayor has Clark released from jail and talks to the students to go home. Clark calls for his students to return to their homes. He is interrupted by assistant principal Ms. Levias who reports that more than 75% of the students have passed the basic skills test. He announces the results over his megaphone. As a result, the school's current administration remains intact, and Clark is allowed to keep his job as principal of Eastside High. The students break into their school song in celebration. The film ends with the senior students graduating high school and Clark handing them their diplomas.

Awards and Honors

1991 NAACP Image Awards

Outstanding Lead Actor in a Motion Picture Morgan Freeman (**Won**)
Outstanding Motion Picture (**Won**)

1990 Young Artist Awards

Young Artist Award Best Motion Picture – Drama (**Nominated**)
Best Young Actor Supporting Role in a Motion Picture - Jermaine 'Huggy' Hopkins (**Nominated**)
Best Young Actress Supporting Role in a Motion Picture - Karen Malina White (**Nominated**)
Jackie Coogan Award – Norman Twain, Producer (**Nominated**)

Television Adaptation

In September 2018, it was reported that a television series based on the film was in development at The CW. The project will be written by Wendy Calhoun, who will also serve as an executive producer alongside LeBron James, Maverick Carter, John Legend, Mike Jackson and Ty Stiklorius. The potential hour-long drama series will be about "when a spirited young black teacher Amarie Baldwin scores the principal job at an Akron, Ohio, public high school, she must dig deep to transform a failing campus into an urban oasis.

In a time when education and school safety have life-or-death stakes, Amarie will take on a broken system that tests her mettle, love life, and family. But can she keep her moxie in check in order to embody the aspirational educator that motivates and uplifts an entire community?

Hazel Clark

Hazel Clark was born on October 3rd in Livingston, NJ. Hazel is named after her grandmother and mother and adopted the nickname Peachy as a newborn. To this day, family, friends, and fans affectionately refer to her by the aforementioned moniker. Hazel is a **seven-time National champion, three-time Olympian and World and Olympic finalist.**

Hazel is the daughter of Joe Clark, who inspired the Warner Brothers Movie Lean on Me and appeared on the cover of Time magazine. She is featured in his book Laying Down the Law and has appeared in numerous television features with her famous father.

Hazel is the sister of four-time Olympian Joetta Clark Diggs. Her sister in law Jearl Miles Clark, is a five-time Olympian and American record holder. Her brother JJ is a world-renowned coach, Hazel's personal coach, and served as the 2008 Olympic coach.

The Clark sisters made history when they swept the 800-meter event at the 2000 Olympic trials. The Clark family is known as the first family of track and field. A member of the Clark family has been on the last seven Olympic teams.

Hazel attended Kent Place School and Columbia High school. She began her high school career reluctantly and did not join the track team until her junior year. As a senior, she was the top high school 800-meter runner in the country, capturing the prestigious Golden West Invitational and National Junior Championships.

Hazel received a scholarship from the University of Florida, where she was coached by her brother JJ. While in Florida, Hazel was undefeated in SEC competition and won six NCAA titles. She also captured the NCAA meet record and won the 1998 800-meter NCAA title by the biggest winning margin in history. Her excellence extended to the classroom, where she was a member of the academic all-American team for three consecutive years.

After college Hazel signed a multi-year deal with Nike and immediately joined the world-class ranks, qualifying for her first Olympic team, advancing to the finals, and winning the 2000 Olympic trials title. At the 2004 Olympics, Clark was eliminated from the first-round heat after she was burned severely in a freak accident.

Hazel rebounded from the disappointment with one of the best seasons of her life, setting a new personal record of 1:57.9.

Hazel has appeared in three global campaigns for Nike. Her likeness was displayed on billboards, storefronts, shopping bags, and storefronts. She also appeared in print ads featured in Glamour, Vogue, and numerous publications. In addition to her work as a spokesmodel, Hazel has appeared in instructional videos, commercials, and advertisements for Hershey and Home Depot. Throughout her career, Hazel has hosted various events, radio, and television shows. Hazel speaks, entertains, and motivates audiences worldwide by speaking about her life experiences and the story of her career. Today she is a sports and education ambassador for the city of Atlanta, and the US embassy appointed sports envoy, founder of Clark Winning Concepts Inc. Nike Run Club director and the executive director of the Georgia Track Club.

Hazel is considered a favorite of the media due to her engaging personality. This quality has given her a platform to represent charities and causes she is passionate about.

Vaughn Mckoy

Vaughn is well known in New York and New Jersey for his 25 years of leadership of corporations, communities, and people. His experience spans federal and state governments, non-profits, law firms, and corporations, where he has earned a reputation as a business-savvy lawyer who is at home in the boardroom and in the trenches. Vaughn is recognized for his ability to inspire, influence and motivate others to achieve their goals, and is known as a straight-shooter and big-picture thinker. Currently, Vaughn is the Business Administrator for New Jersey's third-largest city, where he was tapped by the new Mayor to help lead the city's transformation. Prior to this, Vaughn held various legal and business roles of increasing responsibility with New Jersey's largest utility company and completed his tenure there as Managing Director and Vice President, where he led and oversaw the management of the law department for a company subsidiary. As an Assistant Attorney General and Director of Criminal Justice, Vaughn was one of the state's top prosecutors after stints as an Assistant U.S. Attorney and a lawyer in private practice for several prominent firms. He is currently affiliated with Inglesino Webster Wyciskala and Taylor, LLC.

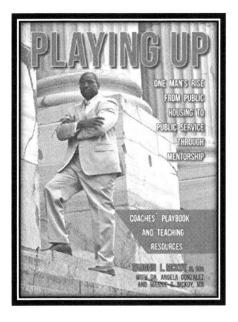

(2013)

Monique Latise

Comedian Monique Latise was born & raised in Paterson NJ. Since childhood, Monique had dreams of becoming an entertainer. She spent the first 14 years of her life entertaining family at gatherings. In 2004 Monique started her own event planning business in which she organized 5 successful fashion shows. In 2010 Monique stepped out on faith, aggressively going after a career in comedy while working two jobs to take care of her family.

Today Monique Latise is a well sought-after comedian. She is the winners of Young Guns of Comedy 2011, Comics Rock Clean Showcase in LA 2018, 3rd place winner at The Apollo theater 2018. Monique Latise is a COMEDY POWERHOUSE with a very nice resume. She has blessed major comedy clubs such as The Broadway comedy club NY, New York Comedy Club, The Governor's Comedy Club NY, Caroline's on Broadway, Stress factory Comedy Club NJ, The JSpot in LA, The Laugh Factory in LA, Downtown Comedy Club in LA. Monique Latise also hosts and produces several comedy shows throughout the tri-state area. Monique had the privilege of performing on the famous carnival cruise ship 2018. She has accomplished 4 self-promoted successful one WOMAN SHOWS And is currently working on her "PRISON MOM'"TOUR 2019...Monique Latise is also the founder of

YOUNG STARZ ROCK mentoring program and talent showcase and have produced 5 successful talent shows featuring the youth in the Paterson community. Monique Latise is a Mother, Motivational Speaker, Comedian, Actress, and Businesswoman with 24yrs experience in banking!

Mike Williams

Mike A. Williams is an experienced senior information technology executive who has over twenty-nine years of technology management and executive experience within global Fortune 500 Companies in the financial services, insurance, outsourcing, and transportation, and logistics industries.

Williams has embraced his non-traditional path of entering corporate America and climbing the corporate ladder. From his start as a low-level computer operator to his rise to Senior Director, Vice President and Senior Vice President ranks reporting two levels down from corporate CEOs; Williams' determination to grow was unrelenting, and his demonstrated ability to learn from failures afforded him the chance to stare down the odds and have what most would consider a very successful career in Information Technology (IT).

Williams has leveraged his diverse skills in technology, strategy, process, business transformation, and operations to give back to his community and enable great people with amazing ideas to develop and initiate programs to support their communities.

As an author, philanthropist, and passionate developer and leader of talent, Williams has spent a good part of his career mentoring and advising aspiring young professionals (millennials), small businesses and nonprofit organizations. To date, Williams has received over 40 community awards and citations across 5 states and has personally helped roughly 35 small businesses and nonprofits across the country from daycare centers to mentoring programs get started. He continues this work through the ThinkNext Foundation, a foundation he started to help support social and community-based causes.

A loving father and dedicated mentor, Williams' most significant accomplishments to date are the birth of his daughter and the legacy of leaders he has personally mentored and helped in some way. Williams enjoys spending time with his daughter, Mikayla, and actively participating in community-based initiatives locally and back home in Paterson, New Jersey.

(2014)   (2014)

Dr. Pinky Miller

Dr. Pinky Miller, a native of Paterson, New Jersey, was educated through the public school system, attending Public School #24 and the famed Paterson Eastside High School. Eastside was depicted in the 1989 movie Lean on Me, in which Morgan Freeman portrayed the controversial principal, Mr. Joe Clark. Dr. Miller received her Bachelor of Arts degree in Communication Studies, and her Master of Arts degree in Counseling and School Guidance, from Montclair State University. In 2011, she received her Doctor of Philosophy degree from Georgia State University.

Dr. Pinky Miller is an author and motivational speaker. In her authentic and enlightening book series Life after Lean on Me, she shares her life experiences and research by articulating the impact (good, bad, and indifferent) that Dr. Joe Clark made upon the students, teachers, and administration during his tenure at Eastside High School. She is also the Executive Producer of the forthcoming documentary Know Our Story, which chronicles the successes and failures of Dr. Joe Clark's kids, the real-life legacy of the bullhorn, and the baseball bat.

Dr. Miller has over eighteen years of experience working in higher education and has held positions as Hall Director/Academic Advisor, Area Coordinator, Assistant/Director of Residence Life & Housing, Assistant Dean of Students, and Vice President of Student Affairs. Dr. Miller loves working with college students, assisting them in times of crisis, and helping guide them toward becoming successful citizens. She has been recognized for her ability to organize and motivate people to achieve their goals. Dr. Miller is a proud member of Alpha Kappa Alpha Sorority Inc. and has four beautiful, intelligent daughters and one awesome son. All books can be purchased at www.Drpinkymiller.com.

(2014)

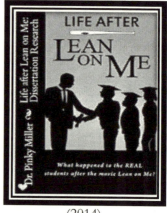

(2014)

(2019)

The Clark Family
123 Wht

The Clark family has made positive indelible contributions to the world in a myriad of ways. Through the legacy of famed educator Dr. Joe Clark to the legendary athletic accomplishments and commitment to community service of Joetta, JJ, Jearl and Hazel, the overarching goal of The Clark Family is to positively impact the lives of others.

Visit **www.clarkfamontop.com** and become a member of team Clark today!

"EASTSIDE"

Is Truman really going to hit me?

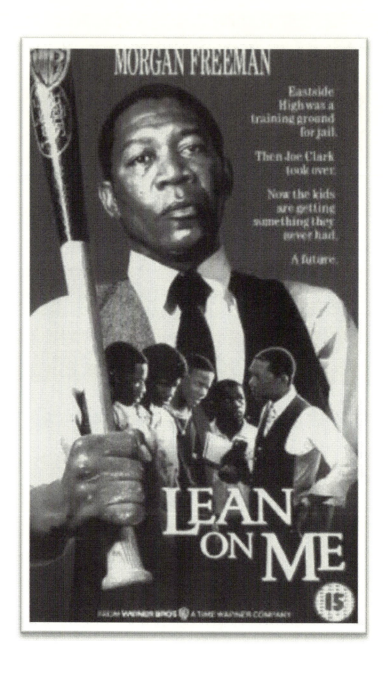

ALMA MATER

Fair Eastside, by thy side we'll stand
and always praise thy name.

To ever lend our hearts and hands to
help increase thy fame.

The honor of old Eastside High bring
forth our loyalty.

So cheer for dear old Eastside High!
Lead on to victory!

So cheer for dear old Eastside High!
Lead on to victory!

Thank You!

This epic event would not have been possible with you! God Bless you! The Paterson Board of Education, Eastside High School, The Paterson City Council, Alpha Performing Arts Center & The Paterson Community

Gloria Clark (Wife of Mr. Clark), Eileen Shafer (Paterson Superintendent of Schools), Dr. Gerald Glisson (Principal, EHS), Hazel Clark, Maritza Davila, Charles Florio, Mike A. Smith, Jermaine "Sams" Hopkins Marcus Debnam, Marylyn DiMartino, Vivian Gaines, Sharon Revoal, Mayor Andre Seyegh, Lilisa Mimms, Mike A. Williams, Benji Wimberly, TJ Best, Thomas Page, Michael Conner, Vaughn McKoy, L. Burns, Denise Hardy, Zellie Thomas, Gee Grier, Michael Best, Steven Capers, Delvis Damon, Anthony Fuller, Lewis Cole, Robert Belmont, Chrystal Cleaves, Darlynn Davis, Verraina Freeman, Elaine Dorsey, John Dixon, Junita Dixon, Alex Clavijo, Janay Boucan, Olandha Miller, Darylynn Miller, Evonne Bazemore, Randy Simon, Elaine Dorsey, Verlena Moss, Keshia Green-Moore, Melissa Rayfield, J'Mar Grayson, William "BigWorm" Blount, Riff, Steve Lenox, George Bodie, Angela Moore, Stacy Watkins, Skip Van Rensalier, Robbynn Chapman, Kenny Simmons, Tonya Ingram, Vivian Thorpe, Eric Zimmerman, Michael McDuffie, Jaime McDuffie, William Cash, Kim Cash, Alfreda Lawrence-Paige, Timothy Tobias, Shanell Irving, Coretta Lawrence, Lewis Cole, Elvis Durham, Cassandra Davis, Marvin Sykes, Carla Williams, Kareem Peppers, Craig Redmond, Ty'Jahnay Reid, Tiajah Brown, Tianna Fletcher, Joel Burt, Na'Asia Harper, Judea Brown, Giovanni Pipkin,

Dorisijiah Hickman, Dah-Quine Warren, Eliana Diaz, Jesus Rosario, Eric Mckenzie, Lisa Webb, Matthew Rodriguez, Tavania Laster, Jestia Hawood, Amorianah Wright, Robertico Alcantara, Robert Wimbush, Janeide A. Matthews-Chillis, Judith Crawford, Jonah Reid, Kyndyl Porter, Charlie Batchelor, Alex Zuniga, Phyllis Riley, Alaa "Al" Abdelaziz, Friends of Al Abdellaziz, Ruby Cotton, Michael Jackson, Shahin Khalique, William McKoy, Flavio Rivera, Luis Velez, Sonia Gordon, Faith Oliver, Tracey Dodson, Debbie Mathews, Brenda Dailey, Tomacinia Campbell, Troy Gillespie, Angelica Gillespie, Tomas Knox, Jeanette Pierce, Janie Young, Deangelo Dangerfield, Oshin Castillo, Nakima Redmon, Emanuel Capers, Johnathan Hodges, Manuel Martinez Jr., Eddy Oliveres, Joel Ramirez, Robinson Rondon, Sharon Allen Pamela Holloway, Tangy Major Susan Peron, David Cozart, Mike Smith, Sharon Allen, Corey Crawford, Ainsworth Jackson, Rosalind Thompson, Center City Mall, Paterson Chapter of Zeta Phi Beta Sorority Inc., Pastor Alexander McDonald III, and the Second Baptist Church family, the dynamic supportive students, staff and teachers of Eastside High School, last and certainly not least Thank You God for giving me the dream, vision and guidance to keep OUR STORY and Dr. Joseph Louis Clarks' legacy alive.

**If I have forgotten your name,
please blame it on my brain and not my heart!
I love you!**

Dr. Pinky Miller

Dr. William "Big Worm" Blount

WILLIAM BLOUNT
The Corporation for National and Community Service named **William Blount**, founder and creative director of the Academy of the Gifted, as recipient of an the honorary doctorate in humanitarianism. The honorary doctorate is awarded to a student in the Global International Online School and Awards program who has completed at least 500 hours of community service.

Blount founded the Academy of the Gifted as a music and arts enrichment program, focused on helping children discover themselves though self-expression in the arts. The nonprofit provides hands-on instruction in drums, guitar, piano, theater, digital arts, music production, visual arts and cosmetology. Blount received a Lifetime Achievement award from former President Barack Obama in 2016. He also received a Grammy and Soul Train award through working with famous artists such as Tyler Perry, Monica, Outkast, Goodie Mob and R. Kelly. ■

Jermaine "Sams" Hopkins

This program is endorsed by
The Grassroots Arts &Cultural Commission, City Of Paterson, NJ
Lewis Cole, Chairman
graccpaterson@gmail.com • 201 667 9016

(Little "Pie" McElveen & William "Big Worm" Blount)

(Robbyn Chapman, Pinky Miller & Adriana Warren)

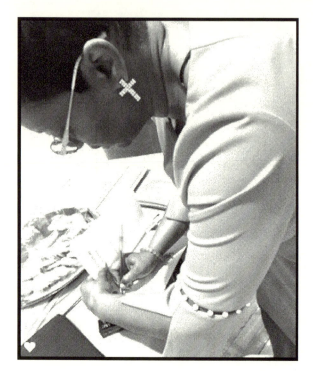

(Pinky Miller signing a book)

The Red-Carpet Event at the Alpha Performing Arts Center

(Thank you, Dr. Thomas Page, for allowing us to utilize your Alpha Center to host our fundraising events!)

"Once a Ghost! Always a Ghost!"

Sunday Morning Worship with Alumni Pastor William and First Lady Kim Cash

Refreshments were served at the Life Changing Word Church. Eastside High School classmates fellowshipped, reminisced, and strategized on how to gain additional support for the students at EHS Paterson, New Jersey. Thank you! Pastor William Cash, First Lady Kim, Brenda Dailey, and the Life Changing Word Church Family!

129

Surplus food from the weekend events was happily delivered to a women's shelter in Paterson, New Jersey. We must pay it forward in everything that we do.

The core team took a break and went to get some Paterson Pizza
Pinky Miller, Robbyn Chapman, Marcy Traylor, Tonya Ingram & L.
Burns

The First Saturday in March of every year is "Dr. Joe Clark - Lean on Me Day!"

Immediately after the weekend fundraising events, Pinky Miller drove from Paterson, New Jersey to Gainesville, Florida, to present Dr. Joseph L. Clark the proclamations that were established by the Paterson City Council. Dr. Clark was filled with appreciativeness and euphoric to receive gifts, letters of appreciation, well-wishes, and love provided by the committee and supporters.

RESOLUTION DESIGNATING "JOE CLARK /LEAN ON ME" DAY TO BE HELD EVERY FIRST (1ST) SATURDAY IN MARCH

SPONSORED BY: Council President Maritza Davila

CO-SPONSORED BY: Councilwoman Ruby Cotton and Councilwoman Dr. Lilisa Mimms

Signed by Corporation Counsel January 8, 2019

WHEREAS, Dr. Joe Louis Clark was born on May 8th, 1938 in Rochelle, Georgia, after which he grew up in Newark, New Jersey and attended Central High School; and

WHEREAS, he is the father of Olympic track athletes Joetta Clark Diggs and Hazel Clark, and the father-in-law of Olympic track athlete Jearl Miles Clark. His son JJ Clark, was their coach, having served as head coach at University of Connecticut; and

WHEREAS, in 1982, he was offered the position of principal of Eastside High, after transforming PS #6 into what many called the "Miracle on Carroll Street; and

WHEREAS, he gained public attention for unconventional and controversial disciplinary measures as principal of Eastside High, with a TIME cover story observing that his while his style was primarily disciplinarian, he focused on encouraging good behavior and school pride; and

WHEREAS, after his tenure as principal of Eastside High, he served as Director of the Essex County Detention House in Newark, a juvenile detention facility; and

134

WHEREAS, he became the subject of the 1989 film <u>Lean on Me,</u> after which his book, <u>Laying Down the Law</u>, became a resource for educators, and more recently, he has inspired an anticipated <u>Lean on Me</u> television series, to be produced by John Legend and LeBron James.

NOW THEREFORE, IT BE RESOLVED BY THE MUNICIPAL COUNCIL OF THE CITY OF PATERSON that the Council hereby designates the first (1st) Saturday in every March as "Joe Clark / Lean on Me" day, in recognition of Joe Louis Clark, and in gratitude for the inspiration that Joe Louis Clark and the film <u>Lean on Me</u> have provided.

STATEMENT OF PURPOSE

The purpose of this Resolution is to designate the first (1) Saturday of in every March, as "Joe Clark / Lean on Me" day in the City of Paterson.

SECONDED BY COUNCILPERSON Luis Velez

RECORD OF COUNCIL VOTE ON FINAL PASSAGE - AYE – Abdeaziz Alaa "AL" Cotton, Ruby, Davila, Maritza, Michael Jackson, Khalique Shahin, McCoy, William, Mimms, Lilisa, Rivera Flavio, Velez Luis

This resolution was adopted at a Municipal Council meeting in the city of Paterson, NJ on January 15, 2019. This resolution must remain in the custody of the City Clerk. No 15 – Res. # 19; 006

These two pictures present a full-circle moment. The top picture was taken in 1986. Mr. Clark presented Pinky Miller with a high school graduation award of accomplishment. The bottom picture was taken in 2019. Dr. Pinky Miller presented Dr. Joseph L. Clark with an award that highlights his life achievements.

Mr. Clark & Pinky Miller (1986)

(Dr. Pinky Miller & Dr. Joseph L. Clark, 2019)

137

(Dr. Joseph and Dr. Gloria Clark)

138

(Hip Hop Artist, Run-DMC, Mr. Clark & daughter Hazel Clark)

(Movie Debut – Paterson, NJ - Fabian Theatre March 1989)

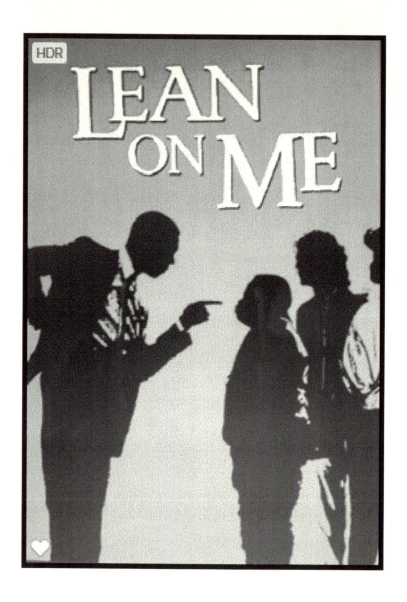

(Morgan Freeman & Mr. Clark, 1989)

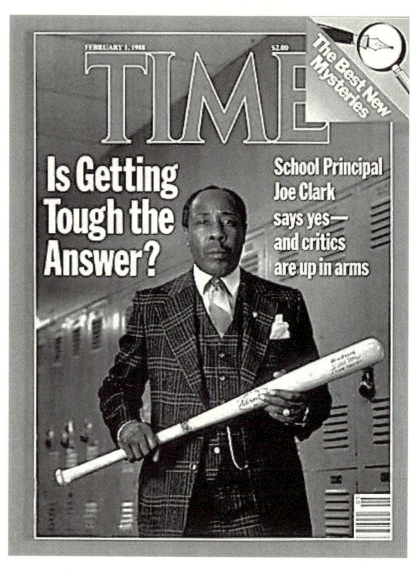

(Dr. Clark on the cover of Time Magazine – February 1, 1988)

(Dr. Clark on the cover of Senior Times Magazine – 2013)

Dr. Clark has a Facebook Page.

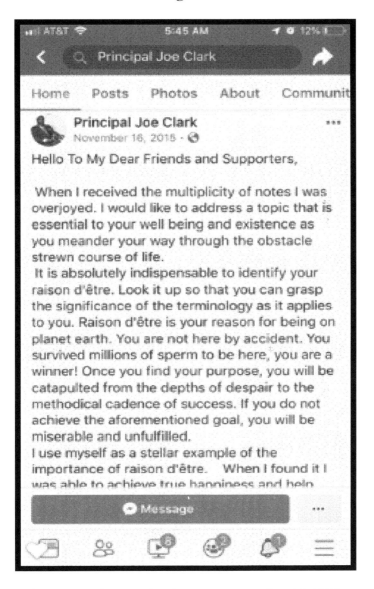

(Dr. Clark's first Facebook post on November 16, 2015)

methodical cadence of success. If you do not achieve the aforementioned goal, you will be miserable and unfulfilled.

I use myself as a stellar example of the importance of raison d'être. When I found it I was able to achieve true happiness and help others become significant products in a most complexed society.

Don't be concerned with what others think about you. Personally, I was born to raise hell! Those who like me as a result, thank you very much. Those that don't, have a good damn day! I would like to reiterate your word for today. Raison d'être!!! Look it up and do not forget it.

Peace,
Joe Clark

OO 51   15 Comments 13 Shares

👍 Like   💬 Comment   ↪ Share

👤 **Principal Joe Clark** shared a Page.   ···

Eastside High School Senior Awards Day – June 5, 2019

The Lean on Me – Dr. Joseph L. Clark Legacy Scholarship applications were created, released, completed, submitted, and reviewed. Deserving students were awarded at the Senior Award assembly on June 5, 2019, at Eastside High School.

The following pictures were produced by photographer Gee Grier –
Thank You, Gee!

(Eileen F. Shafer, M. Ed, Paterson Superintendent of Schools)

(David Cozart, Assistant Superintendent)

(Eastside HS Guidance Counselors Pamela Holloway & Tangy Major)

(Time to present the scholarships to the EHS winners)

(Dr. Glisson, Principal & Dr. Pinky Miller)

(Waleska Valazquez – Valedictorian – GPA – 4.08)

(Keyrin Lopez – GPA 3.63)

(Daniela De los Santos – GPA 3.54)

(Jennifer Portorreal – GPA 3.89)

(Lindsey Marte – GPA – 3.71)

(Diovine Minaye – GPA 2.96)

(Delia Maldonado – GPA - 3.59)

(Anthony Rodriguez – GPA - 4.00)

(Dewar Lausell – GPA – 3.56)

(Dillen Dennis – GPA 3.25)

(Elizabeth Estrella – GPA – 3.75)

(Melinda Guzman – GPA – 2.93)

(Presenters: Trinace Hickson-Grant, EHS Staff, Pinky Miller, Verraina Freeman, Maritza Davila, Robbyn Chapman, EHS Staff, Lauren Nance)

Eastside High School 2019

174

Hanging out with Alumni at an Eastside High School Basketball Game 2019

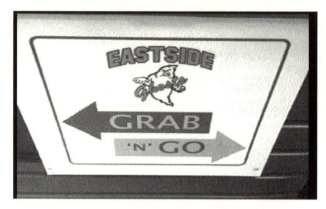

(Eastside Cheer Team, 2019)

(Pinky Miller & Pastor William Cash)

(Pinky Miller and Vincent Edwards)

(Audrey Adams, Stephanie Fletcher and Pinky Miller)

(Pinky Miller and Mark Baker)

185

(Pinky Miller and Lil Pie McElveen)

Eastside High School Class of 2019 Graduation

(Ms. Vivian Gaines and Ms. Marylyn Dimartino)

There were several ***articles written about the Lean on Me 30th*** ***Anniversary*** – Dr. Joe Clark Legacy Scholarship Fundraisers. Noted below are two articles that were written by Editor, Steve Lenox, from "Tap into Paterson" on February 10, 2019.

(Steve Lenox)

By TAPINTO PATERSON STAFF
February 10, 2019 at 10:30 AM

PATERSON, NJ - For many, former Eastside High School principal Joe Clark is little more than the main character in the 1989 movie Lean on Me. Played by Morgan Freeman, Clark, in the movie, is seen as the bat and bullhorn wielding leader of an inner city school besieged by drugs and violence.

However, for thousands of students that attended Eastside during his tenure from 1982-1989, including Dr. Pinky Miller, Clark was a figure that that had a great impact, both positive and negative, on a generation of Patersonians, as well as the education system as whole.

Now an educator, author, filmmaker and motivational speaker in Georgia, Miller is leading an effort to commemorate the role that Clark played in so many lives, including students, teachers, administrators, and the community, and using the 30th anniversary of the film's initial release to organize a weekend's worth of events, March 1-3, that will help to raise scholarship funds for Paterson students.

The weekend's festivities begin with a free screening of the iconic film, as well as a special performance of a portion of "Lean on Me: The Musical" produced by William "Big Worm" Blount and Donald Gray, and starring members of musical performing group Riff and Jermaine (Sam) Hopkins, at Eastside High School beginning at 5:00 p.m. This is followed by an Eastside High School Reunion for all classes with food, fun, and dancing at Alpha Performing Arts, 211 Lackawanna Ave, Woodland Park. The reception, for guests 21 and over, is just $20 and begins at 9:00 p.m. Guests are encouraged to arrive dressed up as their favorite Lean on Me character, or wear something from their high school years.

On Saturday, organizers will host a scholarship luncheon and celebration at Eastside High School beginning at 1:00. Tickets for the event are just $40 and include keynote addresses by Freeholder T. J. Best as well as three time Olympic athlete, and daughter of Joe Clark, Hazel Clark.

Guests who purchase a ticket for just $40 will be back at Alpha Performing Arts for a VIP/Red Carpet Reception on Saturday evening beginning at 8:00 p.m.

Riff will provide musical performances at both the scholarship luncheon and the VIP/Red Carpet reception.

The weekend will conclude on Sunday for a special worship service, potluck meal, and documentary interviews beginning at 11:00 a.m. at Life Changing World Church, 522 W. Broadway in Haledon.

Bundle packages are available and sponsorships for all of the events are welcome. For more information on how to purchase tickets call 404-713-3895 or visit Dr. Pinky Miller online by clicking here.

EDUCATION

Work, and Legacy, of Dr. Joe Clark Live on Through Scholarship Fund

By STEVE LENOX
July 8, 2019 at 6:36 AM

PATERSON, NJ - Eastside High School's School of Information Technology 2019 valedictorian Waleska Valazquez is due to attend George Washington University in September, while graduate Anthony Rodriguez completed his coursework with a 4.0 grade point average will be attending Rutgers University.

Both, Dr. Pinky Miller, a 1986 Eastside High School graduate announced last month, will also have the assistance of a $1000 scholarship awarded by the Dr. Joseph Clark Legacy Fund.

In its first year, the scholarship program, Miller told TAPinto Paterson, seeks to keep the legacy of the principal, who became a household name through press accounts and the major film Lean on Me, alive by "paying it forward."

Most only know Clark from the depiction of him by Morgan Freeman, that of a baseball bat and bullhorn wielding leader of the school that had become overrun by gangs and drugs.

But that wasn't the whole Joe Clark, and that wasn't the whole Eastside experience, several alum recalled during a weekend marking the film's 25th anniversary in May.

"He was kind and gentle to the students," Miller recalled fondly. "He was a hellraiser to the staff," especially those, she added, that weren't willing to put the time in to improve the educational outcomes of those they were hired to teach.

1986 Eastside High School graduate, and now Paterson City Council President, Martiza Davila, also reflected on the life-changing role of Clark when she said that she was "supposed to be a statistic." Raised by a single mother of four it was generally accepted that Davila's life wouldn't lead to much, certainly not to the position of leading the legislative body of the state's third largest city for two years in a row.

"I made it because of people like Joe Clark said 'believe in yourself,' Davila recalled, concluding that thousand of students owe him their thanks because he never gave up on them.

Also being awarded scholarships from the fund that Miller hopes will continue to grow and offer educational assistance on an annual basis were:

Dillen Dennis, School of Government and Public Administration

Elizabeth Estrella, School of Culinary Arts, Hospitality and Tourism

Melinda Guzman, School of Government and Public Administration

Keyrin Lopez, School of Information Technology

Delia Maldonado, School of Government and Public Administration

Dewar Lausell, School of Information Technology

Lindsey Marte, School of Information Technology

Diovine Minaya, School of Government and Public Administration

Jennifer Portorreal, School of Information Technology

Daniela De los Santos, School of Culinary Arts, Hospitality and Tourism

EDUCATION

Work, and Legacy, of Dr. Joe Clark Live on Through Scholarship Fund

EDUCATION

Work, and Legacy, of Dr. Joe Clark Live on Through Scholarship Fund

EDUCATION

Work, and Legacy, of Dr. Joe Clark Live on Through Scholarship Fund

Credits: Gee Grier

EDUCATION

Work, and Legacy, of Dr. Joe Clark Live on Through Scholarship Fund

Credits: Gee Grier

The New Eastside High School – Eastside is an institution of learning that is segmented into three academies; **School of Information Technology, School of Government and Public Administration, and Culinary Arts, Hospitality, and Tourism.**

School of Information Technology

MISSION & VISION

The School of Information Technology is designed to prepare and motivate students to develop, operate, maintain, manage, and integrate hardware, software, and multimedia systems through career pathways.

To create a safe and nurturing, 21st-century learning community where all students develop the necessary skills to compete in a global society. Eastside High School will emerge as a model urban institution that will prepare all students for higher education opportunities as well as effective job placement readiness.

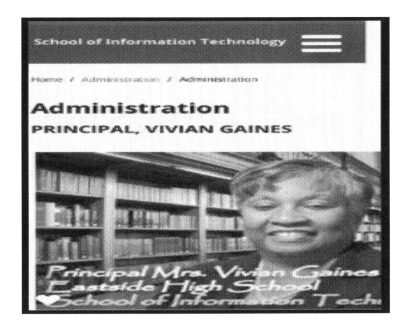

I, along with the Administrative Team of the School of Information Technology at Eastside, am excited about the vast undertakings that have taken place over the last few years. We will continue to use a personalized and proactive approach as we strive toward becoming one of urban education's best. As we move forward, we always remember the words of Dr. Martin Luther King, "The function of education is to teach one to think intensively and to think critically. Intelligence plus character is the goal of education."

The high school experience is what students, staff, administration, and parents make it. With a focused lens from each of us, we can easily expect each student to graduate in four years. Not only will they graduate, but they will be ready for their post-secondary experience. We encourage all to embrace and respect this learning phase knowing that its outcomes will produce more for students than any other identified educational experience. Their education will take them farther than anything else in life. Learning goals have been set that will assist each student in being successful. Now, we, as a collective team, must focus on assuring success. The right focus will assure it happens.

During the time that the students are in school, a nurturing and supportive environment will be provided. Our school doors are always open for you to visit our classrooms, Home School Council meetings, and any other event that involves your child. Questions about the educational process are welcomed and will be answered. Consider our school the informal community school where the community is vital.

Each year brings a new beginning in education. New beginnings allow us to reflect and refine for improved performance. With high expectations, we embrace the 2019-2020 school year. Collectively, we have all the synergy that is needed to transform our school into a leader in urban education. **Let's Do It Together!**

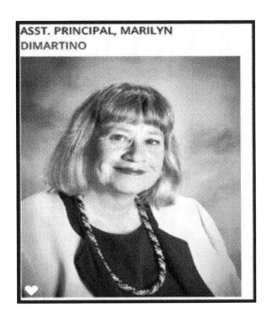

205

Eastside Alums Come Home with College Stories

Eastside High School's School of Information Technology and School of Government and Public Administration recently hosted its second annual college fair. The event featured recent Eastside graduates speaking about their experiences in college. The returning alumni hailed from a variety of colleges and universities including George Washington University, American University, University of Richmond, Rutgers University, Stockton University, St. Peter's University, Seton Hall University, the College of St. Elizabeth, Bloomfield College, William Paterson University, NJ Institute of Technology, Passaic County Community College, Rider University, Kean University, Montclair State University, Caldwell University, Ramapo University, the New School of Manhattan, and New Jersey City University.

The students spoke about their experiences in college. One returning alumnus said that even though he was taking ESL courses, he still had to take academic courses. The audience applauded when he said that he had achieved a 4.0 grade point average in his first semester.

OIT SERVES COMMUNITY

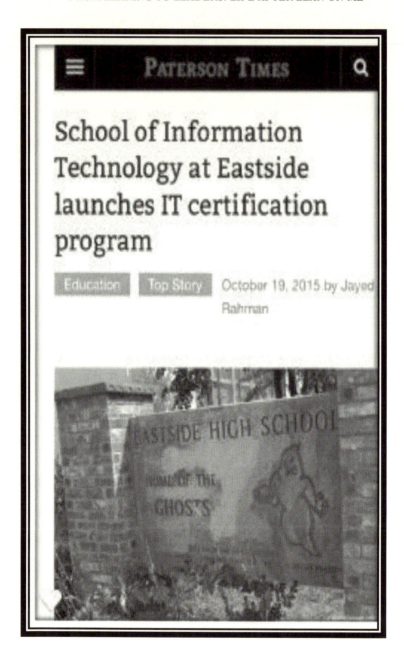

The School of Information Technology at Eastside High School launched an information technology skills training program in collaboration with Cisco Systems to prepare city students for information and communications technology (ICT) careers in the tech industry, announced the district on Monday afternoon.

Students will take the courses through the Cisco Networking Academy, an IT skills and career building program, that helps to prepare pupils for careers in network security, technical support, and network administration.

The program also prepares students for professional certifications and higher education in engineering, computer science, and other related fields.

"These are highly exciting times in Network Security which offer both challenges and opportunity for qualified individuals," said school principal Vivian Gaines. "Recent criminal breaches of world financial and commercial networks show not only the vulnerabilities of the 21st century economy, they also illustrate the need for specialists in Network Security. These jobs are abundant, rewarding, and high-paying."

The program will initially offer essentials like router, switching, and network security courses which will be delivered via the cloud-based Cisco NetSpace Networking Academy. The online courses developed by Cisco and IT experts will offer network simulation exercises, labs, assessments, and feedback to reinforce key concepts.

Certified instructors will provide students with hands-on support in tech labs to further learning and track student progress, according to the district.

"Our twelve high schools offer a choice of a career/CTE [Career and Technical Education] or academic theme, and it is critical that we continue to expand the depth and breadth of these programs – not only by adding more theme-related courses, but through the inclusion of some form of licensure or certification for students to earn at the end of their respective program," said state-appointed district Donnie Evans. "This will serve as a model for all of our high schools."

The School of Information Technology at Eastside High School will partner with local businesses to identify internship and career opportunities for its graduates.

"The School of Information Technology administration and staff at Eastside High are excited to be ahead of the curve by offering these Cisco courses and certifications to Paterson students," said Gaines.

SOIT's own, Dr. Benevento's Black History Mural has adorned the walls of many Paterson schools since 2014. This year, this impressive mural has come to SOIT. This is my tribute to Black History Month, Dr. Benevento said. Dr. Benevento is an ingenious educator with a knack for fusing Art into teaching of Mathematics. Stop by the Art Corridor today to take a look at this colossal piece of art. She gratefully thanks SOIT for giving the Black History Month

School of Government and Public Administration

MISSION and VISION

The School of Government and Public Administration at Eastside High School, in partnership with all stakeholders, instills in its students' core values for academic excellence, leadership, and responsible citizenship.

GOPA aims to create a community of learners through working collaboratively in a safe and challenging learning environment that encourages dignity, involvement, independence, and responsibility through high expectations and cooperation, resulting in lifelong learning and personal growth.

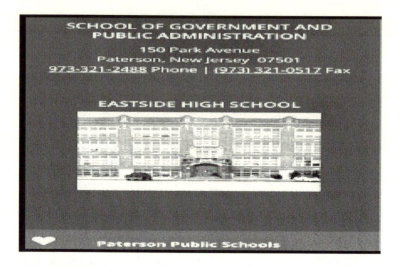

Principal, Miguel Sosa

PRINCIPAL'S MESSAGE

On behalf of our teachers and administrators, welcome to The School of Government and Public Administration (GOPA)! My name is Miguel Sosa, and I am the principal of GOPA (a fellow Patersonian) raised and still living in this great historical city.

At our school, we believe when given the proper nourishment, motivation, and adequate resources to learn, all our students can academically succeed and become leaders in their own rights. We are a diversified school that embraces and respects all cultures with their individual heritage. Students' self-esteem must begin by knowing and embracing their roots.

For this reason, the staff and administration tirelessly believe in building bridges and inspiring students to have the confidence in themselves to succeed in all facets of body, spirit, and mind. We believe our students can reach their true potential through hard work and determination regardless of their personal circumstances.

The School of Government and Public Administration understands that it takes a village to raise a child. We have an open-door policy towards the community and the parents that are committed to becoming partners (bridge builders) towards our students' success.

As the new principal of GOPA, I look forward to leading this school with these uncompromised values and working with all stakeholders to drive academic excellence. May God bless you all and The School of Government and Public Administration.

GoPA Earns National Recognition

U S NEWS AND WORLD REPORT HONORS GOPA

US News and World Report, a National Publication, has recognized *GoPA* as one of *America's Best High Schools in 2016.*

This prestigious recognition validates the efforts of the school administration, instructional staff, support staff, and students at all levels. The recognition rewards the talent, effort, and perseverance of everyone at **GOPA**. This affirmation indicates that the school is living up to the highest standards that State Superintendent Dr. Donnie Evans has placed before it. Dr. Evans's vision is for Paterson Public Schools to be a model for urban education in the state of New Jersey, and **GOPA** is meeting that challenge. As a result, **GOPA** continues to earn a wide variety of recognitions. Factors that led to this selection are:

- Annual increases in graduation and attendance rates
- Annual increases in English and Math scores
- Annual increases in the percentage of seniors admitted to selective universities
- Documented successful academic programs (including National History Day, Mock Trial, Law 2 Life, Debate)
- Successful community engagement programs (including winning the Optimum Challenge)

School Principal, Dr. Karen A. Johnson attributes the success of the school primarily to the dedication of the teaching staff. Says Dr. Johnson: "There is overwhelming research that the most important part of student success is having effective teachers in the classroom. The results of high-quality teaching and a school committed to reaching its goals are rewarded with recognitions such as this and others. Congratulations are extended to everyone in this school."

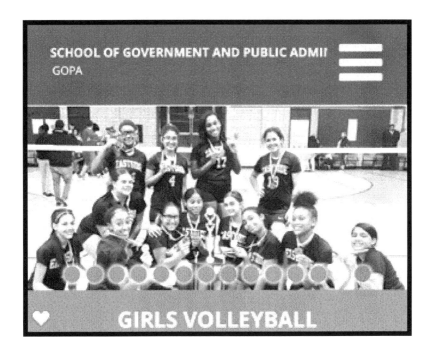

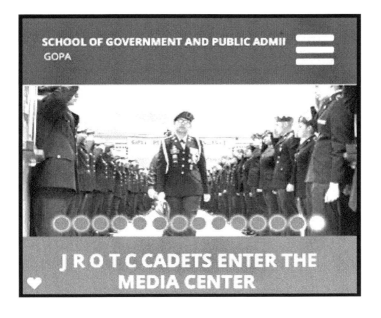

General Abramson, an active general in the US Army, for a special Black History Month presentation.

Vice Principal Hibert with JROTC at Superior Courthouse Black History Celebration

Culinary Arts, Hospitality and Tourism

MISSION and VISION

To provide a rigorous learning environment where student's unique educational needs are met in the classrooms through theme infused academic classes enabling them to grow into responsible, productive citizens, and life-long learners.

To create a safe and nurturing 21stcentury learning community where all students develop the necessary skills to compete in a global society.

CAHTS at the Eastside Educational Campus will emerge as a model urban institution that will prepare all students for higher education opportunities as well as effective job placement readiness.

CULINARY ARTS, HOSPITALITY AND
TOURISM SCHOOL@ EASTSIDE
EDUCATIONAL CAMPUS

150 Park Avenue
Paterson, New Jersey 07501
(973) 321-2354 Phone |
(973) 321-2356 Fax

PRINCIPAL

Mr. Edgard Nieves

ASSISTANT PRINCIPAL

Mr. John Super III

CAHTS 2017 GRADUATION RATE

92.3% - 4th Highest in the District

STUDENTS ACCEPTED INTO STEPS PROGRAM

Four students from the Culinary Arts, Hospitality and Tourism School at Eastside High School have been chosen to participate in the STEPS program (Students Taking an Early Pathway to Success) for their senior year during the 2019-2020 academic school year. Paterson Public Schools have partnered with Passaic County Community College to allow these students the opportunity to complete their senior year on campus, while also obtaining college credits. Stephen Octable, Athziri Castellanos, Emilly Cruz and Algeny Zenon are four of only ten students chosen among Paterson Public School juniors throughout the district.

CAHTS STUDENT SCORES A PERFECT SCORE ON THE NATIONAL SPANISH EXAM

Natalia Almonte, a junior from the Culinary Arts, Hospitality and Tourism School at Eastside High School, scored a perfect score on this year's administration of the National Spanish Exam. This annual exam, taken by students studying Spanish as a second language across the country, measures students' performance in interpretive communication and proficiency of the Spanish language.

CAHTS CELEBRATES THEIR TOP STUDENTS AND RED NOSE DAY AT CITI FIELD

The School of Culinary Arts, Hospitality and Tourism at Eastside High School travelled with their top 40 students in both the junior and senior classes to Citi Field to cheer on the New York Mets. Not only were the top students in the school recognized, but the school also supported "Red Nose Day" in dedication to ending child poverty in our country.

CAHTS SENIOR ACCEPTED INTO AUTO APPRENTICESHIP

CAHTS Senior, Kevin Rivera, has been accepted into the competitive "IAM CREST District 15 Automotive/Diesel Technicians Pre-Apprenticeship Program." Kevin is one of only two students chosen from Paterson, with only 20 students chosen for this program from the entire state! With this acceptance, Kevin will receive the cost of attending trade school, along with earning a wage while learning the trade alongside a Union mechanic. Congratulations, Kevin!

ABR Report Card

District Anti-Bullying Report Card

District Score: 70 out of 78 points

GOPA ABR Grade is 69 out of
78 points

GOPA Anti-Bullying Coordinator
Ms. Verraina Freeman

Photos were garnered from the Paterson New Jersey Eastside High School websites:

https://soit-pps-nj.schoolloop.com/pf4/cms2_site/view_deployment?d=x&theme_id=i32a1yfmcff&group_id=1500178972392

https://gopa-pps-nj.schoolloop.com/pf4/cms2_site/view_deployment?d=x&theme_id=i16a14vzt7ay&group_id=1500178974407

https://cahts-pps-nj.schoolloop.com/pf4/cms2_site/view_deployment?d=x&theme_id=td58i5g1wjtl2o1&group_id=1500178974054

Photographers:

Gloria Clark

Hazel Clark

Joe Clark

Eastside High School

Eastside High School - Yearbooks 1982-1989

Facebook

Gee Grier

Getty Images

Pinky Miller

www.TAPINTO.net

The following research describes Dr. Joe Clark's legacy is garnered from my 2011 dissertation "A Phenomenological Case Study of a Principal Leadership: The Influence of Mr. Clark's Leadership on Students, Teachers, and Administrators at Eastside High School," has been downloaded in 31 different countries almost 13,000 times for academic purposes. The countries include but are not limited to:

United States	China
Philippines	Spain
Saudi Arabia	Jamaica
Nigeria	Netherlands
Pakistan	Bahamas
United Kingdom	Chile
Russian Federation	Germany
Zambia	Egypt
Canada	Mexico
Malaysia	Botswana
South Africa	Nepal
India	New Zealand
Dominica	Virgin Islands (US)
Puerto Rico	Vanuatu
Ukraine	Samoa
Bangladesh	

CHAPTER 1

The Problem

The fundamental problems contributing to the urban-suburban achievement gap include but are not limited to poverty, violence, drugs, alcohol, discrimination, low student achievement, ineffective teachers, lack of strong discipline, overcrowding, gang activity, teenage pregnancy, lack of safety methods, learning disabilities, emotional disorders, family dysfunction, single parents homes, and inadequate education. These "are typically manifestations of larger societal problems related to (1) social inequality, (2) racism, and (3) the deterioration of urban areas" (Noguera, 1999, p.1). It is essential that the complexity of this triple threat facing urban schools is addressed.

Declining urban neighborhoods have negatively impacted students living in these environments. Upon Joe Clark's arrival at Eastside High School, it was plagued with all the issues mentioned above.

During Dr. Clark's tenure as principal at Eastside High School (EHS) 1982-1989, school safety was and continues to be intensely scrutinized in the wake of amplified gang activity in schools. More than half of the gang members surveyed in various studies compiled by federal officials and gang research experts specified that members of their gang have a history of assaulting teachers.

As reported by Huff and Trump (1996), the number of cities in the United States, acknowledging the existence of gangs, had risen from 58 in 1962 to nearly 800 in 1992. Moreover, an estimated 24,500 recognized gangs in 1997 that includes 750,000 gang members in 2000 and 2007 that increased to one million gang members in 2009. Approximately 6.6 million criminal acts occur in the US each year, nearly 370,000 of those non-fatal violent crimes are committed by gang members from urban, suburban, and rural public schools each year. (National Youth Gang Center, 2009).

I can only imagine how the number has vastly increased in 2019. Unfortunately, these statistics are currently accurate regarding my beloved home town of Paterson, New Jersey, because gang violence runs rampant, and there are several senseless killings monthly. Something has got to change!

Some of the students were victimized because others sought after the status symbols that went along with their clothing, and some because of their gang-affiliated colors. Additionally, Dr. Clark was placed at EHS to decrease problematic student behaviors and increase educational achievement.

When I interviewed and asked *John* (who was a student prior to and during Clark's tenure), about the number of drugs he believed was being disbursed at Eastside High School? He stated that everybody he was associated with in his crew brought in about 20 joints (marijuana cigarettes) every day.

He stated that the upperclassmen were dealing and using crack cocaine and angel dust/PCP. "PCP is an addictive drug, and its use often leads to psychological dependence, craving, and compulsive PCP-seeking behavior" (Drugs.com, 2014). He also shared that there were people from different areas and cliques that were also bringing in drugs. "There was a lot of drug activity going on in the school before and after Dr. Clark's arrival."

The Rationale of the Book

The raison d'être (the reason for being) of this book was to determine Dr. Clark's philosophies, strategies, and leadership style as principal of Eastside High School. Moreover, to investigate from the point of view of

Dr. Clark's former students, teachers, and administrators what, if any, affect or impact his strategies and leadership style had at EHS, as well as on the participants' lives during and subsequent to their time at EHS. I investigated the issues regarding Dr. Clark's philosophies, leadership style, controversies, successes, and challenges during his tenure.

The goal of this book is to provide insight for educational leaders and policymakers who want to make an effort to take steps to diminish high school violence, drugs, gang activity and increase academic achievement to assist low-income students.

I intend that the information gained from this book will help educational leaders move students toward a better and more successful life.

This investigation will allow educators at all levels, the opportunity to view and understand Dr. Clark's leadership style and strategies, and to realize the impact Dr. Clark had on his former students, teachers, and administrators. This information could be useful to school principals and assistant principals as they work with students in situations similar to those at EHS. It could also be helpful to school superintendents and school board members as they assess the leadership styles, values, and beliefs of principal candidates. The information collected is retrospective data of past events and is, therefore, subject to the problems inherent to memory that could provide limitations to my research.

I conducted this investigation by giving voice to my high school classmates, teachers, and administrators. I interviewed twenty-three informants (including Dr. Clark) about their opinions on leadership and their experiences, good, bad, or indifferent with Dr. Clark to determine what leadership style(s) Dr. Clark established during his tenure at EHS.

Introduction

The system abandons them and, far worse, they abandoned their dreams, their real opportunities. I cannot, I thought, change the economy or age-old prejudice or the system at large. However, what I can, must, and will stop is the way these young people destroy themselves. I will return them their hope. I pledged myself to show them how to fulfill their better dreams. (Clark & Picard, 1989, p. 18)

In 1982, EHS was one of two large high schools located in a poverty-stricken area of Paterson, New Jersey. Conditions such as high dropout rates, gangs, drugs, prostitution, teenage pregnancy, violence towards students and teachers, racial uproars, political wars, and complicated educative battles with the board of education existed at that time.

In 1982, an attempt to raise the students' minimum basic skills test scores and eliminate the violence and other harmful conditions at EHS, Joe Louis Clark was hired as the new principal (Clark, 2009). Dr. Clark had a leadership style that, while controversial, some would argue was successful.

Much has been written on the topic of practical strategies and leadership styles in America's schools. By taking a look at EHS from 1982 to 1989, this research will add to the literature on the effects of Dr. Joe Clark's leadership style from the point of view of a select group of students, teachers, and administrators who attended and worked at EHS during that time.

Paterson, New Jersey

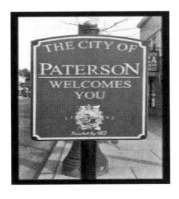 

To further provide the context for the emergence of Mr. Joe Clark, I will give brief historical information about Paterson, New Jersey. Paterson was established as a lively industrial city that supplied the United States with several manufactured goods. Paterson is located twenty-five miles west of New York City and situated within Passaic County. According to American Memory (2009), Paterson was founded as a corporation in 1792 by Alexander Hamilton and The Society for the Promotion of Useful Manufacturers. Alexander Hamilton was an American politician and the first U.S. Secretary of the Treasury from 1789-1795 (Jost, 1997).

(Alexander Hamilton)   (William Paterson)

Paterson, New Jersey was named after William Paterson, an Associate Justice of the United States Supreme Court, a signer of the Constitution, and the Governor of New Jersey (New Jersey, 2009). The city holds the "distinction of being the nation's first planned industrial area" (American Memory, 2009, p. 1). The power for the industries in Paterson came from the 77-foot high, Great Falls of the Passaic River. These industries included textiles, firearms (Colt Revolver), silk, and railroad locomotive manufacturing (American Memory, 2009, p. 1).

(Silk workers)   (Paterson, Falls)

(Photo Courtesy of Richard H. Walter Collection)   (Photo Courtesy of Dr. Pinky Miller)

According to the web site City of Paterson Silk City (2009), Paterson was known as the "Silk City" during its earlier history for producing silk in the 19th century. By 1870, Paterson was the primary producer of silk in the United States (American Memory, 2009). According to Bookrags Staff (2006), "Paterson was also the site of historic labor unrest that focused on anti-child labor legislation. It was also the 'mecca' for immigrant laborers who worked in the factories" (p. 1).

The city has changed drastically since those early years. In the 1970s, there was a significant deterioration in urban areas, and Paterson was afflicted with homelessness, drug use, gang violence, racial riots, high unemployment rates, and low high school graduation rates. By 1980, Paterson was one of the most distressed cities in the United States (Bookrags Staff, 2006).

Eastside High School

According to the 1986 and subsequent yearbooks, the first high school in Paterson was structured in 1860 and was named Paterson High School. Only advanced students from a few elementary schools were allowed to attend this program that would prepare them for college. In 1875 the school acknowledged its first graduating class, which consisted of 13 students, two boys, and 11 girls. In 1911 a fire destroyed the original building that housed Paterson High School, but it was quickly replaced with a new building (EHS Yearbook, 1986).

When this new school became overcrowded in the early 1920s, the city officials decided to build an additional school. The site chosen for this new building was land that had been previously used as a cemetery. Before construction could begin, the remains of the people buried there had to be exhumed and relocated (EHS Yearbook, 1986).

In 1924 this new building was named Eastside High School because it was located on the east side of the city. This was the birth of the present Eastside which population was at least 95% White at that time.

The class of 1986 was the 100th graduating class, as displayed on the commencement invitation of Eastside High School.

Nineteen hundred eighty-six

of

Eastside High School

requests the honor of your presence

at the

100th Commencement Exercises

dnesday Evening, the twenty-fifth of June

nineteen hundred and eighty-six

six o'clock in the evening

to be held at the

Hinchliffe Stadium

Paterson, New Jersey

Although there is no documentation as to how Eastside students were given the nickname of the Undertakers or how the Ghost became the school mascot, it seems only natural since "bodies had to be dug up" for Eastside High School to be built (EHS Yearbook, 1986).

Many traditions have been started and passed on from one generation to the next. Some have changed, others have been forgotten, however, the spirit of the Undertakers in the spirit of every ghost who ever walked the halls of Eastside will remain and be felt forever (EHS Yearbook, 1986).

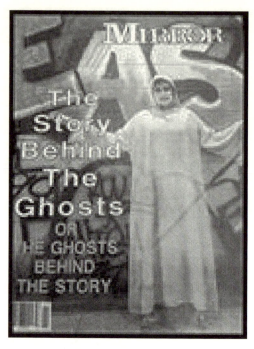

(Photos created by Salvatore Scarpinato, English Teacher - Courtesy of EHS Yearbook, 1986)

Eastside High School is a four-year public high school that serves ninth through twelfth-grade students. EHS is located at 150 Park Avenue, which became a poverty-stricken area of Paterson, New Jersey. The school colors are orange and blue.

Mr. James Bradshaw was the principal before Dr. Clark, and Mr. Charles Lighty became principal after Dr. Clark's tenure. The most prominent feature of the school in the 80s and 90s was the population of the students, which from 1982-1989 was 98% African American and Hispanic and two percent White (Clark, 2009).

On August 7, 1991 (two years after Dr. Clark left), the State Board of Education voted to take over the school district due to low teacher morale, overcrowded classrooms, obsolete textbooks, violence, and ineffective educational approaches. Dr. Laval S. Wilson served as the State District

Superintendent.

EHS is in what can best be described as the ghetto. From my lived experience, before the arrival of Dr. Clark, the interior and exterior of the school were dilapidated and filthy. The inside of the school was graffiti-covered and garbage scattered all over. There seemed to be chaos everywhere, even inside the classrooms.

The student body ran the gamut, from those who were violent, disruptive drug dealers and gang members, to those who were non-disruptive and eager to learn. Some teachers were scared and not able to teach due to fear of the disruptive students. Outside the school, drug addicts, alcoholics, gang members, drug dealers, and prostitutes circled the building walls of the school. This forced students to wade through many potential hazards every day as they traveled to and from school. It was not a safe campus.

According to Clark & Picard (1989), "EHS was an open-air, cash and carry drug market," and his [Clark's] aim was to shut down the "drug business permanently" (p.51). Dr. Clark argued that "the best way to get drugs out of a school is to keep them from getting in" (Clark & Picard, 1989, p. 51).

John (who was a student before and during Clark's tenure), indicated that students spent much time in the cafeteria instead of going to class. He shared that there was a hidden room in the auditorium that students had to climb up a ladder to enter. While in this room, students used to hang out all day, participate in drug transactions and smoked weed regularly.

Dr. Clark also stated that "ghetto youths have been murdered because of the hats they were wearing, Murdered because the hat identified the youth as a member of a particular gang" (1989, p. 43). As Clark began to implement policies and procedures such as increasing security, locking and chaining the doors, and monitoring incoming and outgoing traffic, Dr.

Clark stated that he received "death threats" from the "doped-up hoods" that he began to keep out of the school (Clark & Picard, 1989, p. 45).

From my personal experience, several students were robbed, beaten, and had their fashionable expensive clothing, sneakers, and jewelry stolen from them both inside and outside the school. During that time, there was a mixture of street cliques and gangs, as well as "religious"-oriented cliques/gangs. Some of the student gangs were defined by race, African American, Hispanic, Dominican, and Jamaican descent. There was also a group of students who were known as the Five-Percenters. Five-Percenters sometimes have been considered an offshoot of the Nation of Islam. According to Allah (2007)

> The Five Percent nation believed that 10% of the people of the world know the truth of existence, and those elites opt to keep 85% of the world ignorant and under their controlling thumb. The remaining five percent are those who know the truth and are determined to enlighten the rest of the world; thus, they are called the Five Percent Nation.

The Five-Percenters have also been perceived as posing a threat or as a gang because of some criminal and other anti-social acts committed by a few members (Allah, 2007).

John was a member of the Five Percent Nation and stated that he and his group of friends were called the Be Islam boys. He reminisced about the time in 1982 when there was a major issue between the administration and a group of Five Percent Nation students. He shared the following information. "When the Five Percent women wanted to wrap/cover their bodies by wearing ¾ length clothing, Dr. Clark had a major problem with that."

John believed that the Five Percent Nation was "a culture; it was a way to cultivate their women." He remembered asking Dr. Clark why he disagreed and being dissatisfied with Dr. Clark's response. He shared that information with the leadership of Five Percenters. Some of their members came to EHS from Newark, New Jersey, and New York to speak with Dr. Clark. "this issue became a massive controversy against the administration, and some of the students along with leaders of the Five Percent Nation protested the policy and a riot broke out in the parking lot.

In 1984, there were race riots in Paterson, which began at EHS, involving the Five-Percenters, Hispanics, Dominicans, African Americans, and Jamaicans. According to Clark & Picard (1989), a fight erupted outside the schoolyard gate between a Black male and a Hispanic male. Racial epithets were shouted, and a "near mêlée began" and "several students who were fighting received scrapes and bruises" (Clark & Picard, 1989, p. 110).

There were race riots throughout the night, and the next day in all sections of the city between the youths. Some students were hurt and were arrested by the police. The following day, Eastside High School student attendance was less than half of the 90% that generally attended. Students and teachers were frightened and stayed home as a result of the race riots (Clark & Picard, 1989).

For years, due to the increasing viciousness and gang presence in schools, administrators have looked for ways to safeguard the protection of students and teachers. According to (Clark & Picard, 1989), many of these security measures were costly and were not considered by the Paterson Board of Education because of budget cuts and increased operating costs.

From my lived experience, Dr. Clark had to focus on order and structure. He implemented a plan for keeping the drugs and drug dealers out of EHS, which "involved making the school a fortress that the drug pushers could not penetrate" (Clark & Picard, 1989, p. 51). Specifically, Dr. Clark replaced door locks, old fences, and removed security guards he deemed ineffective. He also kept an eye on the students he perceived as most likely to open the door and let the drug pushers into the school.

Dr. Clark stationed security guards outside the school near the entrance fences, even though some teachers were fearful because they felt the school would be "guard-less" inside. However, Dr. Clark instituted a plan for teachers and administrators to serve as in-school security. Teachers stood in the corridors before and between class periods. In addition, the administrators roved along the corridors until students were settled in their classrooms.

Dr. Clark initiated an Identification Card System that was rigorously enforced. All students, teachers, and staff members had to wear color-coded, picture ID badges that were checked by security guards upon entering the building. The ID badge always had to be worn and visible. Those who did not have their ID were not allowed to enter the school or had to pay a fine to receive another one. All visitors had to stop at the principal's office to obtain an ID for the day. This system was a crucial step in keeping people who were not affiliated with EHS out of the school (Clark & Picard, 1989).

The Average EHS Student Background

My experience with classmates indicated that the majority of the students who attended EHS were recipients of free or reduced-price lunch, welfare, food stamps, Medicaid, and lived well below the poverty level. In 1982, the poverty level was defined, for a family of four, as households living on $9,300 per year or less and was increased to $12,100 in 1989 (U.S. Department of Health and Human Services, 2011).

According to Clark & Picard (1989) the national average for single-parent households living in poverty in the inner-cities was between 50-60% and "it's the same for Eastside High School. More than half the kids come from single-parent homes, and we all know that this parent is almost always the woman. The men are gone, and the children have no fathers" (Clark & Picard, 1989, p. 73).

There were many students who wanted to learn, who were not violent, and who were not gang members or addicted to drugs. Many of those students, including me, were afraid to attend EHS and prayed for a change. Dr. Clark was an answer to those prayers when he was assigned to Eastside, and the transformations began.

The Environment

When asked to describe the outside environment of Eastside High School before, during, and after Mr. Joe Clark's tenure, some of the informants in the study shared their experiences at EHS.

Mr. 13 (who was a teacher prior to, during, and after Clark's tenure), stated that "it was challenging at times, but there are challenges in all school environments."

Mr. Will (who was a guidance counselor prior to, during, and after Clark's tenure), indicated that Eastside "was totally out of control and dangerous."

Ms. Florence Jones (who was a teacher prior to, during, and after Clark's tenure), said that EHS was "filled with gangs, drugs, and poverty."

Coach "O" (who was a teacher prior to, during, and after Clark's tenure) proclaimed that prior to Dr. Clark, "it had more negative qualities than positive. It was pretty safe during the day; it was a different culture at night...crime was prevalent. Drugs and gangs were in existence all the time." Additionally,

Ms. Smiley (who was a teacher prior to, during, and after Clark's tenure), asserted that

The building was standard and hasn't changed, except they took down the 6 foot high wrought decorative iron fencing around the entire school. They had taken that down and recently put up the same type of fence except this time it's made of aluminum because wrought iron is cost-prohibitive during this day. People don't hang out nearly as much as they used to. Mainly, because the entire building is wired with cameras; the doors hopefully are locked now. However, they don't hang out as nearly as much as they did back then.

Furthermore, *Ms. De-Mo* (who was a teacher prior to, during, and after Clark's tenure), stressed that Eastside High School was

Overcrowded, lots of fights, smelled of marijuana in some stairwells and bathrooms, open defiance and disrespect toward teachers, but most students were good kids in crowded classes and unfortunately, taught by teachers who "passed the time" by handing out word puzzles, worksheets and truly not teaching. Some teachers would leave the building and have colleagues take their kids into their classes. The heat never worked in the "old" building, and there were false alarms and bomb scares on almost a weekly basis, sometimes several in one day. Outsiders would enter the building to walk with friends or start fights, and students cut classes – a lot!

John (who was a student prior to and during Clark's tenure), stated that Eastside was a different kind of place; there were race riots that were not included in the *Lean on Me* movie. He thinks the film watered down the violence. He stated that the movie did not show the race riots that were going on at Eastside, whereas the blacks dominated the Park Avenue (front) side of the school, and the Puerto Ricans dominated the Market Street (back) side of the school.

Mr. *Moody* (who was a student during Clark's tenure and currently is one of four principals at Eastside High School), discussed the current changes regarding the restructuring of Eastside High School. "This is a major difference. Dr. Clark had about 3000+ students back then [1982-

1989]. We only have 1600 students, and we have four principals" that help maintain and manage the students.

Eastside is currently fragmented into three separate academies, (1) the School of Government and Public Administration, (2) Information Technology, and (3) Culinary Arts, Hospitality, and Tourism. Each academy has its own staff that is comprised of one principal, two vice principals, secretaries, guidance counselors, and teachers.

Moreover, Eastside has an additional principal position, titled the Principal of Operations, who is responsible for the overall operations of the building; facilities and maintenance; athletics; and student management which includes discipline, suspensions, and different protocols of how students should enter and be dismissed from the school. Eastside has implemented a mandatory uniform policy. The students of each of the three academies wear separate colored uniforms so that the administration is aware of which academy a student belongs to.

Before all of the occurrences above, I must share how Dr. Clark was invited to be the principal at Eastside. According to informant *Ms. Demo*, there were rumors about Eastside that included gangs and violence since 1975, and in fact, EHS was referred to as a "Cauldron of Violence" in the newspaper headlines back in the late 70s. Also, she stated that the New Jersey prosecutors' office conducted a momentous investigation because several teachers were attacked by students, and ultimately this led to Dr. Clark being hired.

She remembered Dr. Clark telling the Paterson Schools' superintendent, Dr. Frank Napier, that he needed "free rein" to "clean up" Eastside High School.

CHAPTER 2

Dr. Frank Napier, Jr.

(Mayor Frank Graves, Frank Napier & Rosa Parks)   (Governor Kean, NJ & Frank Napier)

According to the Napier Academy website, Dr. Frank Napier Jr. was born and raised in Paterson, attended Public School Number 4 and Paterson Central High School. He received his bachelor's and master's degrees from William Paterson Teachers College. Dr. Napier's 37 years of experience as an educator and community leader in Paterson changed the lives of countless young men and women.

As stated by the Napier Academy website, Dr. Frank Napier began his professional career in the Paterson School System as an elementary school teacher and assistant football coach of (Rival) Kennedy High School. In 1972, he was appointed the Assistant Superintendent of Paterson Public Schools and, four years later, became the first African American to serve as the Superintendent of Schools.

Napier Academy website states that in 1984, he earned his Doctorate in Education from the University of Massachusetts and began expanding his work as Superintendent of Schools by returning to the classroom as an adjunct professor at William Paterson University.

According to the Napier Academy website, Dr. Napier's commitment to the community of Paterson extended far beyond the classroom walls. As a district chairperson for the Passaic County Boy Scouts of America, as an active member of the Board of Trustees for the Paterson Public Library, and as Pastor of the Gazaway Baptist Church.

Napier Academy website states that the quest for personal and professional excellence to which Dr. Napier dedicated his life, is a legacy that lives on in each of the students whose lives he touched. In 1982 Dr. Napier hired Joe Clark as principal for Eastside High School, and his three children David, Dina, and Darren, attended Eastside. Sadly, Dr. Napier passed away in 2002. On August 15, 2003, Public School Number 4 was changed to Dr. Frank Napier Jr. School of Technology – Napier Academy. See dedication plaque below:

(Dr. Napier, wife Margaret & children David, Darren & Dina, Photos Courtesy of Napier Academy)

Dr. Joe Louis Clark

(Photo Courtesy of EHS Yearbook, 1986)

The following quote is what governed Dr. Clark's philosophies, actions, methodologies, strategies, and leadership styles during his seven-year tenure at Eastside High School.

> 'God Dammit, Wake UP!' We are not dealing solely with Paterson, we are working within a complex economic, social, political, and cultural entanglement called the inner-city, a deep entanglement that pervades the urban areas of this nation. And despite what some people would like to think, what goes on in the inner-city has a direct effect on what happens in the rest of the country. Dope, crime, taxes, to give you some examples. In the inner-city, youths get killed because of the hats they might be wearing. Black and Hispanic youths cut down by their own kind before getting a chance at life. Maybe one was the next Washington Carver or the next Neruda. And kids have been killed in Paterson too for reasons as horribly absurd as a hat. (Clark & Picard, 1989, p. 43).

My investigation is about Joe Louis Clark, who believed in focusing on order, structure, and firm discipline. Dr. Clark is best known as the bullhorn and baseball bat carrying principal of EHS in Paterson, New Jersey, from 1982 to 1989. Dr. Clark and the EHS story gained notoriety from the movie *Lean on Me,* starring Morgan Freeman, who portrayed Dr. Clark as the high school principal. One interpretation of Dr. Clark and

Eastside High School follows:

> An extraordinary situation calls for an extraordinary leader. At strife-torn Eastside High School, that leader was Dr. Clark. *Lean on Me* is the rousing, fact-based story of high school principal Dr. Clark, who armed himself with a bullhorn and a Louisville slugger and slammed the door on losers at Eastside High School in Paterson, New Jersey. Brought in as the last hope to save the school, he chained the doors shut to keep the trouble-makers out and the strivers in. Parents fought him. Teachers fought him.
>
> Lots of kids loved him. Dr. Clark turned Eastside High School around, becoming a national symbol of tough-love education and appeared on the cover of Time. "If you students don't succeed in life, says Dr. Clark, "I want you to blame yourselves." His message is simple: Don't lean on excuses. Don't lean on drugs, crime, or anger. *Lean on me* and learn. (Blockbuster.com (2007) [Avildsen, 1989].

(Photo Courtesy of Amazon.com & Warner Bros.) (Photo taken by Dr. Pinky Miller, EHS, 1986)

Dr. Clark was born on May 7, 1938, in Rochelle, Georgia. Dr. Clark went to New Jersey when he was 12 years old; he worked while he was in high school to help support his mother and siblings. He received a Bachelor of Arts degree from William Paterson College and a Master's of Arts degree in administration and supervision from Seton Hall University located in New Jersey (Clark & Picard, 1989). Dr. Clark did further graduate work at Rutgers University and received an honorary doctorate from U.S. Sports Academy that he received in 2005 (Amburn, 2012).

According to Dr. Clark, his daughter Joetta Clark Diggs is the president of Joetta Sports and Beyond LLC, she graduated from the University of Tennessee in Knoxville and was a four-time Olympian. His son Joe Louis Clark II is a graduate of Villanova University and also an Olympic athlete. He coached for ten years at the University of Florida and is now the head track and field coach for both men and women at the University of Tennessee. His daughter Hazel Clark Mac is a University of Florida graduate and three-time Olympian, all three competed in the 800-meter races. His daughter-in-law Jearl Miles Clark attended Buchholz in Gainesville, Florida, and Alabama A&M and became a five-time Olympian in track in 2002" (Amburn, 2012).

(Photo Joe Clark, sent to Dr. Pinky Miller - completion of her doctoral studies- "Pinky, Never wait for your ship to come in, row out and meet it" Joe Clark – Lean On Me)

According to Clark Speaks website, in addition to being the main subject of the movie *Lean on Me,* Dr. Clark was spotlighted in a Time

Magazine cover story and profiled on the CBS show "60 Minutes." He was featured in many newspapers and journal articles. Dr. Clark appeared on a considerable number of television news and talk shows in the tri-state area (New Jersey, New York, and Philadelphia).

After only two years of his hard-nosed leadership at Eastside, New Jersey's Governor, Thomas Kean acknowledged the former disorderly high-school as a model school, and Dr. Clark was titled one of the nation's 10 "Principals of Leadership" in 1986 ("Clark Speaks Website," p.1).

(Mayor Frank Graves & Governor Thomas Kean - Photos Courtesy EHS Yearbook, 1984)

Dr. Clark gained national applause for his accomplishments, which resulted in President Ronald Reagan, naming him a model educator. Dr. Clark was offered a White House position as a policy adviser by President Reagan, which Dr. Clark declined (Clark & Picard, 1989).

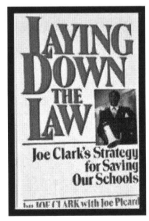

Throughout his book, *Laying Down the Law*, Clark shared his beliefs, strategies, leadership, and success stories about his experiences at EHS, his work as an educational consultant, his speeches, and his activities as Director of the Essex County Youth House. His first message was: "Every day, pride in self and school must be reinforced. Every day, the value of academics must be demonstrated."

Dr. Clark was a former army drill instructor who saw education as a mission and was an elementary school teacher for over ten years in New Jersey. Dr. Clark held enormous expectations for his teachers, administrators, and students. He inspired most of them to develop lifestyles for success, and he challenged them when they did not improve (Clark & Picard, 1989).

From my lived experience, Dr. Clark was not only a caring, father-like, unwavering supporter for students who wanted to learn, but also a charismatic role model and steadfast ally for parents, teachers, administrators and community leaders who believed in his efforts to save EHS from the negative influences of drugs, violence, and a lack of education. Despite his popularity in some circles, Dr. Clark's tactics were not always praised. For example, he came under attack during his first couple of weeks at EHS because he expelled 300 students for fighting, vandalism, drug possession, abusing teachers, or for being fifth-year seniors who were not showing what Clark considered sufficient academic promise.

In response, Clark explained that "kids desire discipline because order is necessary for learning to take place" (Clark & Picard, 1989, p. 193). When there is a lack of discipline, there is disorder. Good citizenship demands attention to responsibilities as well as rights (Clark & Picard, 1989).

Information about Dr. Clark was published in numerous national and local newspapers and magazines, including but not limited to the *New York Times, The Philadelphia Inquirer, The Washington Post, The Record, The Press of*

Atlantic City, and *Ebony Magazine.*

Some of the most notable headlines were chronicled as *Lean, Mean Principal Gets Call From Reagan;* this article talked about how Dr. Clark received a phone call from United States President Ronald Reagan, who applauded Dr. Clark for his tough approach to discipline ("Lean, Mean' Principal Gets Call," 1983).

An article entitled *2 Schools With 2 Remedies For Drugs And Violence: Discipline Stressed In Paterson School,* explained how some of the older faculty members remember the scary, violent days of the past that included chaos in the hallways of 3,200 students, assaults on teachers and administrators, gang violence in the cafeteria with knives, and blatant drug sales during the school day.

However, it was a new day at EHS because students "walked to the right" circumventing fights in the corridors, teachers were boasting about student performance and the clean appearance of the potted plants, couches, and paintings unscathed by vandalism ("*Schools (2) With 2 Remedies for Drugs*," 1986).

Although in the eyes of many, Dr. Clark had much success yet, his success came with many controversies. An article entitled *Clark's Get-Tough View Airs Nationwide* (1986), described how Dr. Clark was profiled on NBC news. The television show opened by introducing "Crazy Joe," a man admonishing students, yet berating administrators with a bullhorn in hand and referring to suspended students as "deviants,"

A newspaper article entitled *Principal Clark Drops Dukes, Gets Big Gift for School* (1988), described Dr. Clark's resolution to cease and desist struggling with the Paterson Board of Education to accept a $1 million generous contribution to EHS ("Principal Clark drops dukes," 1988).

The newspaper article, *Principal in Paterson, is Directed to Reinstate 50 Expelled Students* (1987), described how Dr. Clark was ordered to reinstate

50 students that he expelled out of school for being disciplinary problems and not being productive students ("Principal in Paterson is directed," 1987).

The newspaper article, *Principal Says He'll Relock School Doors If Necessary* (1986), described how Dr. Clark unwillingly removed padlocks from the doors of EHS and stated that he would "take the consequences" because he felt the students were in danger from criminals outside of the school and that he would rather be safe than sorry.

The newspaper article, *400 Students Walk Out, Back Clark* (1987), provided information about the 400 EHS students who left school and marched downtown to the Paterson Board of Education office in demonstration of support for Dr. Clark, who was suspended. Students acquired control of the meeting in the Paterson Board of Education building. The Paterson Police escorted the students back to school later on that day as requested by Mayor Frank Graves (Students (400) walk out, back Clark, 1989).

(Courtesy of Joe Clark website)   (EHS Yearbook, 1988)

According to Clark Speaks website, after seven years as principal at EHS, Dr. Clark resigned and became a noted speaker on the country's lecture circuit. He was eventually nominated in 1996 for the National

Association of Campus Activities, Speaker of the Year Award. Dr. Clark "began his latest crusade on behalf of America's youth in August 1995 when he was appointed Director of the Essex County Youth House, a juvenile detention center in Newark, New Jersey" (Clark Speaks Website, 2010, p.1). He was later released from his appointment for shackling some of the detention center residents together.

Based on my observation as a student at EHS, Dr. Clark seemed to be dogmatic, demanding, arduous, unbending, and very flamboyant in his approach in the public view, yet showed love and compassion to the students while holding them accountable for their actions.

In the final chapter of his book, *Laying Down the Law*, Dr. Clark speaks about leadership and management. He stated that "current management theory, as taught in colleges of business administration, denotes five key, interrelated facets, or functions, of proper management. These facets include preparation, organizing, staffing, guiding, and controlling; every quality manager should perform each of these functions well" (Clark & Picard, 1989, p. 185). Moreover, Dr. Clark (1989) stated that,

> I feel that I have performed all five of those functions well at Eastside High School. The old Eastside High School produced drug addicts and criminals, unwed mothers, and welfare cases. Thousands of underdeveloped youths lacking direction and skills were poured out upon the bleak streets of Paterson and the nation. The new EHS turns out responsible, drug-free young citizens ready to work to achieve their goals and make worthy contributions to society. My management accomplished this (p. 185).

Clark & Picard (1989) also offered that "current theory lists two prerequisites for the successful manager: clear-headedness and the ability to work through people" (p. 185). Dr. Clark added the requirement of *instinct* and placed it at the top of the list. He argued that without this attribute, the other two could not carry the day.

(Courtesy of EHS, 1984)

Dr. Clark described the instinct for leadership, as "the desire and the drive to be a leader" (p. 186). Unlike theorists, who imply that this quality is necessary, Dr. Clark indicated that it should be the most emphasized.

Dr. Clark stated that leadership is a quality that must rank high amongst the superintendent's, and the board of education's employment search committee standards or they will be in jeopardy of ending up with a principal who executes the managerial functions, "but only within the crippling parameters of the status quo" (p. 186).

Dr. Clark was apprehensive that new principals might manage the staff despite the necessity of accurately knowing how to lead the administrators and teachers. Dr. Clark was concerned because he believed that the consequences are more detrimental if the school is in dire need of substantial restructuring because it is in a distressed state of being (Clark & Picard, 1989). Dr. Clark stated that he received firm support from two levels of American political structure, the grassroots support of parents, students, and residents, and the support of the White House. Clark & Picard (1989) stated that

> Minority students, poor youths - I gave them a needed role model, a Black man born in poverty, who rose in a good cause and through his efforts to national prominence. I showed them, and I told them, that the media would surely have exposed me for a knave had I been one. I was not an imitation or fanciful commercial image of a real man. I

was and am! - Through rightful purpose and years of hard work, through building on a strong foundation - a real man. I pointed the way for them, as an educator should (1989, p. 206).

According to Dr. Clark, the problems in education, in this country, are excessive. "We all must confront them, or live with the dire consequences" (Clark & Picard, 1989, p. 206). Many people looked to where they might find solutions, and Dr. Clark gave himself as an example.

(Photo Courtesy of EHS Yearbook, 1984)   (Photo Courtesy of EHS Yearbook, 1986)

I have shown you what one man, a Black man born into abject poverty, can accomplish against the odds. Now it is your turn to act and effect change. Help save our schools, our children, in the future over our civilization. Yes, there is that much at stake. However, together, we can make a crucial difference. I have seen how righteous actions transcend ethnicity and economic class. Such works evoke a deep, rushing river of support, which is nothing less than the flow and the spirit of humanity. We are the solution to the present crisis in education. We can, we must, and together we will triumph (1989, p. 207).

In Clark & Picard (1989), Dr. Clark related the students' lives to a baseball game and explained to the students that they had three strikes held against them in life. The first strike was that they were black and members of a minority group, and the second strike was that they were poor. Dr.

Clark explained they had one more chance at-bat, and their education was the way to hit a home run. Dr. Clark argued that dropping out of school would count as strike three, "you're out of the batter's box, out of the ballgame, and off the team, you're finished" (1989, p. 92).

Dr. Clark believed in communicating real-life examples of what his students had to deal with as a minority in these Unites States.

Dr. Clark demonstrated a culture of power as one of several strategies to connect with his students. Sharing his personal experiences and life stories about his childhood, growing up poor, and not allowing his circumstances to dictate his future was a way to bond with his students. Dr. Clark used his proficiencies as an illustration to be a role model for his students. Dr. Clark allowed his students to see an African American man who progressed, acquired higher education, and used power to help his students succeed in life.

Mr. Joe Clark's Experiences at Eastside

Dr. Clark has been thought of as a hero in his own right. He was faced with the challenge of working with a broad high school demographics of primarily minority students who were from poverty-stricken, drug, and gang-infested areas. Dr. Clark experienced situations and occurrences at Eastside High School that including violence, theft, drugs, teachers impregnating students, lack of student's foundational education, defiant students, criticism, and praise from parents, teachers, community leaders, politicians and educators from across the United States and abroad.

Dr. Clark worked extremely hard to increase educational attainment for his students and wanted the best for them. He had a great desire for his students to obtain a high-quality education, prosper, and go to college. Dr.

Clark focused on those students who demonstrated the willingness to learn and stay out of trouble. He viewed higher education as a way out of the ghetto and believed in order, discipline, sacrifice, and working hard to fulfill their dreams of changing the futures of the students who attended Eastside High School. He was admired by the media and was featured in newspapers, magazines, and appeared on television, news, and talk shows.

President Ronald Reagan (1981-1989) praised him for his awe-inspiring efforts to defy the odds at these poor, dysfunctional, rundown high schools. Celebrating his successes, Dr. Clark was featured in a movie: Dr. Clark's *Lean on Me* starring Morgan Freeman was released nationwide in major theaters in 1989.

Dr. Clark began his tenure in 1982 at EHS. I know from my lived experience that Dr. Clark was very dogmatic and autocratic in his approach and leadership style.

Dr. Clark seemed to be vilified in the media for his tirades and throwing at least 300 students out of school. (although a large number of the students were allowed to return based on a mandate from the school board), Locking the doors, and not backing down from critics (teachers, students, staff, fire marshal, the board of education, or administrators who did not agree with his methods and strategies).

Many teachers and staff quit or transferred to other schools. Due to controversies during his tenure as principal. Dr. Clark, after open-heart surgery in May of 1989, resigned from his position as Principal. Two months later, he advanced to the lecture circuit to speak about education reform, school management, leadership, drug control measures for inner cities, and his experiences at EHS.

CHAPTER 3

Leadership

Mr. Joe Clark was the principal of Eastside High School in Paterson, From my familiarity, Dr. Clark was a no-nonsense, dogmatic, controlling, uncompromising, and demanding principal to anyone including students, parents, teachers, administrators, board of education leaders, community leaders, political incumbents, fire marshals, or anyone who did not follow along with his strategy to reconstruct EHS into what he envisioned as a model institution for learning.

Dr. Clark has expressed himself as well as by the effect he had on many persons while he was at EHS.

You cannot lead your sheep without being a formidable shepherd, a servant leader. Servant leaders place their own needs second. A servant leader rolls up their sleeves and serves the flock. When Dr. Clark put his ego above the school, he was doomed to fail. Toward the end of his tenure, he spent more time on the lecture circuit (*Florence Jones*).

With Dr. Clark, the fatherly concern was shown to students who remained in the school. That concern was not shown to students who were expelled or to those teachers with whom he had differences.

Dr. Clark's paternalistic relationship with his students is demonstrated throughout a conversation he had with a Hispanic student who was in a fight with an African American student. This is one of the battles that began the race riots in 1984. Dr. Clark shared his displeasure with the students' behavior.

That is why the police car is parked outside, as though this was some prison because the citizens of Paterson think Eastside has become a haven for hoodlums! You have dishonored your school. Furthermore, Francisco, it is you who have dishonored your family and your people.

His face flared. "But, Dr. Clark…!" Shut up and listen!

You have given many people cause to think lowly of Hispanics, to think of them as brawlers and delinquents, as uneducable people. That is a disgrace and dishonor to your family and your people. You ought to be ashamed! He was ashamed, as well as angry and confused. He could not respond. I continued. "Francisco, this is our school. This is our opportunity, yours and mine, and the opportunity of everyone else that comes here to prove to the world that just because people are poor or from a different culture, it does not mean that they cannot become decent, productive citizens.

That's what Eastside is all about. But if we damage the school through dishonoring it, we'll eventually destroy it, and then we really will have nothing. Bring honor to your family and your people by honoring your school. It is the difference between civilization and barbarity. In the future, if you have trouble, any sort of trouble, come first to me. We'll get to the bottom of it together. We'll follow the law of civilization, not the law of the jungle. Do you understand me? (Clark & Picard, 1989, pp. 117-118).

Leadership and Power

Several of Dr. Clark's teachers and administrators did not identify with what he was attempting to do at first. However, many others saw his willingness to create an environment that was conducive to learning, followed his lead, and appreciated his methods once they understood what he was striving to do. Most teachers and administrators did not doubt his competence, although many questioned his methods. It was evident that Dr. Clark had formal job authority even though he had periodic disagreements with the board of education and city officials. His power to reward and coerce was demonstrated repeatedly, as he demanded his favor and disfavor upon students and staff.

CHAPTER 4

Principal Leadership and Effective Schools

> I want to inspire youths to work for and truly achieve their goals. I know they can do it if they try. I did. The best way a principal can help is to create for them an atmosphere conducive to learning. That is what my task is, and I diligently perform it. I have locked horns with the board because this task though it should be, is not high on their list of priorities if it is there at all (Clark & Picard, 1989, p. 143).

According to all the informants in this study, promoting school climate was a focus of Dr. Clark, particularly protecting instructional time and maintaining high visibility. Dr. Clark believed that maintaining order and safeguarding instructional time were the necessary foundations for student achievement.

Dr. Clark was interested in reversing that cyclical process and made that quite evident through his words and actions. Not only did Dr. Clark have and discuss high expectations with students, but he also discussed high expectations with teachers and administrators. Dr. Clark advocated for an environment that was orderly, quiet, serious, and conducive to academic achievement.

Dr. Clark was demonstrating these actions and activities at Eastside High School. Based on my lived experience and the experience of most of the informants, Dr. Clark cultivated a sense of pride and community among the students. He reduced vandalism, the appearance of the school improved dramatically, the halls were bright, everyone was aware of the rules and consequences for not following the rules, and he wanted the teachers to focus on instruction.

Impact of African American Principals

According to the informants in this study, Dr. Clark indeed demonstrated confidence in his ability to make a difference in the lives of his students. He also showed compassion and commitment to those students who, in his view, exhibited that they wanted to learn.

Although Dr. Clark did not involve the community in decision making about the school, he showed that he was interested in the well-being of the broader community. Dr. Clark was invited to several churches in Paterson, New Jersey, and was given the opportunity to speak to several parents of the children who attended EHS.

Dr. Clark stated that the first thing he did to reach out to the community was to formally introduce himself and his program at neighborhood churches. Each week Dr. Clark would attend a different church service with the help of concerned ministers and would be allowed to address the congregation. In motivational messages, he shared with the parents he stated,

> If you persist, you will survive, if you work hard and do not give up, though the obstacles are many and the road is hard and long, you can advance. You can succeed. Your life will have meaning, even joy. High regard for education is the surest and the most decent way to advance (Clark & Picard, 1989, p. 71).

Dr. Clark gave the same message to the students at EHS. As mentioned earlier, one of the ways he connected with the students was to talk about his childhood and the importance of community. He also revealed his relationship with the community by providing personal financial assistance to students and parents who were in need.

This insight leads further credibility to Dr. Clark's impact and legitimacy. Moreover, there is a correlation between black principal leadership and Black student achievement:

CHAPTER 5

Researcher Role and Biases

I was a student at Eastside High School during the time that Mr. Joe Clark became principal and a graduate of his first official graduating class in 1986. I have maintained a personal relationship with some of the participants who were selected for the study, and I am aware of my researcher's biases. As a way for the reader to understand who I am. I am the person, who as a student, saved her pom-poms, cheerleading uniform, and jacket from my freshman year in 1982. That is just who I am.

(Pinky Miller, 1983 Cheerleader & 1985 Snare Drummer – Marching 100 Band)

It was incumbent upon me to acknowledge my biases so that I could write this book in a way that takes into account so many other perspectives than my own. I am *Pinky* Miller, I have this personality that is very sentimental in nature, but when it comes to this book, I have taken myself seriously as a researcher.

I understand the importance of separating myself as a former student and from myself as a researcher. Separating me to eliminate the bias was

266

the goal, and that is why I conducted the self-interview. In this regard, I conducted an interview of myself to ensure that I bracketed my experiences from those of the participants. The act of bracketing was an essential activity because, while I experienced the same phenomenon (Dr. Clark) as the participants, my interview revealed how strongly I felt about my experience at Eastside High School.

Bracketing does not remove my experiences from the study. Instead, my interview assisted me in noting areas of bias. Because I was able to bracket my experiences and acknowledge my biases, I was able to conduct the interviews without influencing the responses of the participants. This included avoiding agreeing or disagreeing with the participants; a phenomenologist must listen.

I acknowledge that I believe that many of my fellow students' lives were changed for the better because of Mr. Joe Clark and his leadership, disciplinary methods, communication strategies, and the genuine love and concern I believe he had for his students' well-being. He was a father-figure to me, and I relied on him for stability, and I relied on the stability of Eastside High School.

I suggest that Dr. Clark motivated his students, believed in them, and desired for them to gain an education. The sacrifices that I think he made to ensure his students were educated in a safe environment, further colored my role as a researcher. The beauty of phenomenology is that my experiences are data-driven and can be used to explore further knowledge, rather than having to be obliterated.

Participant Criteria

The twenty-three participants for this study were purposefully selected based on a set of criteria to select students, teachers, and administrators who could provide an information-rich perception of Mr.

Joe Clark's leadership. Mr. Joe Clark, the main subject of this book, students who attended Eastside High School from 1980 to 1992 and teachers and administrators who worked at Eastside before, during, and after Joe Clark's tenure was invited and selected to participate in the study. Each participant chose their pseudonym.

I interviewed twenty-three informants, including Dr. Clark. Both male (13) and female (10) participated in the study. The participants were asked to self-identify their cultural background. The participants are African American (14), Biracial (1), German (1), Italian (3), Jamaican (3), and White American (1) descent.

Participant Characteristics

The participants share the following characteristics: They were a student during the time that Mr. Joe Clark was principal during 1982 and 1989. They were teachers or administrators who worked at Eastside prior to, during, and after Joe Clark's tenure. They had a variety of socioeconomic statuses, and they had a variety of experiences while attending Eastside, more specifically, students who were successful as well as students who may have had challenges academically and behaviorally. They had a variety of involvements while working at Eastside High School, more specifically teachers and administrators who worked well with Dr. Clark and in contrast, others who did not and disagreed with his leadership style.

My purpose in this study was not to generalize its findings to a larger population, but rather to deeply understand a phenomenon. In this regard, I interviewed informants until the point of saturation was reached. The point of saturation was reached when the researcher ceased to learn additional data from participants.

CHAPTER 6

Table 1 - Teacher and Administrator Profiles

Name	Sex	Race	EHS Alum	Years at EHS	Years in EDU	Degree Earned	Job Title
Coach "O"	M	Italian Polish American	No	10	32	Masters	Principal
Coach Rosser	M	Jamaican American	Yes Class 1969	23	30	Masters	Social Worker
Mr. 13	M	African American	No	22	43	Masters	Principal
Mr. "B"	M	African American	Yes Class 1969	35	38	Masters	Assistant to the Principal
Mr. Will	M	Italian American	No	28	39	Masters	Guidance Counselor Dept. Ch.
Ms. Annette	F	African American	Yes Class 1980	23	34	Masters	Principal
Ms. De-Mo	F	Italian Scottish American	Yes Class 1963	38	43	Masters	Assistant Principal
Ms. Florence J	F	White American	No	34	39	Masters	Principal
Ms. Smiley	F	German American	No	27	30	Masters	Science Teacher
Joe Clark	M	African American	No	9	30	Masters	Retired

The detailed findings and support evidence that emerged through the data analysis conducted are included in this chapter. The chapter begins with the participants' demographic information, including their profiles. I will begin by providing demographic information on the teacher and administrator informants that will be followed by information regarding their views of Dr. Clark and EHS. Secondly, I will take the same approach with the knowledge that was gathered from former EHS students. Following that, I will share Dr. Clark's interview and provide additional insight into his leadership, the strategies he utilized at Eastside High School, and the emerging themes garnered from the informant interviews.

Demographic Information of Teachers and Administrators

The participants for this study were purposefully selected based on a set of criteria, as described in chapter 5, to select teachers and administrators who can provide a thick information-rich perception of Dr. Clark's leadership.

Ten individuals, both male (6) and female (4), participated in the study. Four of the ten participants are alumni who attended EHS as early as 1963, before Mr. Joe Clark's arrival. The ten participants were African American (4), German (1), Italian (3), Jamaican (1), and White American (1) descent.

The ten teachers and administrator informants have their master's degrees in various majors, including education, science, and social work. One informant is currently seeking her doctoral degree.

Five of the ten are currently principals. One is an assistant principal. One is an assistant to the principal for discipline. Of the remainder, one is a Guidance Department chairperson, one is a social worker who is working for the Paterson Board of Education Central Office, and one is a science teacher, and Dr. Clark is retired.

Together they worked at Eastside High School for over 265 years and jointly worked in education for more than 350 years. Their current salaries range from $93,678.00 to over $160,000.

Teacher and Administrator Participant Profiles

Coach "O" – an Italian Polish American male, was born and raised in an urban setting in New Brunswick, New Jersey. He volunteered that he is a believer in the Catholic faith. He worked at Eastside for ten years from 1981-1991 (one year prior to and two years after Joe Clark's tenure). He has worked in education for thirty-four years; as a teacher for fifteen years, a vice principal for nine years and principal for ten years. He also coached the male varsity basketball team at EHS. He was a coach at EHS before becoming a teacher.

When interviewed, he talked about how he did not have a choice of whether or not to teach at Eastside High School because, "when Joe Clark became principal, he wanted all coaches to teach in order to control their athletes and to help with overall discipline."

However, "Joe Clark told me that after one year if I didn't like it, he would transfer me... I stayed for ten years. I liked it." He described Paterson in the 1980s and 90s as having a diverse culture that was predominantly African American, a typical urban city with "good areas" and "bad areas." Conversely, currently, predominantly Hispanic/Bengali families have moved in during the last ten years and are the central residents in Paterson, which is still characterized as an urban setting.

Coach "O" stated that he always got respect from most of the students... "If they believed that you were sincere about teaching them... they respected you." *Coach "O"* described his fondest memories... "I loved the interactions of the students... teenagers who cared... most of them did care about their life and their future."

"They could tell if you were not sincere and honest with them." He described his not so positive memories as having to deal with negative students, "although most were just eager teenagers willing to learn... 90%

of them were good, and 10% were terrible but that 10% dominated the papers [news media] making Eastside High School a lousy place.

He also talked about how students were robbed and had items stolen from them by fellow students such as money, sneakers, boots, and Walkman radios. He described Eastside as having more negative qualities than positive before Joe Clark's arrival.

He further stated that learning was not a priority for students before Dr. Clark arrived. It was just a "place to hang out" and be around friends. He described the academic and teaching environment as teachers having to deal with "discipline first and teaching second," and that the teachers' mentality was just "to survive and learning was not number one," and that drugs and gangs were in existence at all times on the outside environment of the high school.

He also talked about the infamous controversy regarding Dr. Clark locking and chaining the doors of the school, and he stated that "he [Clark] did what he had to do; however, it was a safety issue." *Coach "O"* shared some of his accomplishments that he is very proud of, such as being a principal for ten years, vice-principal for nine years, a teacher for thirteen years, a varsity basketball coach with a record with 101 wins versus 37 losses, and two Passaic County championships in 1990 and 1991.

He left Eastside High School in 1991 to become the vice-principal at another public school in Paterson, New Jersey.

Coach "O" described Dr. Clark as being "very pro-student!" He stated that he was very excited when he heard Dr. Clark was the "new leader." He believed that Dr. Clark's leadership style had a direct, positive effect on developing his leadership style and stated that "I became an administrator as a result of my relationship with him." *Coach "O"* described that while he was teaching English and coaching girls' softball and boys' basketball, he was attending graduate school to get his Master's degree in Urban

Education/Administration.

Dr. Clark knew this and provided him with additional opportunities to enhance his experiences in administration. Dr. Clark took over Coach "O's" daily supervision periods and assigned him to other vice principals so he could see their daily routines and help where needed.

Dr. Clark gave him summer school administrative positions, where he supervised staff and students. *Coach "O"* believed that Dr. Clark took an interest in him because he recalls Clark saying, "I see a lot of potential in you because of your commitment to the district and the children of Paterson."

Coach "O" described Dr. Clark's as always being pro-student, and while observing him during his tenure at Eastside, he stated that Dr. Clark "lived by the three F's - he was FRIENDLY, he was FAIR, and he was FIRM if need be." *Coach "O"* stated that he made the students feel wanted, and "gave them the confidence that they can overcome most situations, and yet he gave them the "tough love approach if needed."

He said Dr. Clark made each student feel important in his or her unique way. Additionally, Dr. Clark provided buses for fans and students to away football and basketball games, and he developed a sense of *pride* within the school that was never evident before his time there.

According to *Coach "O,"* Eastside was a better place because of Dr. Clark's guidance and leadership. *Coach "O"* described two situations where Dr. Clark took money out of his own wallet and gave it to students, one, where a student needed money for a prom bid and another where a basketball player did not have money to buy team sneakers. He stated that he was sure that there were many other situations too.

Coach "O" described Dr. Clark's interactions with staff; he stated that Dr. Clark always treated you fairly unless he realized that you were not going to be a positive influence on the students.

Dr. Clark wanted all staff to work extremely hard, not only in the academic areas but also in the social development of each child. Dr. Clark wanted you to make a direct impact on their lives. If you were a staff member who was "going through the motions" in the classroom, he would transfer you.

According to Coach "O," Dr. Clark would document informal and formal observations and collect enough information to validate his rationale for the transfer. *Coach "O"* stated that in time, Dr. Clark created a positive working environment for approximately 250 staff members at Eastside High School.

Coach "O" stated that overall, Dr. Clark did change the culture at Eastside. His leadership skills made both the students and staff feel wanted and cared for." Also, "Yes, I am sure that he wasn't always perfect, *but* he was right for the school and the need for his leadership, which made the school a better place."

Coach "O" described his thoughts about the *Lean on Me* movie as: "The movie was on target! Morgan Freeman played him perfectly. He followed Dr. Clark around the school for three weeks. I never saw him take notes, but he played him perfectly. He was the perfect actor to play Joe Clark." He stated that he still has a copy of the movie, and his children have watched it several times. If he could say something to Joe Clark right now, he would tell him, "A big *thank you.*"

Coach Rosser - *Coach Rosser* is an African American male whose grandparents are from Jamaica, West Indies. He worked at Eastside for twenty-three years from 1981 to 2004 (one year prior and fifteen years after Joe Clark's tenure). He has worked in education for thirty years as a social worker. He also coached football and basketball.

When interviewed, he told me he was a graduate of Eastside and requested to work there because he "wanted to give back to the school that helped him so much." He described Paterson in the 1980s and 90s and currently "an urban setting with many social and economic problems."

He described his students as "motivated to learn and having to deal with so many social issues," and that's because "we live in an urban setting, and they are part of the community, and whatever is happening in the community, they have to deal with it in the school."

Coach Rosser described Eastside (prior to Joe Clark) as "calm and relaxed without the media coverage" and stated that the academic environment focused more on the needs of the students, and as a social worker he was thoroughly "aware of all the facets of the school and tried to be a good listener and a fair adult." He described his fondest memories as the years he attended Eastside High School as well as his graduation. He described his not so positive memories as "in 1969 during the student protests when the police officers removed students from Eastside."

Coach Rosser indicated that there were drugs and drug dealers in the school, and students had their popular items stolen, "it happened but not often." He also stated that there were gangs at Eastside, and the gangs were more affiliated with each neighborhood. He also agreed that there was violence at Eastside, "but it was not as much as the media portrayed it to be."

Coach Rosser felt that Joe Clark was media-oriented and described his relationship with Dr. Clark as "not good" and stated that "I respected him, but I did not agree with him." He described the controversies at Eastside as "too many to recall, but all were really blown up by the media." Moreover, "many routine student issues were turned into media issues."

Coach Rosser stated that Dr. Clark did have an effect on his life and described it as, "how *not* to treat students and their families and that it was difficult to work with Dr. Clark."

He believed that Joe Clark's leadership style was "driven by media coverage and personal gain" and that he thought his leadership was "weak." *Coach Rosser* found that Dr. Clark used "personal appeal" strategies to connect with the students, and does *not* believe Dr. Clark was a good principal, although he thinks Dr. Clark was "a good leader with poor strategies and tactics."

He also stated that he thought Dr. Clark treated teachers and other administrators in "a disrespectful manner" and believed that the *Lean on Me* movie was "a Hollywood version of things that were supposed to have happened. It presented our community negatively."

If he could say something to Joe Clark right now, he would tell him, "enjoy your retirement." He left Eastside in 2004 to become the school social worker for the central office of the Paterson Public School system.

Mr. 13 - is an African American male who worked at Eastside for twenty-two years from 1973 to 1995 (nine years prior and six years after Joe Clark's tenure). He has worked in education for thirty-eight years as a teacher, a department head, coach, vice-principal and principal. When interviewed, he talked about how he wanted to start his teaching career at Eastside because that is where he did his student teaching, and he was assigned to teach there by the Paterson Board of Education.

He described Paterson in the 1980s and 90s as a "city that was economically challenged. White flight had begun. Some of the city's major businesses had left the city." Moreover, currently, the "city is experiencing an economic and cultural revival."

Mr. 13 stated that before his employment at Eastside, "some teachers said that the students did not care, and staff had no expectations for the students." He described some of his fondest memories as his "first day; the opening of a new wing; his appointment as vice principal and working with

Dr. Clark was definitely a memorable experience."

He described his not so positive memories of dealing with some of the student violence, and he called it "unsettling." He described Eastside High School prior to Joe Clark as "never a dull moment" and that "expectations were not as high as they should have been regarding the academic and teaching environment.

Mr. 13 described himself as a teacher and administrator who was "concerned, willing, and able to exceed expectations." Moreover, he was an advisor, coach, and mentor to many students. He described the students as "like students everywhere. They wanted the best life had to offer." Also, "a small percentage of what would be considered, honor students, did well. Teachers were not held accountable to the extent possible for the quality of instruction delivered to students."

He described the gangs at Eastside as "not in the sense of what we have today. Students gravitated to their ethnic groups." *Mr. 13* stated that "Dr. Clark was committed to making the school better. I supported his efforts as a classroom teacher and an administrator. I taught before Dr. Clark arrived. I did not need his presence to raise my expectations of students."

Mr. 13 described his relationship with Dr. Clark as "agreeable at most times." When asked about the controversies at Eastside, he stated that "the denial of due process and the theatrics at times were trying." Moreover, "I learned from them. Dr. Clark was placed in a unique situation, and he made the most of it." *Mr. 13* believed that Dr. Clark had an impact on his life and stated, "Yes, his work ethic was admirable. He truly, at the beginning of his time at the school, placed the interests of the students before his personal ambitions."

Regarding the strategies Dr. Clark used, *Mr. 13* stated that it was "hard to separate the theater from reality at times. He [Clark] used student-centered approaches when striving to connect with students, and he held teachers and administrators accountable for their actions." Concerning Dr. Clark's leadership, he thought it was "puzzling when dealing with staff. If he respected you, he treated you with respect, if not "lookout!"

Mr. 13 stated that Dr. Clark's initial leadership style was appropriate for the challenges he faced and did not believe he would have had the same impact if he would have applied a different form of leadership. *Mr. 13* found that Dr. Clark was a good principal and also thought he was a good leader "at first."

Mr. 13 further described "Dr. Clark as an interesting study of human relationships. He lost sight of his dream when the school became secondary to personal fortune and recognition." He described the memories he had with Joe Clark as "good, some not so good, but most of the memories were good and that Dr. Clark encouraged him to pursue a principal's position." Moreover, that he is "grateful for the guidance and the opportunity that Dr. Clark afforded him."

Some of *Mr. 13*'s accomplishments consist of being Teacher of the Year at Eastside and being a principal for seventeen years at two different schools. He believed that the *Lean on Me* movie was "Hollywood at its best; I did not like the portrayals of our students. There were and still are so many great students at Eastside." Also, when asked, if you could say something to Dr. Clark right now, he would say, "Thank you, what a ride!"

Mr. "B" - is an African American male who worked at Eastside for thirty-five years from 1974 to 2009 (eight years prior and 20 years after Joe Clark's tenure). He has worked in education for thirty-eight years, thirteen years as a history teacher, and twenty-five years as an assistant to the principal.

Mr. "B" was appointed as the first assistant to the principal and special assistant for discipline by Dr. Clark's. *Mr. "B"* is a graduate of Eastside, Class of 1969. While in his first year at Boston College, his father passed away, and due to the financial strain of his two brothers and his sister also attending college, he came home. *Mr. "B"* later transferred to William Paterson University, where he graduated in 1974.

After college, he began to play professional football. He played with the world football league first, then the Philadelphia Bells, and after that league went bankrupt, his football contract was picked up by the New York Jets. His contract ended in 1977 and was acquired by the New York Giants in 1978. He played in the professional league for a total of four years. During the football seasons, *Mr. "B"* took a leave of absence from September to December, and then he returned to work at Eastside in January every year.

Mr. "B" provided valuable information regarding his experiences while working with Dr. Clark. When he first met Dr. Clark several years before Dr. Clark's appointment at EHS, he felt a teaching connection between himself and Dr. Clark because they both were interested in teaching African Studies and history. He stated,

> So naturally, he and I being friends, he asked me about what the situation was at Eastside? Also, being that I had gone to that school, I graduated from the school, and came back and became a teacher there, I had a pretty good knowledge of what was going on there. I had seen quite a bit. Also, I experienced it as well, at that point.

> I was asked by Dr. Napier [Superintendent of Paterson Public Schools] to visit with Dr. Clark at school number six to set up an outline as to what I felt he needed to concern himself with if he wanted to come to Eastside as the new principal and make a difference. Well, we met for quite a few hours weekly at Public School # 6 to dialogue and exchange ideas, and that became the means of him becoming the principal. As a result of that, he took the job.

Mr. *"B"* shared some vital information regarding Dr. Clark's first meeting with teachers and administrators that provided some awareness of how Dr. Clark's initial interaction was when he was introduced as the brand new principal. He stated that when Dr. Clark came to EHS, he "was armed with a whole lot of information about staff, about problems and situations with students. So he addressed them immediately." Mr. *"B"* described the first meeting below

> The information we gathered and shared, he presented it to the staff in the auditorium. He brought me to the stage and announced this is Mr. *"B,"* He is my assistant, he's my partner, and 99.9% of what he says comes from me, do as he says! So at that point, the assistant to the principal position was created. I was promoted from a teacher to his assistant.
>
> Naturally, some of my colleagues felt betrayed, not betrayed, but let down because there were some people there who thought that they had been there longer than I had and assumed that they should have maybe had an opportunity to have that position. However, Dr. Clark knew different, and no one could persuade Dr. Clark once he made up his mind to do something.

Mr. *"B"* stated that Dr. Clark knew about the different little groups and cliques, and the "teacher games because I gave him the rundown on those departments and individuals in those departments who were kind of like the leaders or the heads, or advisers of other teachers." Mr. *"B"* revealed what some of the teachers said because they thought no one would find out.

For example, teachers would say, "I will cover for you, I'll sign-in for you, I'll cover your class until you get back," or, "here are my lesson plans, you know nobody is going to check, nobody is going to know." Mr. *"B"* believed that he was *not* the only one that Dr. Clark was soliciting to gain information about what was going at Eastside.

Mr. "B" stated that Dr. Clark addressed those things. He believed that Dr. Clark put him in an interesting spot because he was the "kind of leader who didn't hold back."

> I mean, he went on the stage and said names! Called out names!... Ms. So-and-so, I know about you taking your fifteen coffee breaks. Mr. So-and-so, I know about this…, and you know people were saying wow! Man, how does he know about all of this? Moreover, of course, they looked at me. So I think at that point, my real role in the Paterson Public School System was established.
>
> Hey, I don't care! If you're not doing what you are supposed to do, then you should be exposed! So that was me. I guess I was known for (Laughs) as a matter of fact, and it was a funny situation because the folks that had the nerve to say anything negative about Dr. Joe Clark or me would say it undercover. I got the title of "Big E Rat" by guys, and so they called me "Big E Rat." Me being the person that I am, I didn't give a hoot about what they said. Because no one said anything to my face, you know, I was the big NFL brute and liked to beat up on people, so nobody said anything. They wouldn't dare say it!

When asked about the 300 students who were kicked out of Eastside, *Mr. "B"* explained that during the first week of class Dr. Clark called a meeting with the guidance counselors and told them to bring all records of every student that was eighteen years old or older that you know cannot graduate.

The list of students was trimmed down to about 300 students who were hanging out and had no intention of graduating. Dr. Clark called a special meeting with all the students on the list, and during the assembly, he shared with them the importance of being in school and what school was about, and at the end of his conversation he told the students that they "were no longer members of the Eastside High School family! Now get up! Also, get out!"

Mr. "B" and the other security guards created a trail of staff members from the auditorium to the exit door, and all of the students had to exit the building. "We marched them to the exit door, as a matter of fact, we marched them from the auditorium out the door and to the curb!"

Mr. "B" explained that "this was done through their actual records because we had kids that were eighteen and nineteen years old who only had enough credits to be sophomore student status. As a result, the expelled students and their parents called the Paterson Board of Education and contacted the news media.

When asked his opinion on how Dr. Clark treated the teachers, he stated that the teachers whom Dr. Clark believed were productive teachers were treated well and liked professionals. However, the ones that he thought were not good were "treated like they acted."

He further explained that those teachers were not good and did not show real concern for and about the students; he [Clark] confronted them by asking, "Why are you not doing this? Why are you not doing that? Do you know John's mother? Do you know his father? Have you ever called them to find out why he's not doing what he's supposed to do?" If the teacher could respond to these questions, then they were in good standing with Dr. Clark.

However, when they did not respond appropriately, the following day, a policy was created to require teachers to be sure they knew each of their students and reached out to their parents using what were called parent log sheets.

Mr. "B" also shared that when Dr. Clark came to a class, he would ask teachers for their roll books and lesson plans while he sat in the class and observed what they were doing. He would read through notes for each student's attendance and assignment record and would ask questions about students who may have missed work assignments or were absent.

He wanted to know if the parents were contacted and wanted to see the communication log sheets to verify that the teacher did, indeed, communicate with the parents of the student. Mr. "B' stated that "he made them step up their game, so that was a good piece. He held everybody accountable for their job and their position."

There were occasions when Dr. Clark and *Mr. "B,"* told teachers to "get their bags, get their stuff and get out!" when they did not comply with Dr. Clark's rules and regulations. Furthermore, *Mr. "B"* stated that Dr. Clark actually "kind of never ejected anyone unless he had his information or little notes to defend the actions."

Mr. "B" believed that this strategy "woke up teachers to get on the ball." He went on to explain that some of the teachers who left, were caught by Dr. Clark when he walked by the classroom and noticed teachers reading newspapers, students staring out the window and chitchatting while they were supposed to be learning, and teachers were arriving late from lunch.

Mr. "B" also stated that at times, students were left in the class by themselves without teacher supervision, and some teachers did not show a genuine interest in the kids. According to *Mr. "B,"* Dr. Clark was disgusted with the unorthodox behavior displayed by male and female teachers who dated students. He remembered that Dr. Clark used to say,

> "The hens are messing with the roosters and the roosters messing with the hens." That was the title of his assembly. He said, "all you hens leave my roosters alone" or "leave my little chickens alone." That was his message to the teachers. He yelled at them, telling them, "you are too old for those kids and you old guys; leave these young girls alone!"

Unfortunately, I have firsthand knowledge that disgustingly, there were several teachers (male and female) dating students while I was a student. I am aware of at least one of my classmates who have three children by one of our teachers, and she had her first baby while we were students. There were also some staff members who married students. I can remember at least three male teachers who made inappropriate comments to me as a student. I also have classmates who shared with me that they were driven to the local Eastside Park and had sex with their teachers in the teachers' car. I am elated that the laws have changed and are more stringent concerning inappropriate relationships between teachers and students.

I asked Mr. *B.* if he could share some controversial occurrences that happened with teachers, he shared two examples that were portrayed in the movie *Lean on Me* that were actual incidences that occurred at Eastside.

> Oh, I can talk about Ms. Green, [pseudonym] she was a music teacher. She was old-fashioned; she was more like a theater-type music teacher, dramatized to music. She expressed through music, and maybe once or twice, Dr. Clark had remarked, "you know black people don't do that."

> He wanted some life, some movement in her music, and you know she kind of rejected him saying that and feeling like that. So I'm not a chauvinist or anything, but her being a woman challenged him. Also, I guess she got the fight she was looking for. He walked her to the door.

He further explained that if you did not see eye-to-eye with Dr. Clark, he would definitely challenge you, and you always had the opportunity to respond. *Mr. "B"* admitted that there were very few opportunities that a teacher's response changed Joe Clark's mind. *Mr. "B"* believed Dr. Clark's tenure was a success he stated,

> It was successful in the sense that he exposed a lot of the teacher's and administrator's shortfalls. He made sure that the negative things that the teachers weren't doing were revealed. Many people work in education think that they are doing what they are supposed to do. When indeed, they are not. They get stuck in their mess. Dr. Clark defined what education should be in high school.

Additionally, he discussed Dr. Clark's philosophy on how teachers and administrators should feel about the students with whom they worked. He stated,

> You should have concern for these kids; you should not just be in the classroom, standing in front of them, making them think that you are better than them, because you went to college; show them why you are better; show them what you know, what they should know. He [Clark] made them come back on Saturdays to watch the kids participate in sports.

> He would say to me; I want the list of everybody, all the teachers who showed up to the games. I would give him a list. He would say I want a list of all the teachers who speed out of here at the end of the day because nobody wants to stay and tutor these kids after school. Also, as a result of that, the bell would ring, and the parking lot would be like school was starting. Nobody would speed out of here anymore.

> You know, because Joe Clark would say, "you don't care about these kids." He exposed a lot, and he enlightened many people on how they should feel about working in the inner-city with our kids. Moreover, some of that I am still working in the public school system, and some of that is still around. So you often hear, "Oh, what are you a Joe Clark? Are you trying to be a Joe Clark?" I hear some of the staff members saying that to administrators.

Mr. "B" shared the story of why he left Eastside one year before Dr. Clark left.

> I left actually before Joe Clark left because he and I at some point kind of well, I will say we had different ideas after the book writing of the story of Joe Clark. You know. I never wanted everybody to know that I was his muscle, and it was said to him many, many, many, many times. You wouldn't do this, and you wouldn't be saying that shit if Mr. "B" wasn't here with you. So I got that a lot. You know. So even with some of my friends, they would say, man, why do you do that? Why do you back that joker? Man, he ain't right!

> Do you know the situation that you saw in the movie with that teacher that picked up the paper in the lunchroom? Mr. "R.?" He and I were

childhood friends. We grew up together, and we lived next door, around the block from each other, up until the 12th grade. So when he [Dr. Clark] went after Mr. "R" about not standing still in the auditorium… The situation really happened in the auditorium during an assembly.

He [Joe Clark] wanted him out! I didn't agree with that. I mean Mr. "R" was my friend, and he was not defiant. However, he didn't hear Joe Clark's instructions, and again Dr. Clark was on the stage, and he said," Mr. "R" you are to be still or be quiet!" or something like that and Mr. "R" was like... "Who are you talking to, man? I am not one of these kids!" and Dr. Clark said, "get out! And go to my office! So he told him to go to his office. And Mr. "R" being the strong black man that he is... said, (Yelling) "I'm not going anywhere! Make me!"

And oh, boy! Now, now, Mr. "R" is my friend. We were colleagues, and we still are to this very day. However, he got him out! Because he was the basketball coach and Dr. Clark said, you will never coach another game in this place! This and that moreover, he was the girls' basketball coach, and that he wanted him out and it got really crazy!

Because Mr. "R" tried to get him! He went after him! And of course, I'm Joe Clark's savior. I stopped Mr. "R" and Mr. "R," said (Yelling) if it weren't for Mr. "B," I would kill you! I'll do this!, and I'll do that! And as I am escorting Mr. "R" to the door… Dr. Clark is following behind me and pointing at him and saying (Yelling). You're done! You're finished here!

I was saying Dr. Clark, please, man! Come on!... because now Mr. "R" is already provoked! Mr. "R" walked out, and he left. He got to the bottom of the steps, and he invited Joe Clark out (to a fight!); he said to Dr. Clark, come out here now! You so bad! Come out here now! *Mr. "B"*: you stay in there! Let him come by himself! (Laughing) Dr. Clark wouldn't go!

So now a few hours went by, and a little bit after that Dr. Clark called me to the office, and he had one of his secretaries type up what Mr.

"R" had said to him, and he put it in front of me and told me to sign it. I would not sign it because that was not the whole story. The man was provoked, and he was responding to Dr. Clark's actions

So Joe Clark said to me that, if you're loyal to me, you're with me! Or you're against me! Alternatively, something like that. You know I said, Dr. Clark, I have been faithful to you all of these years, but I can't sign that. So that was the beginning of my end with Joe Clark. Also, as time went by, things began to change with Dr. Clark.

When the idea of the movie started, and after the Mr. "R" incident, the kids started saying things about Dr. Clark, such as, "you ain't nothing without *Mr. "B"* and that became a little thorn in his side. He called me in the office one day and told me one time that "this place is not big enough for the both of us" and I guess you got to go, and that was kind of it for me.

Later, I spoke with Dr. Napier, and I said look man; I got to go now because you know, I have done a lot of stuff for Joe Clark, and I'm still here now, without his blessing. I was still there with my colleagues so that they felt that I had not betrayed them but changed. So as a result, I was transferred to school # 4, and then the next year, Joe Clark left. Moreover, later, Mr. Lighty, his executive vice principal, became the principal, and he called me back. He wanted me back at Eastside, and I remained there for 20 years.

Mr. Will - is an Italian American male who worked at Eastside for twenty-eight years from 1972 to 2000 (ten years prior and eleven years after Joe Clark's tenure). He has worked in education for thirty-nine years as a guidance counselor and currently holds the position as Guidance Department chairperson in the central office of the Paterson Public School System.

When interviewed, he told me that when he applied to the Paterson Public School system, there was only one teacher of English position available, and it happened to be at Eastside. He described Eastside before

Joe Clark as "it was totally out of control!" Also, the outside environment was "dangerous."

He described his students as "respectful, caring, cooperative, and eager to learn." He described his fondest memories as "the camaraderie among the staff, students and parents," and his not so positive memory was the "tragic death" of one of his students.

Mr. Will stated that there was violence at Eastside before Clark and that it was due to poor management. He also said that he supported Joe Clark when he first stepped into the building and that he believed he used successful strategies and thought about and discussed everything out before acting.

He believed that Dr. Clarks' leadership skills were excellent and described them as "absolutely strong" and stated that "too bad he could not use them to run the district." He further believed that if Dr. Clark's leadership were not as strong, he would not have had the same impact. He thought that Dr. Clark treated all students as individuals, and he always approached them with a positive attitude. Not only does he believe Dr. Clark was a good leader and principal, but he also stated, "he was the *best!*"

He believed that Dr. Clark treated the teachers and administrators "fairly, with honesty and respect." He stated that it was a "pleasure and an honor" to work with Dr. Clark. When asked if he remembered the *Lean on Me* movie he said,

> Of course! I watched the whole movie as it was being filmed. I met Morgan Freeman and Robert Guillaume. The movie was a little exaggerated--not much. I thought it gave a clear perspective of what EHS was like pre-Joe Clark and during his administration. No, I was not in the movie; however, my wife was.

When asked if he could say something to Dr. Clark right now, what would you say? He stated, "You were the best administrator, PPS's [Paterson Public School's] has ever had. Too bad you weren't assigned to the position of the superintendent. If you were, the district would probably be in better shape than it is today!"

Ms. Annette - is an African American female who worked at Eastside for twenty-three years from 1982 to 2005 (she began working at Eastside during the same year Joe Clark started to and worked sixteen years after his tenure). She has worked in education for twenty-nine years. She was an English teacher for twenty years, a vice principal for three years, and currently serves as a high school principal in Paterson, New Jersey. She also served as the advisor to the class of 1987.

When interviewed, she told me that she was a graduate of Eastside, and she decided to work there because she knew Eastside was not as bad as it was rumored to be, and she also felt that it "needed teachers who cared."

She described Paterson in the 1980s and 90s as economically deprived and that "it was safe to be out and about during the daylight, but at night was another story." She stated that Paterson is currently "dangerous in many areas."

Ms. Annette discussed several negative things that happened before her employment, as well as during the time that she worked at EHS. Some of those incidences consisted of, "adults dating students; fights among students, staff assaults and stealing were normal occurrences." She described students at Eastside as diverse academically and economically, and she described the outside environment as a neighborhood that is generally unkempt and drug-infested.

She described her fondest memories as being an advisor to the class of 1987 and described her not so positive memories as having to deal with the "negativity among a few staff members."

Ms. Annette mentioned that Dr. Clark treated teachers and other administrators in such a way that "he seemed to respect those who stood up for themselves and those who were committed to their jobs; for those he did not like, he tried to get them to quit or transfer." She stated that she had a positive working relationship with Dr. Clark.

She reported that she worked well with him, and he was supportive of her endeavors and was concerned about her professional growth. She further stated that he "made life fun, unpredictable, and exciting; I think he was a good school manager who was needed at that time." She talked about one of the controversies that amused her, which was the formation of the "virgin club" that was put together by Dr. Clark.

Ms. Annette believed that Dr. Clark had an impact on her life because she "learned a lot from him" regarding teaching and administration. She thought that Dr. Clark was a strategist and that he was a good disciplinarian who led with wisdom, and he was aware of what he was up against.

She believed that his leadership style was solid and believed that it would not have had the same impact if he tried another type of leadership. She thought that Joe Clark established successful strategies to connect with the students and that "tough love" was the dominant strategy that was used.

Ms. Annette is proud of her educational attainment of one bachelor's degree and two master's degrees; she is currently pursuing her doctorate. She believed that the *Lean on Me* movie "was mostly a Hollywood production that greatly exaggerated what Eastside was like before Joe Clark's arrival. She stated that it was cast well with Morgan Freeman as Dr. Clark. It was good entertainment."

If she could say something to Dr. Clark right now, she would tell him, "Thanks for your encouragement and support; thanks for caring about the students."

Ms. De-Mo - is an Italian Scottish American female who worked at

Eastside for forty-two years from 1972 to the present (seventeen years prior and twenty-five years after Joe Clark's tenure). She worked as a full-time substitute, an English teacher, English Department chairperson and currently serves as an assistant principal at Eastside and has served in this role since 2003.

She has served as an advisor to six classes, 1979, 1998, 1996, 1998, 2004 and 2009 and assisted as an advisor to the poetry club and worked with the school yearbook staff.

When interviewed, she told me that she was a graduate of Eastside and that she "never really left since 1963!" She stated that she just "fell into this job" She was a substitute at Eastside, and later realized that it was not like John F. Kennedy High School because the staff at Eastside was friendlier, more helpful. The staff cared more about the students, and she enjoyed the students as well.

She remembered that there were rumors about Eastside prior to her employment that included gangs and violence since 1975, and in fact, EHS was referred to as a "Cauldron of Violence" in the newspaper headlines back in the late 70s. In addition, she stated that the New Jersey prosecutors' office conducted a significant investigation because several teachers were attacked by students, and ultimately this led to Dr. Clark being hired.

She remembered Dr. Clark telling the Paterson Schools' superintendent that he needed "free rein" to "clean up" Eastside High School. She also remembered the student protests that were being held in 1969 to bring about changes in the curriculum, and the need for the culture of the school to reflect the increasingly growing black population.

As a result of the student protests, courses such as Black poetry, Black drama, Black literature, and Black history were introduced into the curriculum. She also shared one story about how the students conducted a "power to the penny" protest, where all the students paid for their lunches with pennies, and as a consequence, this slowed down the serving lines in the lunchroom so that lunch was not finished before the bell rang.

As a result, new food selections were added with parent and student input. An African American vice principal was assigned the next year, and staff integration took place as vacancies occurred.

Ms. De-Mo described what Eastside was like prior to Joe Clark. She stated that it was overcrowded, there were lots of fights, the smell of marijuana was in some stairwells and bathrooms, and there were open defiance and disrespect of the teachers and students, although the majority of the students were good kids. She indicated there were overcrowded classes (sometimes up to 47 students per classroom, where students had to sit on the floor, on radiators and shared desks), and unfortunately taught by teachers who "passed the time" by "handing out word puzzles, and worksheets and not truly teaching."

She also stated that some teachers would leave the building and had their colleagues take their students and put them into their classrooms. She reported that the heat never worked in the "old" building, and there were "false alarms and bomb scares almost every week and sometimes several times in one day, and the outsiders [non-students] would enter the building to walk and talk with friends and start fights, and the students cut class a lot!"

Ms. De-Mo shared that she did not have a relationship with the previous principal during that time, although he lived down the block from her in Paterson, and she only knew him by sight. She stated that,

> It turned out later that he was "blamed" for the violence and out-of-control school (by the press, parents, and some staff), and I was vocal about my attack and some situations. He did not look too "favorably" on me during his last years…

Yes, prior to Dr. Clark. In 1978, several staff attacks caused the teachers to protest by sitting out in an in-service presentation. Teachers all met in the cafeteria and refused to leave - we wanted the administrators to spend the time addressing the attacks, and other issues of "no control."

She described what the academic and teaching environment was like prior to Dr. Clark and stated that,

> Good teachers taught; others got by, and a few were disgraces to the profession. One colleague in math never recorded a grade – Never! – He gave report card grades out by memory. I remember him, in late June, making upgrades to fill his grade book that had to be submitted in June. That was probably the worst example.

> Teachers, who break the law, are placed on administrative leave until the results of the case are final. If guilty, they are dismissed, and the district can petition the state to end the staff member's tenure. I can think of four teachers at this school who were in this position during my forty-two years here.

When asked if there were drugs or drug dealers at the school, she stated,

> Yes! I saw one of my students, Terry, selling marijuana out of a plastic bag in the hallway during class travel time – right out in the open. He was killed a few years later, found dead in a local housing project. I also entered the violence and vandalism reports for the school, so I am aware of drug selling that took place, there have not been many cases in the last several years here.

When asked if students were robbed and beaten up for their popular items? She stated,

> Yes! Years ago, coats were taken (fleece and leather). More currently, it has been iPods and cell phones. Sneakers are also taken. While walking home, students were/are jumped (beat up) for cell phones, iPods, and money. It doesn't happen in school, but items left unattended like the cell phones and iPods are now stolen.

When asked if there were gangs at Eastside, and what was the status of security? She stated,

> We are located in the middle of the inner-city; we dealt with street life. There were gangs, lots of street noise coming in when windows were opened, outsiders going in and out since the thirty-eight doors did not lock, and we had no guards for all of them. When I first started in 1973, there were two guards – one male and one female.
>
> During the late 70s, more were added. In our school now, we have five board hired guards, and fifteen privatized guards. We did have six police officers for the last six years, but this year they were all cut due to budget cuts. Because of recent police calls to the schools, two officers were brought back to the city high schools.

Ms. De-Mo shared her fondest memories about working at Eastside that included,

> Meeting and working with several wonderful teachers/colleagues, many of whom are still close even though they have retired or left the district. Moreover, touching the lives of thousands of students and many remaining in touch. Along that line, encountering students in their adult lives and seeing that they have gone on to careers such as teaching, law enforcement, fire department. For example, one student is now a principal in Paterson. Others are my colleagues. She also shared great memories of the Clark years, which included entertainers such as Run DMC [Famous rap group], The Winans [Famous gospel music group], and Morton Downey, Jr., [Famous talk show host] appearing and walking through the halls. There are too many to count!

Famous People Who Visited EHS

(Dr. Clark 1988 - Rap Group Run DMC)

Jam, Master Jay.

The kings of rock begin to rock.

(Photos Courtesy of Joe Clark website and EHS Yearbook, 1988 - Rap Group Run DMC)

Is Truman really going to hit me?

Thank you for being a great audience.

(Comedian - Chris Rock & Various Artists – Photos Courtesy of EHS Yearbook, 1988)

(Actor – Ralph Carter – *Good Times* Sitcom – Photos Courtesy of EHS Yearbook, 1988)

(Mr. Berdy & Dr. Clark, Photos Courtesy of EHS Yearbook, 1988)

(Mayor Frank Graves - Photos Courtesy of EHS)

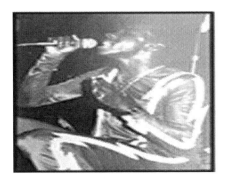

(R&B Artist Bobby Brown)

 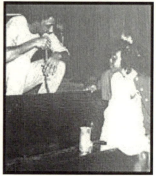

(R&B Artists – New Edition – Photos Courtesy of EHS Yearbook, 1984)

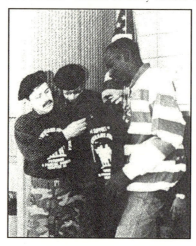

(Founder of the Guardian Angels, Curtis Sliwa – Photos Courtesy of EHS 1984)

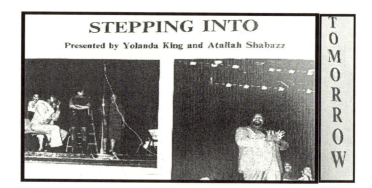

(Civil Rights Activists - Daughters of Dr. Martin Luther King Jr. & Malcolm X – Yolanda King & Atallah Shabazz – Photos Courtesy EHS Yearbook, 1984)

(Professional Basketball Player & Alum – Rory Sparrow – Courtesy of EHS, 1987)

(Civil Rights Icon – Rosa Parks being served lunch by students – Pinky Miller, Derrick McDuffie, Gwen Melvin, Dr. Clark – Photo Courtesy of Pinky Miller)

(Middle photo - Civil Rights Icon – Rosa Parks, Dr. Frank Napier & Mayor Frank Graves – Photo Courtesy of Napier Academy) (Bottom photo - Civil Rights Icon – Rosa Parks, Dr. Clark, Dr. Frank Napier & other city officials – Photo Courtesy of EHS Yearbook, 1983)

(Educator, Lecturer, Author, Dr. Gwendolyn Goldsby Grant & EHS administration & students – Photo Courtesy EHS Yearbook, 1983)

(Photo Courtesy EHS Yearbook, 1983)

(Governor Thomas Kean – Photo Courtesy EHS Yearbook, 1983)

(Governor Thomas Kean & Mayor Frank Graves – Photo Courtesy EHS Yearbook, 1983)

(Governor Thomas Kean & Mayor Frank Graves – Photo Courtesy EHS Yearbook, 1983)

(New Jersey State Commissioner of Education, Saul Cooperman - Third from the left Photo Courtesy EHS Yearbook, 1983)

Ms. De-Mo also talked about her not so positive memories such as "being physically assaulted by a student, and seeing a security guard stabbed in the abdomen," learning of other attacks on colleagues, reading the negative press day after day in the news, and TV cameras and trucks all over the streets as they exited the school every day.

Ms. De-Mo discussed her relationship with Dr. Clark; she stated that she knew him one year before his appointment as principal and that he recommended and pushed her into pursuing her graduate degree in educational administration and supervision.

She also stated that she liked him because he "knew who taught, and who really cared about the students," and he "cleaned house with the teachers," and then he did the "same thing with the students." She mentioned that there were "many students" who had attended Eastside for "five years with less than twenty credits" and were still at a "ninth-grade status." She stated that Dr. Clark tried to find alternative schools and got them out.

She also talked about several controversies that included four male teachers who refused to wear ties (Dr. Clark wanted all males to wear ties and dress professionally). Forcing them to wear ties was against the teachers' contract, and since they refused, they were transferred. Some parents were protesting that their kids were kicked out and "hanging on the streets," and Dr. Clark told the parents to "get jobs themselves!"

Additionally, the fire department would continuously come to the school to check to see if the doors were locked and chained and administrators (she was one of them) who had to take the locks and chains off the doors when they called a "code" over the walkie-talkies.

Furthermore, "Dr. Clark got orange jumpsuits from the Sheriff's Department and had students who wrote graffiti on the walls to wear them and clean up the school grounds." Although she laughs about the controversies now, she used to worry about the firemen showing up and having to keep everyone on point.

Ms. De-Mo believed that Dr. Clark had an impact on her life because she became an administrator as a result of his encouragement. She believed that Joe Clark used successful strategies because he knew how to build public support, among other things, by attending a different church each Sunday and by purchasing coats for students who had none, as well as purchase gym uniforms for students who needed them. He referred families to social service agencies to help them to get food and other things that they may have needed.

She liked Dr. Clark's leadership style because she felt that he was omnipresent; he was always in classes; in the hallways; and the lunchroom. He delegated the office work to his vice-principals and was very well informed about the staff members' families and kept up with birthdays and marriages. She thinks his leadership style was forceful and does not think he would have had the same impact if we would have used a different type of leadership style.

She also stated that "he was able to clean up the school because he had the support of the superintendent. She believed that he demonstrated successful strategies to reach and connect with students by knowing many of their names, and students were always perplexed as to how he knew their names.

He started the ID process in the city of Paterson. He could see the student names on the ID badges. However, he also read the student files and made a point of connecting with them by going to their churches, helping them if there were fires in their homes, or had other problems at home. He was very well aware of students who had babies as teenage parents. He also helped connect students with scholarships and financial aid and wrote recommendations for several students as well.

Ms. De-Mo thought Dr. Clark was a good principal and was very happy that he cleaned the school up. She remembered how he treated teachers and other administrators and stated that he had little respect for central office administrators, and he felt that they were "part of the problem." She remembered that there were times when Dr. Clark had some of the administrators whom he felt did not "work" perform "hall duty" (sit all day) until they learned to follow the chain of command.

Dr. Clark was able to transfer staff members who did not want to work at the school as well as the ones that he did not want to work at the school. She stated that he "stretched the law" to get what he needed and that administrators could never get away with all he did today, but "he was what the school needed at the time."

People either "got on board or got out of the way!" She described that it was an "adventure every day working with Dr. Clark," and you never knew who was coming into the building (celebrities), and there were always controversies going on at the school.

When asked if you could say something to Joe Clark right now, what would you like to say? She stated that what I have said to him, "You were right. I was administrative material!" and she thanked him because she had been ready to leave Paterson to teach elsewhere to get away from the turmoil in the school. She did not want to go, because as she stated, "I loved my students and the school itself, but it was out of control."

Finally, she stated that she remembered the *Lean on Me* movie, and she worked as an extra and was in one large group scene. They cut out all of the scenes that she was in except her left arm!

She believed that it is a great movie – it gets you involved emotionally, and you root for Dr. Clark and the kids. "A lot is true, but much is not, such as the young man on the roof." It is "still a great money maker" always on, "but the school, Dr. Clark, and the district make nothing from it!"

Ms. Florence Jones - is a White American female that worked at Eastside for thirty-five years from 1979 to the present (three years prior and thirty-two years after Joe Clark's tenure). She has worked in education for thirty-five years as a physical education teacher, vice-principal, and is currently one of four principals' at Eastside High School.

When interviewed, she told me that she did not have a choice in her assignment; that she was assigned to Eastside, and that she entered blindly and knew nothing of any rumors prior to employment. She stated that

Paterson had teaching opportunities, and "I was happy to have a job."

She described her fondest memories as becoming a principal at Eastside, and her not so positive memory was and still is the gang violence at Eastside. She described Eastside as "chaotic" before Joe Clark and that "the previous principal was a non-factor."

She described the [Pre-Clark] academic and teaching environment as "teachers survive... no one thrived." When asked about students who were beaten up or had their popular items stolen, she stated that "fights occurred periodically. Students do not always make good choices when trying to resolve their differences.

When altercations occur, punishment is necessary, and parents are involved. Most of these situations require out of school suspension." She stated there were drugs and drug dealers in the school, and gangs are present in the school.

She feels that Dr. Clark improved the atmosphere tremendously and immediately. She stated he had a great working relationship with students yet "was grossly obnoxious toward staff. He bullied teachers to a point. That's why many transferred."

She also felt that he did not want to have a relationship with staff members; he was only concerned about the students. She also talked about the controversies at Eastside during Dr. Clark's tenure and felt that "transferring 125 teachers during the 1982 to 1983 school years was a travesty.

He also dismissed fifty students for lacking credits and offered no educational options." She believed that Dr. Clark had an impact on her life because she "closely observed him for seven years. I learned from "many mistakes, not from his successes." I learned what *not* to do." Concerning the strategies that he used, she feels that he "typically "shot from the hip." He was "self-serving." Also, that "he bullied his way through his tenure.

He had many grievances against him!"

She believed that his leadership style, "It was immoral. She believed that leadership is not a position in life. It is the behavior. His style of leadership was one of intimidation." So that "Dr. Clark was a self-serving leader. He placed his own needs first. Once he was on the front cover of *Time Magazine* in 1988, it was all about him!"

Regarding Dr. Clark's strategies, he made it a point to connect with students at Eastside, and she believed that "If he did anything well, it was his relationships with students. He prided himself on knowing the names of all the students.

The students loved him, and the staff disliked him. Developing interpersonal relationships with students was his expertise." About Dr. Clark's leadership style, she believed that "He was great towards the students but a bully toward staff. He was always yelling and screaming at some staff members. He was disappointing." She further mentioned that,

> You cannot lead your sheep without being a formidable Shepard. Servant leaders place their own needs second. A servant leader rolls up their sleeves and serves the flock. When Dr. Clark set his ego above the school, he was doomed to fail. Toward the end of his tenure, he spent more time on the lecture circuit.

Ms. Smiley - is a German American female who was raised in an affluent suburban area in New Jersey. She started at Eastside in 1985 and retired in 2011 (two years after Dr. Clark began working at Eastside and twenty-six years after his tenure). She has worked in education for approximately thirty years as a science teacher. When interviewed, she told me she was assigned to Eastside and was told that if she did not like it, they would put her somewhere else, but once she walked into the building, she decided she liked her coworkers and students.

She mentioned that once she was hired, some of her acquaintances asked her if she "were nuts" because when you are "white and live in a suburban affluent area. Most people didn't want to go into urban areas, which were in turmoil." Although, on her first formal day of employment, she was chased out of the parking lot by striking teachers and remembered being on the picket line for an hour and marching with the other teachers because, in 1985, the teachers were on strike.

She could not describe what Paterson, New Jersey was like in the 1980s and 90s because she said she "did not pay that much attention to the town itself." She stated that she would "go in, go to work, and get into her car and go home." However, she described Paterson currently as a typical urban setting with some affluent and some poor areas.

She stated that the biggest problem Paterson is having now is budgetary concerns and that they had to lay off at least 125 police officers. So that while certain areas are being refurbished and built up, others are becoming more crime-ridden.

Although she was unaware of the negative occurrences that happened at Eastside prior to employment, she mentioned that her colleagues told her about the fights that occurred regularly as well as a "huge fight in the main office" five years earlier, and "there was blood all over the place!" and that the high school was in major disorder.

Ms. Smiley described the teaching environment, where the teachers did not have enough books and resources, and they had to continually write notes and information on the board because the students did not have enough books to take home for studying. Unfortunately, this lack of resources travesty lasted for the first two years that she taught in Paterson.

Ms. Smiley described her fondest memories as "somehow Joe Clark got the carnival on the grass at Eastside as a fundraiser." She remembered that Dr. Clark had an international luncheon for teachers and students in the cafeteria where everybody could bring something to eat (including students), and all types of ethnic and cultural foods were available for all to taste and learned about different cultures.

She described her not so positive memory as being physically assaulted by a student (after Dr. Clark's tenure); the student rammed and shoved her in the hallway when she asked him a question about a hall pass as he came out of the bathroom.

Ms. Smiley also shared that she assumes there were and are drugs and drug dealers in the school because when you "see them [police officers] hauling teachers down in handcuffs, and you hear that you know, "teachers were caught with drugs on them, and they saw those teachers buying drugs from the students; that's why I assumed that."

When asked if there was violence at Eastside, she stated that every school has a certain amount of violence, because when you have 2500 to 3000 students in the building, they will have tiffs with one another. "After Joe Clark left, things seem to have gotten worse," and the attention had been brought to the newspapers and television news.

However, things have gotten considerably better because they are paying more attention to it now. She stated when "Joe Clark was in the building, we didn't have cops in the building. Now we have cops in the building." Also, okay, so "things were not as nearly as bad when Dr. Clark was around."

She also mentioned that about fifteen years later, the violence was intolerable with "maybe 100 kids were rioting in the hallways."

Ms. Smiley stated that the students were robbed and had their popular items stolen. She described one incident that occurred in her classroom.

Yes. Because I remember one of my young male students, my first year in school, he got jumped on his way home and had stuff stolen. And he came to school with weapons and when I noticed the weapons. I said to him, "Give it to me," and I called him out in the hallway, and when he came back into the classroom, his friends had hidden the weapons in the class. And he said 'no,' I have to give them to her, or I'll get in more trouble. So he gave me the weapons because he had gotten jumped and just wanted some protection. You know, so the same things have happened then, and they still happen today. You know. The streets are cruel.

She also told me the story of an incident that happened several years later (after Dr. Clark's tenure).

I remember a group of our football players. One of them had a younger brother who got jumped from somebody attending Kennedy High School. Also, a couple of days later, weeks later, they thought they saw this kid that jumped their brother. A group of football players, varsity football players, jumped this other kid. One of Eastside students took out a knife, and they stabbed the kid, and he ended up dying, and I think six of them ended up going to prison. You know. These were the so-called good and smart kids that were taking chemistry and going to college.

Ms. Smiley described her relationship with Dr. Clark, as "he was the principal, and I was the teacher," and she described Dr. Clark as being "a Black Hitler!" when asked to elaborate, she stated,

He was definitely a dictator! He definitely let you know if he was not happy with what you were doing. He took no prisoners. He would kick you out! He would lock you out! Have you transferred! If he thought you were screwing up. So in that respect, he was like a Hitler!

She also stated that Dr. Clark reminded her of her mother, because, "He was off the hook! He was a yeller and a screamer! Acted out terribly, and he tried ruling with a firm hand. Moreover, so he reminded me of my mother."

When asked, have you ever had any experiences with him that would make you feel that way? *Ms. Smiley* said she never had a negative experience with Dr. Clark. She mentioned how he wrote her a very nice letter because of an outstanding job that she had done, and she still has the letter in her memoirs.

Although she had not experienced a negative encounter with Dr. Clark, she feels disconcerted with him because Dr. Clark would dismiss the students and have the teachers meet in the gym, and then he would let non-tenured teachers go home early like the day before Thanksgiving.

Then he would "yell and have hissy fits and jump up and down, threaten teachers with their jobs and their livelihood if they did not do what he wanted...." She tells a story of how Ms. English, [English teacher] would, "take her shoe off and throw it at him down the stairwell to hit him with it because she would get so pissed off!" Okay?

"He was just... he was definitely a dictator! Wanted things his way, and it was his way or the highway!" She observed and did not appreciate the interactions that some of the teachers had with Dr. Clark because "if he didn't like you, he got rid of you." She also talked about some of the controversies at Eastside; she explained it in the following manner,

> Oh yeah, he used to always chain lock the doors. His big thing was running around with the bat and keeping fire departments and anybody else he could stay out of the building! He always had the doors chained and locked, which was a huge fire hazard. That really was a safety issue!

> Probably, the worst thing he ever did was to convince the board [Paterson Board of Education] to allow them to shoot the movie *Lean on Me* in the school when school was in progress. Allowing actual students to star in the movie when they were supposed to be in class; they are not in class; they are participating in the film and failing their classes.

> That's absurd! Now how are you supposed to be an educator and thinking that education is the most important thing, and you are allowing the students not to go to class because they are making a film? Because you're egotistical, and you want the film made!

> Do you follow the concept? So, it's okay to keep these kids out of

class and let them fail every subject for the year so that they could go in and make a movie? It does not make sense to me! That is not educationally sound!

When asked about why she thought Dr. Clark locked the doors, she stated, "He did it so that the kids couldn't go to the doors and let their friends in and wreak havoc in the school!" She also stated that he did it to "keep the bad element out! So you keep the kids that were supposed to be getting their education in!"

I asked, what do you think Joe Clark could have done other than locking and chaining the doors? She stated, "Yeah, he could have totally locked all the fences around the school and anybody who came on school property, who didn't belong there, maybe the townspeople or whatever, he could have had them arrested."

When asked if Dr. Clark had an impact or an effect on her life, she stated, "if anything it was more of an annoying effect on my life" and when I asked her to explain she stated,

> Everybody and their mother-in-law have seen the movie *Lean on Me,* including you! Every place I go, if somebody finds out that I'm a teacher teaching at Eastside in Paterson, they reflect what they saw in the movie; think it's gospel, and considers how bad Eastside High School is; and how could I teach there? Now I've never felt insecure or intimidated one day; one hour; one-minute teaching at Eastside in Paterson.

> So I think the movie actually helped tear down the reputation of Eastside rather than build it up! Also, so that Joe Clark could have one egotistical fifteen minutes of fame in the sky!

> So the making of the movie was more detrimental to both the school and the staff which worked there because where ever you go; just like yourself; they will find out you attended Eastside High School in Paterson and people who have seen the movie will ask "was it really

like that." So that's not a very positive thing. Why? Because he was the great Black hope for some school? To turn it around? I don't think so!

Because before he was there, this is going back thirty years before him; Eastside was one of those top ten schools in the state of New Jersey. Neglect, it doesn't happen overnight; neglect; change in clientele in the neighborhood; allowing it to be run into disrepair; many things happened.

Okay, and I will say this…I'm working there now, and I still see on Horatio Day, where a lot of ex-graduates that are 60, and 70 years old, come back to the school and act as speakers to classes.

They talk about the multitudes of professions that are out there, and these are the people that were successful and graduated from EHS when it was one of the best schools in New Jersey. So did Joe Clark turn it around? I don't think so. All right, he probably did more damage by the making of the movie than anything else because he was egotistical!

When asked do you think Dr. Clark made use of [successful] strategies in how he did things at EHS, she stated, "I don't think so. I think it was more of flying by the seat of his pants." When asked about her thoughts regarding Joe Clark's leadership as being strong or weak she stated

That's a tough question. I could say his leadership was strong because he made people fearful. Just because you made people fearful of doing what you want doesn't make you a strong leader. You could be a very weak person, and that's just how you compensate for it.

Ms. Smiley also believed that Dr. Clark tried to establish camaraderie as a strategy as well as trying to be nice. However, she believed that the bottom-line was "It was about what he wanted to be done, and if you didn't do it or couldn't do it up to his particular standards, then he would take retribution on you." She also mentioned that more teachers left Eastside during Dr. Clark's tenure than any other time in the history of the school, and she blames Dr. Clark for "the mass exodus of teachers."

She also stated that he had a multifaceted personality and that he wasn't a "mean S. O. B. [Son of a Bitch] all the time. However, it was in his nature." She also stated that there were times that "He would be fine. He wouldn't be yelling at teachers!

Teachers wouldn't be being threatened. Teachers would be left alone to teach their class;" however, "if you got on his bad side, he would be calling you down to his office, humiliating you in the general staff meeting, or in front of your colleagues, and screaming and berating you!"

When asked what the difference between her and the other teachers was who may have had an issue with Dr. Clark, she stated that she was very secure in who she was, and she has "never been a quiet and demure person that somebody could take and shit on."

She also stated that "I can tell you now; I can enjoy this conversation reminiscing because "I put in for my retirement!" So no matter what anybody says, it doesn't make a difference!" I asked about her thoughts in regard to Dr. Clark expelling students, and she stated that "he did expel them, but he probably did not go about it the right way," and she believed that, "students should be expelled for doing certain things such as being a hazard to other students and staff."

She believed that the most important thing is to have a safe, educational environment so the students can feel comfortable and so that they can learn. She also believed that if somebody is a hazard to the environment (mental or physical) of others, then they don't deserve to be in that type of educational system.

She believed that the students, who were expelled, were expelled with good reason, but chances are Dr. Clark did not go about it legally; he went about it in the most expedient way. To get them out, he told the parents, "here's his hat; his backpack; go find someplace else for your child because we're not letting him back in here! So maybe he didn't expel enough of them."

She believed that Dr. Clark was a good principal, and that "he tried to make a difference, which means that he did the best of his ability with sincerity in his heart, and you can't fault him for that. She stated that he was omnipresent in the school because he was always in the hallways, on the floors, and in the building and walking into classrooms, and he was out there with the kids, and they could see him all the time. She also believed that "walking to the right" was a good practice, and she wishes it was still used today.

If she could say something to Mr. Joe Clark right now, she would tell him, "Joe, I know you did your best, but I don't think it worked out as well as you had hoped. Then I would ask him to have a drink, and we would sit down, and I would tell him I think that he was a Black Hitler, hypothetically."

CHAPTER 7

Student Profiles

In this section, I will begin by providing demographic details on the student informants in Table 2, which will be followed by information from those contributors regarding their views of Dr. Clark and Eastside. To support the context regarding EHS and the students who attended, I have included significant material about the participants' background to help gain a better understanding of each informant.

Demographic Information of Students

The thirteen student participants for this study were purposefully selected based on a set of criteria, as described in Chapter 5. My goal was to select students who could provide a thick information-rich perception of Dr. Clark's leadership.

These participants, both male and female, are alumni who attended EHS between 1980 and 1993, were solicited, and self-selected to participate in the study. These participants are African American (10), Biracial (1), and Jamaican descent (2). Eight are male and five females. Eight out of the thirteen are married with children, two are currently divorced, one is engaged, and one never married.

Eight of the thirteen were members of Dr. Clark's first graduating class in 1986. One participant was expelled. Two participants were nearly kicked out of EHS by Dr. Clark. Two graduated in 1984; one graduated in 1987, and one graduated in 1993. Four of the thirteen were students prior to Dr. Clark's arrival and provided additional rich, thick descriptions of what EHS was like prior to Dr. Clark

Table 2 - Student Profiles

Name	Sex	Race	EHS Grad Year	Years At EHS	Highest Degree Earned	Job Title	Age
Anthony	M	Jamaican American	1986	1982 to 1986	Masters	Physical Therapist Neurological Musculoskeletal	46
Beautiful	F	African American Caucasian	1984	1980 to 1984	Associates	Disabilities Claims Agent	47
Cheeks	F	African American	1986	1982 to 1986	Bachelors	Revenue Specialists Real Estate Officer	46
Dilligaf	M	African American	1986	1984 to 1986	High School Diploma	Garage Door Distributor	46
Flash	M	Jamaican American	1987	1983 to 1987	Masters	Executive Director of a charter school	45
John	M	African American	-	1980 to 1982	GED	Entrepreneur	45
Karimah	F	African American	1986	1982 to 1986	Masters	Clinical Manager for a major pharmaceutical company	46
Kid Fresh	M	African American	1984	1980 to 1984	Bachelors	Territory Technology Specialist -E-Commerce	48
Moody	M	African American	1993	1989 to 1993	Masters	Principal, Eastside High School	42
Pinky	F	African American	1986	1982 to 1986	Doctorate (Ph.D.)	Vice President of Student Affairs	46
Reggie	M	African American	1986	1981 to 1986	High School Diploma	HVAC Project Director	47
Ruth	F	African American	1986	1983 to 1986	Juris Doctor	Lawyer	46
T-Bird	F	African American	1986	1982 to 1986	Bachelors	Facilities Project Integrator for the CDC	46

Five of the thirteen reside in Georgia, five reside in New Jersey (four in Paterson), two reside in North Carolina, and one lives in Florida.

With the educational attainment of the participants: three of the thirteen have a Bachelor of Arts degree. Two have a Master of Business Administration. One has a Law degree. One has a Ph.D. in Educational Policy Studies. One has a Physical Therapist degree. One has an Associate in Arts degree. One attended business school and graduated with a Business Certificate, one took some classes at Passaic County Community College, one served in the army for three years, and one received his GED in prison.

The participants have taken thirteen different career paths that consist of: Lawyer, Physical Therapist, Vice President of Student Affairs (University), Revenue Specialist, Pharmaceutical Clinical Manager, Social Security Claims Agent, Facilities Project Director for the CDC (Centers for Disease Control), Foreman/Technician HVAC (Heat, Ventilating and Air Conditioning), Garage Door distributor, Territory Technology Specialist/Manager of E-Commerce, Executive Director of a new charter high school, Entrepreneur. Moreover, one was a freshman student in 1989 during Dr. Clark's last year as principal and served as one of four Principals at Eastside High School.

Student Participant Profiles

Anthony - is a forty-six-year-old Jamaican American male, born in Kingston, Jamaica, and married with two children. He works as a physical therapist for neurological and musculoskeletal impaired patients. He "evaluates patients on addressing those deficits to maximize their function to provide mobility and ability to regain their activities of daily living." His salary is within the range of $90,000-$120,000, which affords the opportunity to create his work schedule.

He currently resides in Orlando, Florida, and considers himself to be middle class. He attended Rutgers University in New Brunswick, New Jersey, and The University of Alabama in Birmingham, Alabama. He majored in physical therapy. He attended EHS from 1982-1986 during Dr. Clark's tenure and was a member of Dr. Clark's first graduating class in 1986.

During *Anthony*'s high school days, he lived in a home along with four siblings and both parents and considered himself to be middle class during that time. He remembers being a frightened freshman who had to attend EHS because there were no other options. The violent reputation, perceptions of the school, and the surrounding drug-infested neighborhood concerned him.

Anthony perceived EHS as a stepping stone to help him reach his goal of attending college. He wanted more role models to help guide him through particular challenges he had as a teen. When he was accepted into college, there were some areas in which he felt he was ill-prepared and had to take remedial courses to be successful in his studies.

Anthony described Paterson as a low, deficiency-stricken income area. As he walked to school every morning, he noticed beer bottles, beer cans, and empty plastic vials that were used for crack cocaine. He explained how it was typical for physical fights to break out regularly.

At that time, Paterson had a Jewish Temple downtown in the heart of the city. Jewish people worshiped at the temple, but as far as he could tell, they did not live in that area. That was very thought-provoking for him at such a young age.

He thought the people living in Paterson lacked morale and were not happy about residing there. He spoke about his experiences attending Alabama University and living in Alabama, where he was expecting to be called the N-word because of all the racial history in Alabama. However, to his dismay, the only case where someone called him a nigger was in Hawthorne, New Jersey, which is a suburb of New Jersey.

Anthony remembers Dr. Clark as someone who created attention for himself. He believed that Dr. Clark was seeking public media attention way too much, and the use of the bullhorn and some of his other disciplinary tactics (such as toting around a baseball bat) were just for media attention.

He believed that Dr. Clark had good intentions, and his most significant contribution was enforcing the rules and making the classroom environment more conducive to learning. According to *Anthony*, Dr. Clark was available to students before, during, and after school, although he did not take advantage of it. *Anthony*'s mother seemed to be very pleased with Dr. Clark. Although it [EHS] was an extremely violent place, she was happy that *Anthony* did not get stabbed or killed. She credited that to Dr. Clark.

When asked, *Anthony* described his definition of a good principal as

Someone you know who seeks the needs of teachers, students, and whatever the school board is expecting of him. I don't know the teacher's perspective. I don't know if it is based on what the school board wanted him to do. I think by far as the students go, he [Dr. Clark] did, the one thing I will give him the greatest credit for is making and creating an environment conducive for learning, and that was his big thing. Addressing and getting rid of the people who weren't making the school conducive to learning.

Beautiful - is a biracial (African American and Caucasian) forty-seven-year-old woman who was born in Paterson, New Jersey. She is the youngest of seven children, and all of her siblings except for one brother attended and graduated from EHS. She remembers hearing harsh stories about Eastside and did not want to attend because of all the stories of students being beaten up, bringing razors to school, and all the violence she heard about the school.

She remembered stories from her brothers and sisters who talked about fights in the cafeteria and students being bloodied up or cut up by other students. *Beautiful* described her family situation as poor, and she lived with both parents in the home. She described her mother as being very strict and stated that "she ruled with an iron pan and an iron stick."

Beautiful shared a story detailing her only fight in high school. A female harassed her by stepping on the back of her shoes as she was walking away. This student also hit *Beautiful* in the face with her jacket. *Beautiful* then pulled out the cutting shears that she had in her purse (that she carried for protection) and began to stab the antagonist.

She stated that she blacked-out, and when she came to, amid this fight, she realized that two teachers were trying to break up the fight. *Beautiful* punched one of them in the eye by mistake, and he sustained a black eye. The student assailant was cut and bloodied with the scissors and was sent to the hospital. *Beautiful* received a 15-day suspension for the incident.

Beautiful believed that Dr. Clark had a high impact on her life. She felt he prepared her for what life had to offer. He encouraged her to strive for the best, and she believed he was a great principal. She wished there were more principals around like him and feels that the school system would improve with leaders like Dr. Clark.

She believed that Dr. Clark's methods to reach the students by using the bullhorn to get the students' attention and getting to know students' names were noteworthy ways to engage and connect with his students. She believed he was a fantastic leader, and she thought those good leaders are people who take charge and show great initiative when leading others; they are not afraid to stand up and take charge when a problematic challenge comes along.

Beautiful thought that Dr. Clark truly believed in academics and always told his students that getting an education would help them to be successful in life. She assumed Dr. Clark had a significant leadership role regarding extracurricular activities because he attended basketball and football games and other sporting events with and for his students.

She believed Dr. Clark was serious about school safety and keeping his students in a safe environment so they would not have to worry about violence or the threat of violence inside or outside of the school. She would like to thank Dr. Clark for his time and commitment to the school and the students of Eastside High School.

Cheeks - During her interview, *Cheeks* was very excited to share memories of her high school experience and was thrilled to talk about Dr. Clark. The inflections of her voice appeared as if she was very enthusiastic. She laughed a lot, yet she seemed gloomy at times as she reminisced about her high school days. She desired to be interviewed because she felt that she had a great deal of information that she wanted to share regarding Dr. Clark. She attended Eastside from 1982-1986 during Dr. Clark's tenure and was a member of his first graduating class.

Cheeks is a forty-six-year-old African American female who was born in Paterson, New Jersey. She married a fellow student from EHS and is currently divorced. She has three children and was an eighteen-year-old high school student when she had her first child. During her time as a student, she received financial and emotional support from the staff at EHS, including Dr. Clark.

Cheeks works as a revenue specialist's real estate officer. Her salary is within the range of $40,000 to $70,000. She resides in Charleston, South Carolina, and considers her family to be poor "within today's economy." After attending Central Piedmont Technical College in Charlotte, North Carolina, *Cheeks* finished her degree at Emory's Middle University in South Carolina. There, she received a degree in Technical Management with a minor in Homeland Security.

Cheeks heard of rumors and witnessed violence at EHS as well as in her elementary school, Public School Number 6, where Dr. Clark was employed as principal before working at EHS. She had a relationship with Dr. Clark, and he knew her family very well.

Cheeks shared a sorrowful story about her pregnant older sister, who was killed when "one of her "friends" fed her rat poison." This death, which happened when *Cheeks* was in elementary school, affected her life. Dr. Clark supported her, and she appreciated him for what he had done for her and her family by providing emotional and financial support.

Cheeks lived in the poverty-stricken area of Paterson, New Jersey, and had several stories to share about it. During her time in high school, she considered her family to be deprived, and despite the limited financial resources, her immediate family cared for and supported one another.

Cheeks shared many positive interactions with Dr. Clark. She was a member of the EHS Marching 100 band and was an outstanding student who "did not like to hang out too much," because that was how her pregnant sister was killed.

She was not involved in any illegal activities or gangs. However, she did have one fight during her high school years outside of school grounds, knowing that fighting in school would have disappointed Dr. Clark, and he would have suspended her for ten days. She believed that Dr. Clark played a significant role in her life, as she was his student in elementary school and high school.

During her teenage pregnancy, there were several problems in her home, and Dr. Clark was influential in helping her family in times of trouble. The young girl named Kenisha in the movie *Lean on Me* was basically about her life and that of many other female students. Dr. Clark helped *Cheeks'* relationship with her mother and helped *Cheeks* financially when she was pregnant. She is very thankful to Dr. Clark because her daughter is now a very successful gospel artist in Atlanta, Georgia.

Dilligaf- is a forty-six-year-old African American male who was born in Paterson, New Jersey. He is married to a fellow alum of Eastside High School, and they have two children; a daughter who is a graduate of Spelman College and currently pursuing her law degree, a son who was class president at his high school and now attends Georgia State University. *Dilligaf* is also a very proud grandfather.

He is currently employed as a garage door distributor. His current salary is within the range of $27,000 to $47,000 and has been a homeowner for over ten years. He enrolled in some classes at the Passaic County Community College, and when he realized that college was not for him, he enlisted in the army for three years and encountered some of the same racial problems that he encountered previously while attending Don Bosco Tech. There he faced racism and fought often. He was later transferred to Eastside because of the fighting.

While enlisted in the Army, he realized that he needed to be patient, humble, and wait for the other guy to make the first move, but once the other guy made the first move, he would "come out like a Jack -in-The-Box on them. And I'm going to turn into that guy!"

When asked the meaning of his pseudonym *Dilligaf*, he told me that it meant "Do I Look like I Give A F_ _K?" *Dilligaf* lived in the "Alexander Hamilton housing projects, known as the Alabama Projects or the Dog Pound," located in a poverty-stricken section of Paterson.

Dilligaf described himself as "a bully and a troubled youth like everybody else" however, he "managed to escape practically unscathed." He stated that he attended Eastside, and he "did not apply himself academically." He just floated because it was a "total different contrast" from his previous high school, Don Bosco Tech.

Dilligaf's daily transformational [Don Bosco Tech] routine included waking up at five o'clock in the morning, walking three blocks because the bus would not come to pick him up in the projects. He had to wear a tie and was in a class by approximately 6:15 AM. He was doing math assignments by 6:30 AM and had completed three classes by the time the students at Eastside started classes at 9:00 AM.

He stated that when he transferred to Eastside and walked into the classroom and saw "people hanging by the window and smoking cigarettes and chilling'" he thought that was good for him. He said, "this is heaven," and this is where he felt "at home, freer, and where he belonged."

He believed that attending Eastside was going to be a breeze and started to cut class and hustle (sell drugs) on the streets and ended up missing twenty-one days of school and was almost not allowed to graduate. However, he petitioned Dr. Clark and was told that he could not miss any more days out of the four months that were left in the school year. As a result, he had to "dig deep" and go back to the discipline that he had at Don Bosco Tech, and he made it graduation.

After graduation, *Dilligaf* began to indulge in illegal activities and was sentenced to three years in jail in 1985. By the grace of God, *Dilligaf* was accepted into the Total Lifestyle and Support program, which is an alternative to incarceration program for juveniles. The purpose is to reduce the number of commitments of the Passaic County Juveniles to the State Home for Boys and Girls. This rigorous life-changing program was created by Mr. Alonzo Moody.

Dilligaf described Eastside as an animal house before Dr. Clark got there; he stated that there were "food fights every day with knives and guns" [exaggerating a little] and he said that was the mindset of the students who attended, and that students went to Eastside because they didn't have any other choice. He stated that the "educational processes and the curriculums" were easy for him and that all he had to do was "show up" and pass the test.

He remembers that students were beaten and robbed for their popular items. He also mentioned that is why Dr. Clark had to get rid of those who were "hustling all over the school, and not worthy, and did not want an education." When we discussed if there were street cliques or gangs at Eastside High School, he stated

> Absolutely! It was like wherever you were from, your block, and that's what you represented! So whatever the block was doing, you were basically doing too. It was either going out to someone else's hood to do damage [fight] or to stick up for somebody who came in and was violating [disrespecting someone else's hood].

He also referred to Eastside as being like the "old-school *West Side Story* [movie] gangs, type of scenario back then; you know what I'm saying?"

Dilligaf discussed that he was a great student at Eastside; was and still is a member of the Five Percent Nation, and that Dr. Clark loved him because his academics were excellent and the only reason he came under Dr. Clark's radar was that "everybody was running around wanting to be called god [Five Percenters], and trying to wear kufi's and hats in school. He reported that Dr. Clark said,

> Ain't nobody wearing no hats in here! Ain't nobody wearing no hats in my school! But I tell you what; if you can get your grades up like my man *Dilligaf* over here, then you can do that. Dr. Clark would put you on front street [out in the public eye] if you were worthy, but he would not put anybody who wasn't worthy on front street. How do you get on front street? Being very good academically, doing something that's going to benefit other people.

That's what Joe Clark was about; take in some type of pride, stand up young men! Hey, that's what I'm talking about. It wasn't anything else but that. Academics! That's it! I was one of the guys who wore the kufi in school, but in a public building, nobody is supposed to wear hats to cover their heads up, unless it was for religious purposes. The Five Percenter Nation is not a religion; it's a way of life.

The kufi thing was a part of the Five Percenter Nation. So people would wear a kufi, and Dr. Clark would not let them wear it unless they were academically successful.

Dilligaf discussed his thoughts about Dr. Clark kicking the students out of school. He stated that,

> Honestly, he did what he had to do! He really didn't kick anybody out. He just got rid of the people who didn't belong. That's all! Everybody knew they weren't supposed to be in the damn school. They know damn well the people he kicked out were at the school doing the things that I alluded to earlier. Causing confusion, causing confusion, causing confusion, okay that's it; getting in trouble, polluting an environment, polluting the atmosphere.

> Before Dr. Clark got there, it was a hangout spot, the cafeteria. It was everywhere. It was just a big hangout; it was a place where you can go get things; it was a transaction place. You could get everything. So when he came, when Dr. Clark came, he looked in the roll book first, you got to understand that, he didn't just say, you ugly, your big barracuda, I don't like your hair, you got a kufi on, I don't like you, get your ass out!

> No! Dr. Clark went in there, and he got all student transcripts, and he started in alphabetical order because he's just precise like that! Do you know what I'm saying? He looked at your attendance, how old you were, and how long you've been going to this school. And he decided with his team of course, of advisers, that these individuals need to go in this list in a pile over there. We only have enough room for this amount of people. We'll have enough books for them, and he had to get the budget right. So he had to get rid of people.

He went to the book, and if your name was by some 200 or 82 days out [absent], then your ass is getting kicked out! And now you're mad because you can't come here and hang out anymore. Beat it! If you were teetering, he would work with you and give you some alternatives, and he would tell you, you would have to do this. Using my example, you got twenty-one days absent; if you miss one more day, I'm not let [letting] you back in my school. That's it!

If you do what you're supposed to do, then you are good with him. You earned some trust with him. He was cut and dry, not backing down.

He also believed that Dr. Clark had a big impact on his life because he instilled pride along with his teachings of the Five Percent Nation, and the confirmation that Dr. Clark provided to him when he was a student. He believed that Dr. Clark taught him so much by letting him see a father figure, someone who can instill positivity in him as well as that, "can-do attitude," and that's how Dr. Clark inspired him to change.

He believes that Dr. Clark was proactive in his approach and helped others to see that education was important and that anyone who came across Dr. Clark's path would receive assistance if needed; "even the people that got thrown out of school," because he heard some of them say (brothers, cousins and friends), "I'm glad he did that to me man, because I had to get my life together…because they were not doing anything with their lives."

Dilligaf also stated that he believed that Dr. Clark was a great principal and his definition of a great principal is someone who "cares about his students" and who "is hands-on" with the students; who "will go far and beyond the call of duty" for his students, and someone who "has a vision and knows what young people need," and that is positive reinforcement. "That's what Joe Clark was all about!"

When asked to elaborate more on Joe Clark being a father figure to him, *Dilligaf* stated that

> He would take time to listen to anybody. And then he would give you fatherly advice, whether he was telling you to pull your pants up! Comb your head! Calm down; take that cigarette out of your ear! Then you might be able to start getting an interview for a job! Until you do those things, get out of my face! And you know that's what you needed! And now you're (saying to yourself) like damn, now I've got to go brush my teeth, Joe Clark done went off on me. Man, I got to step up my game. Let me pull my pants up.

> And then when you saw him coming down the hallway, you would tighten yourself up. That was the father figure in him. He always wanted more for you. He didn't want any harm to come to you. Any father who wants his kids to do bad or fail and not fulfill their full potential is not really a father.

> He's probably [a] daddy, but it's not really a father. Joe Clark was a father figure because he did those things! I believe 95% of his students were from a single parent relationship, whereas the father was not at home. And there were some households with the father raising his children, but that was far few and between.

> He was an inspiration. You can have both parents in your house, and he could still be a father figure. He may not be your father but is a father figure because [he] is just like your father. Dr. Clark would tell me the right things to do, and he would encourage me to better.

Dilligaf also stated that he thought Dr. Clark's leadership was definitely strong and anybody who says different. He considered them the enemy in regard to not appreciating Dr. Clark for being able to get into the minds of troubled youth, poor youths, who needed some guidance. He also stated there was no reason to dislike Dr. Clark if you understood that he was an educator who loved his people. He also stated that if Dr. Clark had employed a different type of leadership, it would not have had the same impact.

He believed Dr. Clark was a good leader and believes that a good leader is "somebody who was a good follower; someone who won't lead his people astray and someone who is going to stand up and fight for what's right regardless of the forces that are against him."

And if given the opportunity to say something to Dr. Clark, he would like to tell him, "I appreciate everything you did for Eastside, the spirit of the school, creating traditions and how you came and showed us the real meaning of change." And "you affected me. You inspired me, and I'm glad that I've transferred so that I can be a part of history and to be honored to be under your tutelage. I've got nothing but love for you, Dr. Clark!"

Flash - is a forty-five-year-old West Indian male and was born in Kingston, Jamaica. He was married and divorced twice and has two children. He currently lives in Duluth, Georgia, and is working as an executive director. He was in the process of chartering a high school for media and recording arts in Atlanta. His current salary is within the range of $150,000 - $200,000, and he has been a homeowner since 1994.

Flash considers himself to be the middle class. He attended the United States Military Academy, Seton Hall University, and the University of Maryland, and received his MBA in 2000, majoring in Information Systems/Technology. He described his family as poor during his high school days and stated that he was very close with his siblings, mother, and father.

Flash said he felt as if he was never challenged academically in any way, and that he had to go outside of Eastside and attend different academic programs to get the motivation that he needed to be successful. One of his fondest memories of high school was when he ranked number one for high school track athletes. He remembers Dr. Clark being a strong supporter of the track team, and he and his family had a very good relationship with the principal.

Flash remembered that there was a lot of violence, gang activity, and fights among the African Americans and Hispanics that not only happened at EHS but even in the elementary and middle schools. He remembered constant fighting and how it was scary to walk home or to school because he did not want to get caught in the crossfire.

Often fights occurred after basketball games, where the visiting team resented losing the game. He told the story of how students were being beaten up for their sneakers and jumped for leather coats and gold chains.

He also described how he personally knew some of the drug dealers in high school, but he focused on his academics, sports, and felt safe in high school. It was a different story on the outside of the school. He was aware of the gang members in the schools as well as the race riots and was thankful that his father shielded his family from that.

Flash recalled several of the controversies during his years at EHS, including but not limited to: the fire department, the locking of the doors, multiple disagreements between the mayor and Dr. Clark, and Clark's suspension of the group of students and then being ordered to bring them back by the board of education.

Flash believed that though Dr. Clark did not have the authority to do some of the things he did (e.g., chaining the doors and firing teachers), that Dr. Clark still created an environment where students could succeed if they put their mind to it.

He remembered how Dr. Clark dealt with the teachers by calling them out in the open and firing them or demoting them in public. His [Dr. Clark] personality dominated everyone, and he didn't care who didn't like it. "Maybe the teachers didn't like it, but it gave us [the students] a glimpse of what can happen when a Black man is really in command, especially when he called himself the head N-word in charge." This type of behavior was inspiring to *Flash* because this was unusual for him to see.

Flash defined a good principal as someone whom people follow. A leader is compassionate. A leader is someone who understands the problems that you face, is willing to listen, to change, and adapt. A leader is someone who can give advice, get advice, and command respect from inside and outside.

Flash believed that some people probably were disrespected by Dr. Clark and that some of them "needed to be disrespected." He believed that Dr. Clark ran the school with the mentality of being a military drill sergeant. That is how he could get the teachers and staff to understand what needed to be done in order for him to be able to succeed and operate because he could not do it any other way.

He believed it was a gift to inspire students on a regular basis because a lot of students did not have a father figure or someone in their lives that would inspire them routinely. By doing this, *Flash* believed, Dr. Clark showed students he was in command, and that his strategy was to make things right, relevant, and work for the majority of the students at EHS. He feels that the students respected Dr. Clark more for these reasons stated above. He attended EHS from 1983-1987 and was a member of Dr. Clark's second graduating class.

John - is a forty-seven-year-old African American male who was born and raised in Paterson, New Jersey. He is single and currently resides in Paterson. He is the father of three sons. He was a student two years prior to Dr. Clark's arrival and was a member of the class of 1984. He was kicked out of Eastside High School due to missing more than 21 days (a new policy set by Dr. Clark). He was a sophomore in 1982 when Dr. Clark became principal and made tremendous changes in the school.

Prior to Dr. Clark's arrival, *John* described EHS as a place where he bought and sold drugs. He was also a member of the Five Percent Nation and stated that he and his group of friends were called the Be Islam Boys. He began "to study/practice "Islam" through the gods and earths."

During his interview, he reminisced about the time in 1982 when there was a significant issue between the administration and a group of Five Percent Nation students. He shared the following information. "When the young Five Percent women wanted to wrap/cover their bodies by wearing ¾ length clothing, Dr. Clark had a major problem with that." He stated that he believed that Dr. Clark did not think it was proper clothing to be worn in school, and the students could not understand why it was a problem.

John believed that the Five Percent Nation was "a culture; it was a way to cultivate their women." He remembers asking Dr. Clark why he disagreed and being dissatisfied with Dr. Clark's response. He shared that information with the leaders of Five Percenters, and they came to EHS from Newark, New Jersey, and New York to speak with Dr. Clark. He remembered this issue becoming a massive controversy against the administration. Some of the students, along with leaders of the Five Percent Nation, protested the policy, and he remembers a riot breaking out in the parking lot of the school on mischief day, the day before Halloween.

He also remembered that on mischief night after the earlier riot (he laughed as he told this story). He recalled that there was a house that had a pear tree in the backyard next to the parking lot of Eastside on Park Avenue. *John* stated that "normally people would throw eggs at people as they are passing by" however, this particular day he and some other students had picked up all of the rotten pears that had fallen from the tree and put them in a bucket; they noticed Dr. Clark, security officers, administrators and teachers in the parking lot and they began throwing the rotten pears at them. They pelted them with rotten pears hitting them continuously as if they were "throwing hand grenades," he stated, "We fired them up! like rockets!'"

John recollected that Dr. Clark hired a Paterson Police officer named Roy, who was a very tall man who used to ride a motorcycle, was familiar with most of the students and also worked at the very popular Fabian Theatre. This was Paterson's only movie theatre, and at that time it was a very dingy theater where students would hang out, smoke weed, and fight while others were trying to watch a movie. *John* stated

I am not saying Dr. Clark was wrong for what he did or the methods he used, but we knew we were going to get kicked out soon, so we were even more defiant because we knew we were getting kicked out! That was our chance to get back to the principal, security guards, police, and the teachers. I can remember all of them running and ducking for cover! We got back at them!

John explained that a lot of his friends were expelled because of violating the new attendance policy of having missed more than 21 days of school. He stated that the *Lean on Me* movie, "didn't do it [the EHS story] justice" he recalls being involved in some significant food fights in the cafeteria that they were "outrageous" and that the school was "off the chain" it was "wild," and he stated that "it was something else!"

John told me that during his freshman year, he tried to be a model student by going to all of his classes, however in his sophomore year "it was a wrap," and as a result, he was "kicked out." He expounded that "there was so much going on during school hours where students could get easily sidetracked."

He indicated that students spent a lot of time in the cafeteria instead of going to class. He talked about the fact that there was a hidden room in the auditorium that students had to climb up a ladder to get into. While in this room, students used to hang out all day, participate in drug transactions and smoked weed on a regular basis. He stated that students would go to homeroom but hung out in the hidden room during school hours.

He stated that "Dr. Clark had reasons for doing what he did, but his methods were unconventional by carrying the bullhorn and the bat around." Although he believes, Dr. Clark used them as a fear tactic that may have worked for some of the "lame students who feared him, but those things did not work for his crew." He stated that,

> Dr. Clark's methods actually pushed us more over the edge and caused us to be more disruptive; it gave us a reason to be more disruptive. I came from 12th Ave. you know, the hood! Coming from that section of town, we were renegades. When we would see someone "boast up" as he did, it just made us fight back even harder. We became even more defiant.

He further stated

> Once Dr. Clark decided to get the bad seeds out of the school, then he had his way. He was able to contain the freshmen when they came in because he had already set up the examples of what you should and what you should not do and the consequences that could follow. I'm not upset with Dr. Clark at all because if he did not come in the way he did and instituted a lot of those methods that he used, the school probably would have never turned around.

John stated that Eastside was a different kind of place; there were race riots that were not included in the *Lean on Me* movie. He thinks the film watered down the violence. He stated that the film did not show the race riots that were going on at Eastside, whereas the Blacks dominated the Park Avenue (front) side of the school, and the Puerto Ricans dominated the Market Street (back) side of the school.

(Market Street Entrance, Photos Courtesy, EHS Yearbook, 1988)

He further stated that,

> I don't think they [Warner Bros.] told the real story because it was worse than it was in the movie, and a lot of the teachers did not know what was going on. A lot of things were kept from the teachers because they were in the classroom teaching, and they were not in those hidden spots where students hung out. The teachers did not have on-site experience because if the students saw a teacher or administrator, they would stop what they were doing, so of course, they didn't see what was going on!

John described his crew,

> Our crew was named the Be Islam Boys we were between the ages of 15 and 17, and we had just begun learning the lessons of the "Nation the gods and earths" that was our crew from 10th Ave., 11th Avenue, and 12th Avenue and the majority of us attended public school number 21; it was about 10 of us, and we were a rough group. We were intelligent young brothers, but we were defiant.
>
> Just like anything that starts out good; there's always a few bad seeds; actually what happened was we came in the group young; when I went

into the nation of gods and earths, I was 11 years old, and you know those years are the most curious years of an adolescent. I was so excited and energetic, and I studied a lot, I studied really hard, but growing up in a rough city like Paterson, at some point in time you just drift off, and we started doing other things. We began using and selling drugs, snatching pocketbooks, and stealing cars.

John explained that,

there are a lot of brothers that actually didn't go our route. There were a lot of brothers who continued to study, and some of them eventually became Muslim and followed the Hon. Elijah Mohammed and Minister Farrakhan.

But for his group, they "were just a defiant group." *John* described himself as a young man who grew up in a single-parent household where his father left his family when he was 12 years old. He was left without any male guidance or discipline, and he wasn't steered in the right direction that he would have been if his father had not moved.

He shared that the streets became a big brother to him, "the older brothers who were standing on the corner selling drugs, and wearing British Walkers" (a popular shoe), and "shark skins" (shiny pants) "these brothers became idols and mentors to the young brothers and they were idolized by the younger brothers who wanted to be just like them. That's what happened!"

Today *John* is still affiliated with the nation of gods and earths and asserts that there were just a few bad things that happened, which "casts a dark shadow over them. But for the most part, we were a good group of brothers that really wanted to educate themselves."

John attended Public School Number 21 from kindergarten to eighth grade, and he had two brothers who grew up in a single-parent household.

He remembers attending Eastside, and he remembers his first day of high school.

John remembered leaving eighth-grade and hearing stories of what students would do to freshmen on their first day of school. He was told that as freshmen walked in to the school, the upperclassmen were in the hallways and the freshman they would get smacked hard on the back of their head and called "freshies" however, he and his crew were ready; they were prepared for what was to come and because he and "his crew were well-known for fighting by the upperclassmen, they knew not to mess with the Be Islam boys!" He remembered helping some of the other young boys from his block and pulled them into his crew just for that day to give them some protection from the upperclassmen.

During his freshman year, he attended all of his classes, and he did well. He looked forward to hanging out in the cafeteria "because that was a release, a place where you could go and let your hair down, a place for them to hang out." This was also a place where "students could go and see some action such as fists fights or food fights." If a student did not appear to "wear nice clothing, that student would be picked on or bullied, and a fight would break out."

John described that if someone was on the cafeteria line and if the food looked terrible, someone would throw their food tray and yell "food fight!" and a food fight would begin. He remembers students ducking under the tables trying not to get hit with food because students would go to school with their "fresh" clothes on and did not want to get their clothes messed up with food.

He stated that he couldn't remember many days where there wasn't a fight, and there were many fists fights in the cafeteria on a regular basis. He also remembers that the cafeteria was a place where a lot of drug transactions took place.

He remembers that he began to sell drugs during his sophomore year and he remembers that every evening or the morning before attending school he and his friends would roll up (marijuana) joints to get prepared to sell them in the cafeteria or in the hidden room in the auditorium for one dollar.

He stated that there was a door outside of the cafeteria, whereas students had to walk up the stairs to get inside, and that was a door where various drug transactions took place. This was a place where students were allowed to smoke cigarettes; however, some would smoke weed. This was also the door where outsiders were allowed to come into the school. "It was a crazy time!"

When asked about the amount of drugs he believed was being disbursed at the school every day? He stated that everybody he was associated with in his crew brought in about 20 joints every day. He stated that the upperclassmen were dealing and using crack cocaine and dust/PCP. He also shared that there were people from different areas and cliques that were also bringing in drugs. "There was a lot of drug activity going on in the school prior to and after Dr. Clark's arrival."

During his sophomore year, he stated he became "thugged out" and participated in various fights in school. He stated that he and his brothers were fighters; they learned how to fight at the local boxing gym. They were known for "using their hands," he stated that as a child, he created a reputation for himself and that he was "not one to be messed with!"

When asked what happened to the teachings/lessons that they learned from the 5% nation and how that played a part in his defiant behavior, he stated that he and members of his crew continued to study; however, he believed that some of the lessons were misinterpreted by them.

He stated that they were provided various lessons; one of the first lessons that they learned was that the Black man was a god; this was a science/doctrine that they truly did not understand.

He remembered that the young black boys' egos became very large because the students literally believed the lessons. He recalled many times, whereas he believed, expressed, and thought he was a god of his own universe and the god of himself, which inevitably gave him excuses to act out. He exclaimed,

> There was no one there; no elders available to provide us with a proper understanding and interpretation of what the lessons/teachings were really about, so we took them for face value. One of the lessons asked the question who the original man? And the answer states that the original man is the Asiatic Black man; the maker; the owner; the cream of the planet earth; father of civilization and God of the universe. The young brothers believed this lesson literally and believed that they were gods of their own universe.

John stated that it wasn't until he was older and wiser than he began to truly obtain a respectful true understanding of the lessons. Whereas he learned he was a god with a small g. versus a god with a capital G.

John realized he was expelled from Eastside by attempting to go to homeroom one day and realized his name was not on the attendance sheet; he went to the office and found out that he was expelled due to missing 21 days of school. He attended Kennedy High School to finish out his sophomore year and the beginning of his junior year; however, it did not last long. He was 16 years old, and his high school education was over.

He explained that he didn't have anything to do, so he began to hang out in the streets along with some of the other students that were also expelled. They began to buy and sell drugs and traveled to New York City to Delancey Street to buy popular clothing and would then hang out by the Public-School Number 21 playground where they sold drugs.

He stated that his mother owned a soul food restaurant business on North Main Street in Paterson, and he helped his mother out a lot with her business; however, he was now 17 and 18 years-old and began selling drugs full time.

He was incarcerated when he was 19 years old and stayed in prison from 19 until he was 25 years old. He believes that his prison experience was a good experience for him because that's where he learned how to be a man. He educated himself while in prison; he received his GED; became a certified behavior modification teacher and was as an assistant teacher in the Rahway State Prison located in New Jersey.

He believes he changed a lot after his six-year prison experience; he matured and returned home with different aspirations and motivations; he opened up a business next door to his mothers' soul food restaurant. He stated that when you're young and out there selling drugs, you learn how to have an entrepreneurial spirit.

He stated that Dr. Clark was not wrong for coming in and changing the school; however, he believed that Clark's ideology was on point, but his methods of doing it irritated a lot of us, students. In thinking back, in retrospect, he stated: "I wish I would have conformed."

John believes Dr. Clark "did a great justice for the students at Eastside because there probably would have been more students who would have went ashtray had it not been for Dr. Clark." He got parents and the community involved in what he was doing; you know it takes a village to raise a child and the avenues that he took to correct some of the things that were going wrong in the school. *John* stated,

> I am glad that I was able to get a hold on my life. Prison slowed me down, and it gave me another perspective on life! I am glad Dr. Clark did come to implement the changes that he did. He saved a lot of lives. I have no ill will against Brother Clark; I just wish he would have

gotten there a little sooner!

Viewing the situation from a youth's perspective, seeing his older guy walking around with a bat and a bullhorn, we were thinking, "get the hell out of here! Who do you think you are?" *John* asserted that if Dr. Clark was a little less aggressive, he would have gotten his attention.

I think he would have gotten the attention of more students; we were very educated yet defiant brothers. His intimidation tactics just pushed us to the edge. We were used to certain things being a certain way, and I don't think it was feasible; I don't think it was good for him just to turn it around right away; I think he should've been a little more subtle; I don't think he should have forced his intimidation tactics on us. You can get more bees with honey than with vinegar.

I think he should have put some satellite/alternative schools downtown Paterson and give students options to go to other places to finish their education. Dr. Clark should have understood that prior to him coming there, there were things that were going on that kept us corrupt.

If our fathers were around, we would have had better examples of what a man should be! There would have been more structure! My father left when I was 11 years old, and I think if my father had been there, things would have been a lot different. My mother did the best she could do raising her sons; she provided for us, and we came from a good family; we had the most popular clothing and had everything we needed; however, the discipline factor was missing. If I would have had that, possibly I would not have gone the route that I went.

Boys who don't have a father figure in a household will gravitate toward the streets. I gravitated towards the nation of gods and earths, and I began learning things; I had a thirst for knowledge, and they became my father. I wish my father was there to teach me these things.

John mentioned that as a parent of a high school student, he would kick his sons' ass if he knew or found out his son was participating in such activities while in high school. *John* has three sons, 28, 18, and eight-years-old.

Karimah - is a forty-six-year-old unmarried African American female who was born in Paterson. She has no children. She works as a senior clinical manager for a major pharmaceutical company in New Jersey. She "prepares the drug protocols for the FDA." Her current salary is within the range of $80,000-$100,000.

She is a homeowner, still lives in her hometown, and considers herself to be middle class. *Karimah* attended Passaic County Community College and received her associate's degree, and then attended Bellevue University, where she received her bachelor's degree in Healthcare Management. She is currently seeking her doctoral degree.

Karimah described her family situation while growing up as being underprivileged. She was the fourth child out of her family of eight siblings and is the only child that graduated from high school. Unlike most students who did not have a choice of which high school to attend, *Karimah* chose to attend EHS. At first, her parents were adamant about not sending her to EHS because, at the time, the school was being overrun by students, there was much violence, and her parents did not want her to have any part of it. Four of her older siblings attended EHS but dropped out.

Once her parents realized that Dr. Clark was going to be the principal, they decided to allow their daughter and her three younger siblings to attend. Her parents were familiar with Dr. Clark because he had been the principal at Public School Number 6, and they were aware of his reputation of changing a negative school environment into a positive one.

One of *Karimah's* fondest memories of Dr. Clark was when he performed one of his strategies to decrease the chaos in the hallways by requiring students to "walk to the right." She stated that, to this day, she "still walks to the right side of any hallway, no matter what."

One of her not so positive memories of high school was the negative feedback from the outsiders, who were looking in, and they did not understand the scope of what EHS needed at that time, nor did people try to understand what Dr. Clark was attempting to do. She also remembered Dr. Clark's strong discipline and no-nonsense attitude, holding students accountable for their actions, as well as students receiving ten-day suspensions for all infractions. She described Paterson as a poor town with lower-income families.

During that time, EHS's population was approximately 90% African American, around 9% Latino, and Mexican, and one percent White. She remembers that Dr. Clark was very stringent and very active in the community. He focused on education and bettering the lives of his students. She feels that he was the best thing that happened to EHS and her family.

Karimah was very familiar with Dr. Clark because he was the principal at her elementary school as well, and she feels that he implemented the same strategies and methodologies at EHS that he applied at the elementary school. Some of the controversies that she remembers were when Dr. Clark's chained the doors and how he kept the outsiders out of the school, and how Dr. Clark was given a tough time about doing that from the administrators at the board of education.

She feels her life had changed tremendously from when she was growing up poor as a child and not being able to take care of herself. By becoming a homeowner, she could not fathom the idea or the fact that she is living her dream and being able to accomplish what she has accomplished. She believed that Dr. Clark has made a high impact on her life and that he was like a father figure; he was extremely adamant about having respect for you and demanding respect for yourself from others.

She believed he knew all the students by name and that he was more like a father than a principal. She remembered Dr. Clark constantly walking the halls with his bullhorn and calling upon students to sing the alma mater or to correct you if you were doing something wrong.

Karimah believed that a good principal is someone who is genuinely interested in the lives of his/her students inside and outside of the school. She remembered that her parents loved and adored Dr. Clark for what he had done. She believed he was a good leader because he not only talked the talk, but he walked the walk; he taught by being a great example.

She remembers he was very hard on the teachers and administrators because he felt the students needed guidance and support, so he demanded that from his teachers and other leaders of the school and expected them to also lead by example.

Karimah believed Dr. Clark needs to be recognized for the work that he did at EHS because a lot of people came down on him because of his harsh ways, and people were just looking from the outside. She believes that they truly did not understand what was going on in the inside.

"My attending Eastside High School has provided me the opportunity to learn and experience that it doesn't matter what kind of environment you're from as it relates to the goals you want to achieve in life." *Karimah* attended EHS from 1982-1986 during Dr. Clark's tenure and was a member of his first graduating class of 1986.

Kid Fresh - is a forty-seven-year-old African American male who was born in Paterson, New Jersey. He works as a Territory Technology Specialist and is the manager of e-commerce. He works in the corporate office and manages business-to-business online applications.

Primarily, he prepares web applications for the company in addition to providing support for the customers and staff through training, development processes, and provides guidance to the sales field management team. "Fundamentally, it is a technology-based, print business/print industry career opportunity."

He has worked in this position for the past three years, but has been with the company for seven and served in other roles. He currently resides in Matthews, North Carolina, which is a suburb of Charlotte, North Carolina. He has been a homeowner for the past ten years. His salary is over $100,000 and considers himself to be middle-class. He's married with three children and attended Rutgers University - Mason Gross School of the Arts.

He was a student at EHS prior to and during Dr. Clark's tenure from 1980-1984 and graduated in 1984. He attended EHS two years prior to Dr. Clark and two years during Dr. Clark's tenure, and he could not remember who the principal was prior to Dr. Clark.

Kid Fresh described his family life as hectic, sometimes due to his father being addicted to drugs and alcohol. Being the eldest son, he experienced some difficult times that he did not wish to share.

Moody - is a forty-two-year-old African American male who was born and raised in Paterson, New Jersey. He is married, a homeowner, and currently resides in Paterson, and works as one of four principals at Eastside High School. *Moody* is the principal of operations, and he is responsible for the overall operations of the building, the facilities, athletics, and management for all students.

He is responsible for the discipline and overseeing different protocols of how students should enter and be dismissed from Eastside High School. He implemented a uniform policy where all students are 100% in compliance with wearing uniforms. His current salary is within the range of $100,000 and $120,000. He attended the University of Pittsburgh and received his Master of Arts degree in School Social Work. Prior to becoming the principal of Eastside High School, he was the administrator of an alternative school in Paterson for nine years.

Moody stated that as a youngster, he had the opportunity to go to a Catholic or another private school, "but to us, my family, my brothers, and me, there was no other school. It was Eastside or Kennedy, and we grew up on the east side of town.

You wouldn't dare to go to Kennedy." *Moody* shared how, as an elementary school student, he and his family were very supportive of Dr. Clark and what he was striving to implement during that time. He mentioned that his father and Dr. Clark were very good friends and that he and his older and younger brothers were all on the honor roll and played sports for Eastside.

When asked if he remembered any negative rumors about Eastside prior to attending, he stated that "my brother and other family members attended Eastside; I don't view them as rumors. I know them as facts." He also stated, "I was there. I attended basketball games, and I could smell the weed in the bathroom, and saw people get beat up and/or jumped after the games. It was just a way of life."

He also mentioned that yes, there was fighting, drugs, disrespect towards teachers and staff, truancy, low performance, and all of those things. However, at the same time, there was an honor society, and the athletic program was top-notch. "So, there were both negative and positive things happening at the school."

Some of his fondest memories had to do with the relationships that he built with his friends who were on the sports teams and attending a peer leadership program, where teachers would take them away to a leadership camp every year and teach them social and survival skills. He stated that "those experiences were the things that had a lasting impression on me."

He discussed his not so positive memories of witnessing the violence and kids being attacked viciously and feeling helpless and hopeless because you are not able to help them because it could easily happen to you, and if you snitched on someone, retaliation could be worse. He also mentioned that he never had a fight in high school because he was well protected because his older brother and cousins were well known.

Moody also mentioned that during his freshman year in 1989, the movie *Lean on Me* was being filmed, and he was an extra in the movie and was paid $50 per day to sit in the auditorium and act like they were listening to the speeches, smoking cigarettes from approximately 8 o'clock in the morning to seven o'clock at night, and they had to do the same scene over and over again until the film producers were satisfied with the footage.

Moody discussed how the expectations for him to succeed at Eastside High School were "very high and already set." These were the types of messages he received from his parents, teachers, and Dr. Clark. "you better be good," "you are going to college." "I already know what you are about, so you will be getting an A in this class."

He believed that these are the types of messages he received that helped him strive to be a better student and to remain in honors classes. *Moody* remembered that "Dr. Clark would bend over backward for students and do what he could to help students." And that he genuinely cared and that if a student had a problem or if something was in the way, "he moved it out of the way to get you what you needed."

He remembered that Dr. Clark did not tolerate nonsense such as fighting and would allow students to borrow money from him if they really needed it and that he was a student-centered principal and administrator. He also remembered that he was pretty hard and had high expectations of the staff. He believed that Dr. Clark used [successful] strategies as principal and described it as

> I didn't know this at that time. I mean again, you are a student, and you just go to school. However, as an administrator now, 100%, he used some strategies! He had to with a building this size and of this magnitude! This is a major difference. He had about 3000+ students back then. We only have 1600 now, so I'm looking at it and saying we have four principals now. How can one man, really with a team of vice-principals, really effectuate the change he did without having some strategies in place? He had to! He had to!

When asked to elaborate on the strategies that he thought Dr. Clark used, he stated

> He was sensitive to the needs of the students. With the understanding that in this field, it's easy to blame the victim, and it's easy to say, all of these kids are not passing because kids have not been exposed, they don't have exposure to this... kids are not up to grade level on this their parents are messed up; their parents are on drugs; they are homeless; they are poor, so it's easy to point the finger at the victim.

> I think Dr. Clark understood all those things, and despite those things, he understood that we still have an obligation to teach these kids. So, he had to change the thought process and the mindset of our adults! So, his strategies were student-centered; his strategy was high accountability, holding adults accountable.

> If you are getting a paycheck, you have a job to do! You have a group of thirty students in your class; all thirty of them need to be up to par regardless of what level they are on. If you can't get them up to par, then you need to at least show growth from when they started until when they move to the next grade. In my mind, and I don't know this

for sure. He had to have some data. He had to be data-driven to show success other than just the school culture, which was evident.

When asked about Joe Clark's leadership style, he stated that he believed Dr. Clark was very directive in his leadership style approach, meaning that he was highly confrontational and told people what do; he set expectations and goals and expected people to meet those goals. He believed that Dr. Clark raised the bar and level of expectations, and he did not get the consensus from the group if he felt something should be done a certain way.

He believed that Dr. Clark's leadership was "definitely strong" because he had people buy into what he needed to have done, although everything was not always agreed upon. He thinks that the "situation that Dr. Clark walked into was so bad" that he "had" to "shock the system" and that he didn't have time to be nice and get a consensus from the staff. "He needed it done now and demanded a change." He does not believe Dr. Clark would have had the same impact if Dr. Clark would have utilized a different type of leadership style. He stated,

> No, not at all! If he was wishy-washy on any of his stances, I mean he came in, and he put some students who did not display a willingness to adhere to the school regulations, he just put them out! If he was wishy-washy or if he was a weak leader, he would not have any success because the culture of the school was so strong and so dominant at the time.

> If you did not meet that force with an equal, equal, but opposite force with the same strength, you would've been rolled over in a building like this. This was the case, of course, before he came. Who ran the school? The students ran the school! It took a strong leader to do that, to reestablish some order!

> The majority of his work was done there, and that's in terms of being a leader. Because that's the reason, he had to deal with it that way because the major issues and problems that we have in our schools are discipline

problems! That is one major aspect.

When asked about his own leadership style and how it compared to Joe Clark, he stated that,

> My approach is not like Dr. Clark's, and a lot of people may have "thought" I was going to be like a Dr. Clark and be demanding. I am not a directive leader. I'm collaborative. I get my... I am from the community;

> I have more resources in the community, in the school and in this town than most, I would be a fool to just challenge and fight people for the things I want. No, I want to get them to buy into this is why we need to do it, and this is the best thing for all of us and get the team to push the agenda. In contrast to me being the target, if you ever noticed...

> Dr. Clark was always the target. They were always saying, Oh, he can't do that! He can't. No, it's not "he" with me. It's "we," if you fight me, you're going to fight me and the entire community which I have behind me... That's the difference in my approach.

Moody believed that Dr. Clark had an impact on his life as a very strong African American male whom you can see, touch, and can communicate with while in high school.

> This was not the experience for other Black kids growing up because the elementary school staff did not reflect someone who was African American, who can take the leadership role and take control of the school to make a drastic change as Dr. Clark did. To be able to see someone who looks just like you (African American) and leading the way, having someone in your corner who was in charge was major for me.

Moody said, "I had the opportunity to know him personally and to be encouraged by him. Additionally, and for him to have the same values as my parents made what he was doing right for me." *Moody* believes that Dr.

Clark was a good principal and that his parents were probably some of his strongest supporters, and he and his brothers were forced to wear the school uniform back then. He also believes that Dr. Clark was a good leader and described a good leader as someone who "has the ability to take people to a place where they never thought they would never be able to achieve on their own."

Pinky - I am a forty-six-year-old, African American female who was born in Paterson, New Jersey. I was married, had two children, and divorced. I am currently married to a fellow alumnus of EHS; we have five children together. During the time of this research, I worked as an Assistant Dean of Students, and my salary was in the range of $50,000-$80,000. My responsibilities included: caring for the health, well-being, and social development of the students who lived on campus. I was responsible for responding to crisis situations, providing counseling for diversity-related topics, and assisting with the leadership advancement of more than 2,000 students who attended the university. I consider myself to be middle-class.

I attended Montclair State University where I was very active on campus and involved in various organizations; I was the president of the Black Student Cooperative Union; A director of the gospel choir; I was a Resident Assistant and I and became a member of my beloved Alpha Kappa Alpha Sorority Inc.

I graduated from Montclair State University in 1992, where I received my bachelor's degree in Communication Studies. In 1995, I received my master's degree in counseling from Montclair as well, and I graduated from Georgia State University in the summer of 2011 with my Ph.D., in Educational Policy Studies. Higher Education was my major. I graduated from EHS in 1986 and was a part of Dr. Clark's first graduating class.

My description of a good principal is someone with whom students can connect and laugh with; someone who disciplines fairly, and holds students accountable for their actions; someone who is able to connect with teachers, hold them accountable, and keep order among the teachers, students, and other administrators.

A good principal should also foster, create, and maintain a safe learning environment for students, in addition to incorporating a very strong teaching, supportive environment for teachers and administrators.

In my personal interview, I remembered the violence, financial struggles, and fun times in my family. I recalled stories of my siblings that included teenage pregnancies, dropouts, expulsions, and, most of all, graduations from EHS.

I am a product of an adulterous affair. My father did not tell my mother he was married. They dated for a short time, and the one and only time they had sex, I was conceived. My mother told him she was pregnant, and he then told her he was married with four children.

When I was born, my mother showed me to my father, and he said I could not be his child because my skin color was too light. (He was a dark-skinned man) She asked him to help her financially, and he said no! As a result, I grew up not having a relationship with my father. When I was ten years old, my mother took me the bowling alley where she met my father and introduced me to him, and he denied being my father to my face. I was deeply saddened by his response.

I was molested as a child by cousins, elementary school security guard, classmates, and my mother's friend beginning at age 5 until I was 13.

> Molestation is defined as the crime of sexual acts with children up to the age of 18, including touching of private parts, exposure of genitalia…inducement of sexual acts with the molester or with other children, and variations of these acts by pedophiles. And any unwanted sexual acts with adults short of rape (The Free Dictionary, 2013).

I wish I would have been able to have a relationship with my father. I wish he would have played a more significant role in my life. Maybe some of the bad things that happened to me would not have happened.

My mother worked two full-time jobs to take care of her six children. She was a single mother and raised her children by herself and did the best job that she could. My mother also helped raise and take care of several of my male cousins who came to live with us. All my siblings attended Eastside High School. See photos below:

(Brent Keys - Brother & Evonne Seldon - Mother)

(Brother - Lonnie Seldon)

(Brother - Brent Keys)

(Olandha Pinky Seldon)

I described the poverty-stricken, drug-infested areas in Paterson, New Jersey, and about how I really enjoyed my high school days, although, in the beginning, I cried because I did not want to go to Eastside because I was scared. I was terrified of gangs and chose not to get involved in that lifestyle.

I participated in extracurricular activities, such as DECA, yearbook photographer, softball and cheerleading, and drumming (I was the first female snare drummer in the EHS Marching 100 band and encouraged other young ladies to participate). I am Miss Paterson 1986 and represented my beloved city of Paterson well.

(Photos Courtesy of Pinky Miller)

I was encouraged to play the snare drum by music teacher and band director Mr. Peter Nelson. He was another very inspirational father figure to numerous students at Eastside. Mr. Nelson was the band director for 14 years, beginning in 1974. He held students accountable for their actions and helped students achieve their music and life goals.

Though I did not want to attend EHS, I later developed a good relationship with Dr. Clark, and he knew my name. I had several interactions with him and felt that he supported me; he was like a father to me.

My personal interview revealed my belief that Dr. Clark was a good principal and leader, and that he used notable strategies and methods to change the high school for the better. My mother and Dr. Clark inspired me to be who I am today. I was very excited to share memories of my high school experiences. The interview exposed how strongly I felt about Dr. Clark and the violence in my neighborhood.

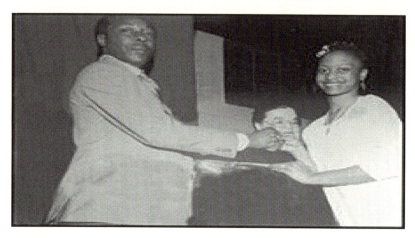

(Mr. Joe Clark & Pinky Miller, 1986)

I understand that my life has been truly blessed by God. I have been through some tough circumstances that hurt me to my core. God has been with me through it all. Prayerfully my trials, tribulations, and triumphs will help someone else realize that your current circumstances do not dictate your future! I am fearfully and wonderfully made! Amen.

Reggie - *is* a forty-seven-year-old African American male who was born in Paterson, New Jersey. He is married to a classmate from EHS. *Reggie* has five children and had his first child when he was eighteen-years-old as a student at EHS. *Reggie* works as an HVAC Foreman, and his salary is in the range of $50,000-$60,000. He lives in Georgia and considers himself to be poor. *Reggie* has three older siblings who attended EHS. Unfortunately, none of them graduated. Reggie was raised in a single-parent household and never met his father. He shared that some of his siblings were addicted to and sold drugs.

When Dr. Clark came to EHS, *Reggie* was a sophomore. *Reggie* who then became a fifth-year senior, was one of the students who Dr. Clark initially kicked out of school. However, he petitioned Dr. Clark to come back to school and graduated with the class of 1986.

Reggie shared some detailed descriptions of what EHS was like prior to Dr. Clark's arrival because he was a student one year prior. *Reggie* remembers that "there was a lot of violence and drug activity inside and outside of the school." He described the school as "a dirty school, where people were allowed to come in and roam the hallways" and cause disruptions. He said, "It was not a good place to learn."

Reggie attended Passaic County Community College and graduated with his associate's degree. *Reggie* believed that "the guidance of Dr. Clark is what helped him become the man he is today." He remembered Dr. Clark's strict discipline, and his three strikes rule that he shared with the students: "The first strike against you is you are Black; the second strike is you are poor and the third strike, is what the people outside think of you… they think you can't make it. You can't do it. You must show them something "different."

Reggie's fondest memory was his fifth year when, as a senior, he really and truly understood what Dr. Clark was doing and came to realize that education was very significant. He also was reminded of his not so positive memory of his first day at EHS.

Reggie stated that he was standing in the lunchroom, getting his food, and a guy came and punched him hard in the back of his head and kept on walking. His books fell, and he was thoroughly embarrassed. He did not do anything; he just picked his books up and was very humiliated.

Reggie does not remember the principal prior to Dr. Clark. He does remember that the school was unorganized and that "the teachers didn't care about the students." People were coming into high school and just hanging out.

People would hang out in the cafeteria, and some were not students. He described Paterson as a poverty-stricken area where there were violence and drug dealers. Students would get beaten up, and their items were stolen from them. He remembers situations where "students would come to school with sneakers on, but when they left school, they didn't have sneakers and had to walk home barefoot."

Reggie remembers many of the student gangs such as, "Black Spades," "Five Percenters Nation of Islam," "17th Ave," "The Master Ground," "Alabama Projects," "10th Ave," "12th Ave.," "Governor Street," "Ellison Street," and "Hamilton Ave." These groups of kids represented particular neighborhoods and were very similar to gangs. He recalls that these groups were not necessarily gangs like the "Bloods" and "Crips," but nonetheless, if one group had a "beef" with another group, then they would fight.

He remembers the violence, and he heard about people getting stabbed, raped (guys and girls) at EHS. *Reggie* had one fight in high school, and he was suspended for ten days.

Reggie's family background was poor, and *Reggie* was a member of the group called the Five-Percenters, which he described as a Muslim religion/organization where you had to learn lessons about the Muslim culture. The Five-Percenters started out as something positive, but as they became more popular, they became almost like a gang, alienating and fighting those who were not members, and potential hazing recruits.

Reggie felt that Dr. Clark is someone who changed his life because he always remembered the three-strikes rule, and he never wanted to get to the third strike. He thought Dr. Clark did the right thing and agreed with how he controlled the "school with strict discipline, and he stopped it from being like a zoo." *Reggie* feels he is successful now because he has a wife, a home, and children. He believed that first, God and his mom contributed greatly to his life and believed that one of his role models is Dr. Clark.

He remembered Dr. Clark said to him, "there are five of you; the statistics state that one of you guys is going to be successful, one of you will die. One of you goes to jail, and the other two will probably be strung out on drugs." He remembered this from twenty-five years ago because as he lived his life, out of his five closest friends, one is in jail. One is deceased, and two are on drugs, and he considers himself to be the successful one. He thinks that it is very significant that Dr. Clark planted that seed in him not to follow in the footsteps of his other friends.

Ruth - was very excited to share her memories of her high school experiences and to talk about Dr. Clark. She laughed a lot and spoke very fast. *Ruth* is an African American female; she is forty-six years-old and was born in Paterson, New Jersey. *Ruth* attended Delaware State University, and her major was English. She got married in 1997, to someone from the rival Kennedy High School in Paterson, New Jersey. She has three children and was twenty-nine years old when she had her first child. She currently works as a corporate attorney, and her current salary is over $100,000.

She lives in Georgia and considers herself to be upper-middle-class; she attended a private Catholic elementary school and high school prior to becoming a student at EHS. She is the oldest of three children. She was a college preparatory major. She had a lot of acquaintances, but not necessarily friends.

Ruth believed, "Dr. Clark was the right man for the job at the right time!" Dr. Clark called her name, "*Ruth*" out loud over the bullhorn and would make announcements such as, she was the president of the "virgins' club." She had a very good relationship with Dr. Clark. He would come into her classroom and check on her to make sure she was doing what she needed to do to be a successful student.

She feels he was a very good principal, one who was involved with the lives of his students and not just involved in the administrative bureaucracy. She described Dr. Clark as one who would have day-to-day hands-on contact with students, investing in the student lives. She also stated that she respects anyone who has a vision, and Dr. Clark had a vision!

Ruth described Dr. Clark as an excellent principal. "He made sure teachers were accountable, and he made sure that the students were accountable. I think that is what created the environment; he made sure that the school was clean. He made sure that the teachers were doing their jobs, and he made sure that you would do your part as a student."

T-Bird - was quite enthused about sharing his memories of his high school experience. He laughed a lot as he reminisced. *T-Bird* is a forty-six-year-old African American male who was born in Paterson, New Jersey. He is currently married. He has three biological children and four additional step-children from his current marriage. He had his first child when he was twenty years old, and the mother of his first child was a student at EHS.

He is currently employed, and his salary is between $60,000 and $70,000; he and lives in Georgia. *T-Bird* felt that Dr. Clark used several good strategies, tactics, and leadership skills to have such a strong effect on the students at EHS. He spoke about numerous good experiences that he had as a student at EHS. *T-Bird* was a very accomplished musician who played the trumpet.

He had a very good relationship with Dr. Clark. As a matter of fact, Dr. Clark used to "pull him out of class so that he would play his trumpet for programs in the auditorium assemblies." *T-Bird* was a member of the EHS Marching 100 band.

T-Bird spoke of the Five Percenters organization of students who attended EHS and was very informative about their activities. He spoke of his living situation when he was a student at EHS. He considered his family to be poor. He was an only child and had to fend for himself in many cases, "having to make a meal out of nothing." He lived in the projects and had two parents in his household. However, his parents had to work very, very hard just to make ends meet.

He spoke of many instances regarding drugs, and how "crack had just come on the scene," and he noticed how many of his friends became drug dealers and drug addicts, and he noticed how many of his friends became rich and made a lot of money from participating in the drug activity. He spoke about the people on the outside of the gate at EHS and about the poverty-stricken area.

T-Bird discussed how Dr. Clark came in and made a dramatic change in the school and with the students. He feels that "we [former EHS students] are, and we were a part of the revolution." "We are part of the evolution of the new EHS."

He spoke about the teachers and the relationship that Dr. Clark had with the teachers. He believed that Dr. Clark respected the teachers if they were teachers who had a passion for their jobs and were available to the students. He spoke about Dr. Clark's methods and strategies and how he worked closely with students.

He shared information about two instances to describe some of Dr. Clark's strategies. He remembered an incident when Dr. Clark gathered all the young people who were spraying graffiti inside and outside the building.

Dr. Clark got them together to share his thoughts and ideas on how they could do something more constructive with their graffiti talents. Dr. Clark encouraged them and allowed them to paint and spray murals on the inside of the school, and that is how he engaged the students into doing something positive, versus something negative.

"EASTSIDE"

(Photos Courtesy of EHS Yearbook, 1988)

T-Bird also spoke of the Five Percenters who was a group of "students who were learning some of the Muslim philosophies and teachings/lessons but were not learning the basic skills, the school lessons."

He stated that Dr. Clark challenged these students to learn the school lessons as well as the Five Percenters lessons, and he told them that if they were to meet their end of the bargain, then he would call them by their Five Percenters names versus their given names. The students bought into that strategy and began to take their studies more seriously, resulting in Dr. Clark calling them by their Five Percenter names." *T-Bird* was not part of any of the cliques or gangs but was very aware of them and had many friends who were a part of the gangs.

T-Bird attended college and graduated with his bachelor's degree in Music Entertainment Management. He described the city of Paterson as a violent city. He also spoke of Dr. Clark in the highest regard and felt that Dr. Clark was like a father to him and was there for him if he ever had any problems.

T-Bird described a good principal as someone with a sincere passion for the students. "You know he [Joe Clark] was able to relate." He wasn't on the outside talking down to you, and he was there grinding (working hard) with us, "He was going through it with us, and we later found out that he was also dealing with his own personal struggles and trying to get us right all at the same time. It wasn't easy. To me, he was definitely a great, great principal."

CHAPTER 8

Dr. Clark's Leadership in His Own Words

The following candid dialogue is from the interview I conducted with Mr. Joe Louis Clark. This was Dr. Clark's opportunity to share his thoughts and feelings about his leadership style, Eastside High School experiences, philosophy while working with students, and his viewpoint on education. I believe his information was an important part of my research as it briefly explores his leadership and purpose in life from his perspective.

(Photo Courtesy of EHS Yearbook, 1989)

I was Born to Raise Hell!

I'm doing what God sent me here to do *Pinky*! The big problem is you have to be focused! *Pinky*, you got a find your raison d'être! Your reason for being! When you find your reason for being, then our Creator has already equipped us with the mechanisms to endure all the hostilities that you're going to encounter.

But if you have found your reason for being, the forces of nature take over that, and you begin to do things that you never thought possible because you're doing what God put you here to do!

I found my raison d'être! I know what it is! I walk down the street, and the dogs stopped barking! Now we all have different personas. That was my task! Principals today are scared. I just didn't care! Because I was doing what God put me here to do! And thus, He became my bridge over troubled waters; He became my battle-ax; He made my enemies my stepping stones!

All that stuff falls into place once you find your raison d'être. 85% of Americans are in jobs they hate. You can listen to them on the weekends. Oh, I can't wait until Friday. When Friday came, I was sad, because that disrupted my management at East High School!

See, when you had that type of instinct, then it's contagious; people see it. It's not about Black. It's not about White. It was not about any of that. Kids know that if you're Black or White or polka-dotted [it's] where your heart is. If your heart is in the right direction, everything is cool.

(Photo Courtesy of EHS Yearbook, 1989)

By getting the students focused academically, getting the teachers and the guidance counselors off their butts, and making sure that they also were motivated, stimulating to students, and telling the students the truth. You are inferior! Academically! And they didn't like that inferior stuff, and they said we could do better than this. We can change it! And we gave them objectivity; this is where we are, and this is where I want to be.

I wanted them to know that there were many opportunities that existed for them and that they needed to take advantage of them. And it's better to be prepared for an opportunity and not have it, [than] to have an opportunity and not be prepared.

Which led them to another level, then I was able to tell them okay you are academically inferior, so they didn't like that, and the parents went crazy, they said that I was off the chain, going nuts! But they missed the point. The point was American Blacks, and even today, American Blacks are academically inferior; there's no question about that in general. Not intellectually. And in order to become intellectually competitive, you have to position yourself academically to be able to compete.

(Photo Courtesy of EHS Yearbook, 1989)

And even today until such time as American Blacks are able to show other cultural and ethnic groups [such as] the Asians, the Africans, the Whites that we are able to compete academically, we will always be looked upon as an inferior people. And that's one of the reasons why I don't like affirmative action and quota systems. I think James Brown said it best 'Don't open the door for me; just give me the opportunity, and I'll get it myself!"

One of the most memorable events was when I went to Eastside High School, even though there were like maybe ten or fifteen Whites in the school. Every year out of about 3000 students, ten Whites; the Whites were the valedictorian. I said something is wrong with this picture. It's not skewed. It's not logical, and it was my desire by design to make Blacks know that this was a clear example of their suggested inferiority, and it proved intellectual inferiority. I had to change that, and that was changed. That was a memorable thing.

So we need to be aware of all of this. Crutches and victimization of those things possibly eradicated from the premise of American Blacks, especially as a people, if we are to explicate ourselves from the stagnation that has actual weight as the basic fabric and soul of American Blacks today.

It's a shame and pathetic that out of all the cultural and ethnic groups in America, American Blacks have the lowest SAT scores. That's demoralizing to me. As American Blacks, we have to deal with it and correct that.

(Photo Courtesy of EHS Yearbook, 1989)

Our leadership, Black leadership, most of the people are nothing, but a bunch of hypocritical little gnats who are out to self-aggrandize them [themselves] as opposed to really uplifting a race by giving our young people goals and objectives and holding them categorically responsible for their behavior patterns. Of course, the most damaging thing amongst American Blacks is the fact that our family structure has been decimated. We cannot, and I reiterate with great gusto, we cannot have a vibrant country, a vibrant cultural group, a vibrant race when you have a 75% illiteracy rate! That's a dog that would not bark!

And as a result, some people liked me, and some people literally hated me with a passion. That's beyond my ability to articulate. But I loved that because I knew that if people like you, if most like you, then there's something wrong. As a leader, you are a dramatic entity in our society. So, I did things that would enhance the zeal and the enthusiasm of students, such as wearing the uniforms, and secondly, a sense of pride in the school.

Teaching the alma mater was a strategy in which I did some research and found that it's one of the hallmarks of success and of zeal and enthusiasm in an institution at the higher level, college, specifically, was credited upon the use of the school Alma Mater. My focal point to bring about unity and camaraderie amongst the students, getting them involved in that aspect academically, of course.

Academically of course, because that was the primary concern, and I had to expose them to the fact, the Blacks and the Hispanics and the poor Whites, who were there [EHS] because they could not escape, they couldn't get out, that's the only reason why they were there! I had to expose to the Blacks and Hispanics, especially and make them aware of the fact that they were academic...that they were academically inferior. Not intellectually but academically.

(Photo Courtesy of EHS Yearbook, 1989)

I didn't care! I was... the students loved me. They saw a guy, a Black man...they would...and they called me crazy Joe! They knew I wasn't crazy; what they were saying was... that this guy, you know in the Black neighborhood... this saying is... "Man you crazy" and that's a good thing! (Giggles) you know. That's a good thing! So, they called me crazy Joe.

They saw me stand up to a bureaucracy that was tainted and rotten to the core, and they liked that! Charisma is a crucial element. That's one thing that I had was charisma. I was able to get in front of the students in the auditorium and get them pumped up! They loved charismatic individuals good or bad. They liked that.

The one element of administration that is essential is that the leader possesses charisma. So, I went to various churches every Sunday. I would go to a different church. Solidifying their support of this combative, combative crusader, and after about a year or so, I had the support of many, many churches and the power in the Black community fortunately emanates from the church, and I knew then that as long as I had the support of the church politically, the bureaucracy couldn't touch me. I solidified my relationship with the church, and like anything else, a wise person needs to know when to exit at the appropriate time.

I found that my worst adversary and I say this chagrins me, were Blacks and Black women, specifically to my dismay. This made me also understand that Black women are... played a crucial role in the development of a group of people, women period! Whether you're Black or White or polka-dotted, that doesn't matter; they play a crucial role. But it should never be the success of the eradication of the male in the community!

We have become a race that's matriarchal, which saddens me that Black men have not arisen to their responsibility as fathers. I admonish them constantly; if you can't get along with your old lady, I understand that you know, I can deal with that, but take care of your children! Take care of your children! I have found that disproportionately American Black men don't!

This again catapults our youth situation in the state of total desperation, frustration, confusion, and that's when they to go to gangs. They walk around with pants, booty chokers hanging down behind below their behind. Not realizing that's just a drug syndrome, not a drug syndrome, a jail syndrome!

Well, almost everything I did was controversial, like kicking out... well, I called them a bunch of leeches and parasites, leeches and parasites, young people who were seventeen and eighteen coming to school with no credit, just exploiting the system. I felt that they didn't belong there. They needed an alternative mode of education. And I was not going to let 200 to 300; I called him pathological deviants, to stump the educational process, so I threw their asses out!

Uniforms, that was the epitome of controversy, because it was antithetical to what people knew. I had seen through casual observation, and I noticed that most of your countries, school systems, many of them, anyway, were wearing uniforms. And I found out pretty quickly that newly arrived immigrants understood the concept of uniforms because that's what they wore.

From Europe, Asia, Africa, the Caribbean, and South America ...so those individuals who were at the school who were immigrants responded to that notion with enthusiasm. The ones who fought it the hardest were again American, American Blacks who wanted to come to school looking fine and wanted to be the best dressed in the class.

I always told them you show me the best-dressed person in the classroom, and I'll show you a dummy! Because you can't be... you can't do all things, if you spend all your time shopping and trying to look fine, you've left the crucial aspects of the educational process which is learning. And I wanted to get rid of that stigma of trying to compete from a clothing perspective.

Another thing that I created was camaraderie with our athletics, I used athletics as a crucial point, and we all went to support the teams. We all went to the games on buses. People would see us coming in the yellow buses supporting our football team and our basketball team. And I would go to all sports games, cross-country, track, golf, tennis; I went to every single sporting event to let individuals know that I was supportive of them.

In that, Socrates said it best "a sound mind has a strong sound body," so an intellectual perspective and a physical perspective are inextricably interwoven. Those are two or three things along with a multiplicity of others.

(In 2008, Dr. Clark received an honorary doctorate from the US Sports Academy.
Photo Courtesy of *Senior Times* magazine)

Well, I coined the idea; I had the luxury of traveling throughout the United States, primarily to universities. The one thing that I do know for sure, and that is, you need to change the paradigm; you must take the educational process away from the bureaucrats and "educrats" and get our teachers, our administrators, our parents involved in the educational process… making them the important cog in the evolution of a system!

And I do also believe that in the American educational system, there are many good systems in public education and there are many, many bad ones, especially as it relates to the inner-city!

We must get back to the basic premise of the educational process [which is] antithetical to the premise of a democracy which is based upon free enterprise.

American public education is a monopoly, and if you have a monopoly, you have no accountability! American education is the only monopolistic agency that exists in this country. All of the other agencies have competition, but there is no competition, and there's no accountability! I say that we need to have a variety of different types of schools for our children and for our parents to choose from; charter schools, the voucher system, tax credit system, etc.

To look at the elite in our society... and I don't understand why Americans are so intellectually derelict; all of your rich and wealthy... most of us... Barack Obama too, will send his children to prestigious white institutions. Why? Now [if] those institutions are good enough for their children, then what about the poor, the downtrodden, the weak? Should not they be afforded the same opportunities?

If public education is in a good area, then that will survive; it will flourish. And the sad saga about this whole thing is that 70% of American Blacks want a voucher system, they want choice, and they want to be able to choose where they send their children.

But the bureaucrats, and the NAACP, and the rest of the hypocrites, who send their children, by the way, to private schools, refuse to give the downtrodden the position where they can get a quality education which will enable them to be intellectually competitive.

And I tell people constantly... that... am I... was I a success? Was I a failure? Look at the school... if it's better off now than it was when I was there, then I failed... if it's worse, then I succeeded. Because no one is going to get to school at five o'clock in the morning, stay all day, working 14, 15, 16 hours a day! No one is going to do that! I knew that the school would fall apart! They tell me that the school today is an absolute disgrace relative to what it was.

I may have done some things that due to hindsight that I could have done a little differently, but that's life, I did what I felt was right and did it without any mental reservation whatsoever! And if I had it to do it all over again, I would do it with even more zeal and enthusiasm! I would tell teachers, the community, and America if [you] like me thank you very much! If you don't, have a good damn day!

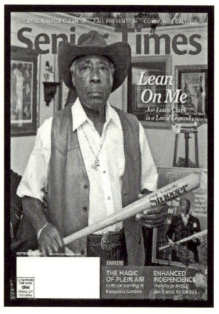

(Photo Courtesy of *Senior Times* magazine Photo by TJ Morrissey / Lotus Studios)

Dr. Clark continues to keep a sharp eye on America's schools, which he still finds not much improved. In 2012 Dr. Clark was on the cover of a *Senior Times* magazine, Dr. Clark is wearing a cowboy hat, a leather vest, over a white short-sleeved shirt with a gold chain and a gold horse medallion, holding a Louisville Slugger baseball bat resembling the 1988 picture of him on the cover of *Time Magazine*, displaying his ever-present bat and a sophisticated suit. The headline: "Is getting tough the answer? School Principal Joe Clark says 'yes,' and the critics are up in arms".

According to Senior Times magazine, Dr. Clark stated that he loved the media when they were writing about him, and he was profiled in over 260 media reports (Amburn, 2012).

(Photo Courtesy of Senior Times Photo by TJ Morrissey / Lotus Studios)

Dr. Clark's Advice to Parents

In the September 2012 article in the *Senior Times* magazine, Dr. Clark offered the following advice to parents: "make certain you provide adequate direction, guidance, and leadership to your progeny. I told my kids, "its college or death" -- facetiously.

The essence of success is interwoven with pertinacity, determination, and never giving up, continuously trying to find your raison d'être (the reason for being). Success wasn't something you'd expect of me, a poor, downtrodden welfare boy from Georgia, but achievement came because I knew my raison d'être and I went from the depths of despair to the methodical cadence of success" (Amburn, 2012).

(Photo Courtesy of *Senior Times* magazine Photo by TJ Morrissey / Lotus Studios)

Dr. Clark's Recent Thoughts on Education

In the September 2012 article in the *Senior Times* magazine, Dr. Clark offered the following advice about education; he believes that as a nation, we are in dire straits in many areas of the educational process. So often the blame for the deterioration is put on the teachers.

But like all other professions, there are a few geniuses, most are average, and there's a liberal sprinkling of fools. Teachers do a hell of a good job and by and large under the circumstances that most confront. They are overworked, underpaid, and maligned for the tragic state of affairs in our educational system. Our teachers perform in an exemplary manner" (Amburn, 2012).

"A large portion of the educational demise is directly related to the deterioration of the family structure. It would help immeasurably if children had parents who were dedicated and committed to the development as young, vibrant Americans.

I believe that children who are born out of wedlock with no father and no mother are put in a precarious situation as relates to becoming productive citizens. If individuals choose to have children out of wedlock, it should be their moral responsibility to take care of their children. It is not the government's responsibility to take care of children brought into the world by individuals" (Amburn, 2012).

Dr. Clark stated that his goal in life is not to make friends but to confront problems that are deleterious to the fate of our country. Poor family structures will be felt and high crime rates, on productive citizens, and gradual breakdowns of all values that have made America great" (Amburn, 2012).

Concomitant with the aforementioned is a need to re-think the educational format. We must take the system back from the legal minded, condescending bureaucratic louts and involve teachers, principals, parents, and educators in the process of rethinking the educational paradigm. A very important factor is to acknowledge specifically that American blacks are academically inferior, and this must be corrected.

This, in no way, is the responsibility of educators; it must be corrected by those individuals adversely affected. It requires massive efforts by a myriad of groups such as churches, sororities, fraternities, businesses, etc. Failure to react fervently will result in a needless societal calamity. A glance at the state of affairs relative to some talented young people such as music, dress, and deportment clearly indicates the exigency at hand. These vicissitudes must be confronted and changed" (Amburn, 2012).

How much change can be implemented as suggested by Kenneth Tewel, a former high school principal and school administration teachers at Queens College, who asserted in TIME'S article on Clark, "you cannot use a democratic and collaborative style when a crisis is rampant and disorder reigns. You need autocrat to bring things under control"

(Amburn, 2012).

Alternatively, celebrated and scorned as a disciplinarian, Dr. Clark's secret weapon is love. "If the kids didn't love, they would have taken my baseball bat and megaphone simultaneously wrapped them around my neck" (Amburn, 2012).

Joe Clark's Leadership

In this section, several leadership theories will be explored in relation to how the informants interpreted Dr. Clark's leadership. "Great man theories focused on identifying" the characteristics and qualities such as intelligence, alertness, initiative, and self-confidence possessed by the renowned military, political, and social leaders, such as "Gandhi" and "Abraham Lincoln" (Northouse, 2007).

It was assumed "that people were born with these traits, and only the "great" people possessed them" (Bass, 1990, p.15). This is emblematic of Dr. Clark's beliefs regarding leaders, as demonstrated by his statement that "real leaders are born, not made" (Clark and Picard, 1989, p. 186).

Regarding directive leadership, Glickman (1990) argued that the directive leadership style is utilized by a principal who interprets his position as one in authority of the school. This principal believes that the administrator knows how to better serve the students than the teacher. *Moody* is one of my informants who believed that Dr. Clark employed the directive style of leadership and stated,

> Dr. Clark was very directive in his leadership style approach, meaning that he was highly confrontational and told people what to do; set expectations; set goals and expected people to meet those goals; It raised the bar and level of expectations, and he didn't get the consensus from the group, if he felt something should be done a certain way.

Dr. Clark's leadership was definitely strong because he had high expectations, and he had the buy-in from most of the people in the community. The situation that Dr. Clark walked into was so bad that he had to shock the system, and that he didn't have time to be nice and get a consensus from the staff. He needed things done now and demanded a change. Dr. Clark would not have had the same impact if he had applied a different type of leadership style

Ms. Smiley was another person who viewed Dr. Clark's style as being directive. She stated,

> He was definitely a dictator. He took no prisoners. He would kick you out! He would lock you out! Have you transferred! He was like Hitler. He was a yeller and a screamer. Acted out terribly, and he tried ruling with a firm hand.

Mr. Joe Clark could be viewed as a transformational leader with his students and authoritarian leader with his administrators, teachers, and staff. Dr. Clark's leadership style was also eclectic as well as situational in the sense that it appeared that he would take tidbits from several different leadership styles, theories and piecemealed them together to fit whatever situation he faced at that particular time.

According to Bass (1999), "Transformational leadership is related to and includes a charismatic leadership style in the sense that its leaders encompass four factors that include (1) Intellectual Stimulation, (2) Inspirational Motivation, (3) Individualized Consideration and (4) Idealized Influence" (p. 20). During his interview, Dr. Clark referred to himself as a charismatic leader and saw that as one of the reasons for his success. He stated,

> Charisma is a crucial element. That's one thing that I had was charisma. I was able to get in front of the students in the auditorium and get them pumped up! They loved charismatic individuals good or bad. They liked that. The one element of administration that is

essential is that the leader possesses charisma.

Another leadership theory that aims to create positive changes in followers that enhances motivation, morale, and performance is Transformational leadership. According to Bass (1999), Transformational leadership is related to and includes a charismatic leadership style. As stated previously, this style of leadership was not exhibited by Dr. Clark relative to how he worked with teachers and administrators. Rather than utilizing facilitative or consensual approaches, he employed dominating approaches along with his charisma to obtain results.

Participative theory was certainly not one of Dr. Clark's usual ways of leading. Participative leadership consists of leaders who consult with and invite staff members to share in the decision-making processes. This type of leader obtains ideas and incorporates its recommendations into the decision processes on how the organization will advance (Northouse, 2007).

Although there were a few examples of Dr. Clark seeking input from others, this type of leadership was not a usual part of how Dr. Clark worked with the teachers at Eastside High School. According to *Ms. Smiley*, "It was all about what he wanted to be done, and if you didn't do it or couldn't do it up to his particular standards, then he would take retribution on you."

Northouse (2007) stated that Fiedler's (1964) contingency theory is mostly renowned because it involves a leader-match theory that strives to match leaders in applicable situations. Dr. Clark and other informants referred to Clark's style as doing what was needed based on the setting and situation. *Ruth* said, "Dr. Clark was the right man for the job at the right time!" *Moody* said he thinks that,

> The situation that Dr. Clark walked into was so bad that he had to shock the system, and that he didn't have time to be nice and get a consensus from the staff. He needed it done now and demanded a

change. If he was wishy-washy or if he was a weak leader, he would not have any success because the culture of the school was so strong and so dominant at the time.

If you did not meet that force with an equal but opposite force with the same strength, you would've been rolled over in a building like this.

As with many aspects of the beliefs about Dr. Clark's leadership, there was disagreement on whether or not he was a servant leader. Greenleaf (1991) purported that servant leadership is unselfish and is profoundly ingrained in the precedence of serving others' needs before one's own. Further, a servant leader strives to develop the skills of others, assisting them to become more independent, focusing on service rather than focusing on the results.

According to the informant Florence Jones, "a servant leader rolls up their sleeves and serves the flock. When Dr. Clark placed his ego above the school, he was doomed to fail. Toward the end of his tenure, he spent more time on the lecture circuit."

Coach "O" viewed Dr. Clark differently. He described that while he was teaching English and coaching, and he was attending graduate school in order to get his Master's degree in Urban Education/Administration. Dr. Clark knew this and provided him with additional opportunities to enhance his experiences in administration.

Paternalistic leadership was another aspect of how Dr. Clark operated. Westwood and Chen (1992) described this leadership style as one, "which combines strong discipline and authority with fatherly benevolence and moral integrity couched in a 'personalistic' atmosphere..." (p. 84).

Paternalistic leadership is a father like leadership style in which clear and strong authority is combined with concern and elements of moral leadership. Redding (1990) described paternalistic leadership as having fatherly concern for subordinates' and 'sensitivity to subordinate views. This style of leadership is practiced in the context of authoritarianism and is expressed in a patronizing manner and may not be extended to all subordinates uniformly.

Certainly, many of the informants saw Dr. Clark's leadership as fatherly and as a strong authority figure. According to *Flash*, Dr. Clark's personality dominated everyone, and he didn't care who didn't like it. *Karimah* believed that Dr. Clark made a great impact on her life and that he was like a father figure. *Moody* stated, "Dr. Clark would bend over backward for students and do what he could to help students, and that if a student had a problem or if something was in the way, "he moved it out of the way to get you what you needed."

CHAPTER 9

Strategies Dr. Clark Used to Transform Eastside High School

A thorough analysis of the data from the interview transcriptions identified ten strategies used by Dr. Clark. The following set of strategies was created by way of recurring clusters of significant meaning statements (Creswell, 2007);

(1) Cleaning of EHS: utilizing students in positive ways, (2) Supporting and encouraging the Five Percenter students to learn more than their group's lessons, (3) Lessons/intimidation/accountability for adults, (4) Walking to the right: creating order out of chaos, (5) Removing students who were disruptive, keeping the drug dealers out of the school, (6) Creating a sense of community, garnering support for reform, (7) Being omnipresent, (8) Enforcing strong discipline, (9) Being a father figure and role model; engaging the three strikes and you are out philosophy: encouraging students to do better and, (10) Creating a strong school spirit by incorporated the singing of the alma mater.

All the informants discussed at least four or more strategies during the interviews. In addition, Dr. Clark mentioned most of these strategies in his book *Laying Down the Law*.

Cleaning EHS: Guiding Students in Positive Ways

According to Dr. Clark, he wanted to give EHS the appearance of decency, respect, decorum, and order. He wanted to create an atmosphere that maintained discipline and was conducive for students to learn. Dr. Clark described his first visit to EHS, during the summer of 1982, where he noticed that there were shattered windows with jagged edges, gang signs, graffiti, and vulgar language on the inside and outside of the school walls.

He also noticed the bathrooms had toilet seats that were ripped out; shattered glass and mirrors were present, and lights were broken. He observed that the blackboards in the classrooms had been split and that the desks were in major disrepair (Clark and Picard, 1989).

Every informant described the aesthetics of EHS (inside and outside) and the poverty-stricken environment where it was located; participants talked about how dirty and graffiti-filled the school was before Dr. Clark. They also talked about the appearance of respectability, respect, orderliness, characterized by framed paintings, posters, drawings, and murals after Dr. Clark's arrival.

(Photo Courtesy of *Senior Times* magazine, via Joe Clark website)

Informant *Kid Fresh* stated, "The equipment wasn't working. The chairs were kind of raggedy." The loudspeaker electrical outlets were damaged, the cafeteria tables were torn apart, and the entrance doors had been propped open from the outside. Dr. Clark stated that the school smelled like alcohol, marijuana, and urine (Clark and Picard, 1989).

Dr. Clark incorporated different strategies in order to clean up EHS; he rented a sandblaster to assist the custodial staff in removing the graffiti. He told the staff to clean it off every day, and Dr. Clark used an unconventional way to involve the students in an effort to remove the debris. He told the custodial staff that they could get some of the detention students to help remove the graffiti.

Ms. De-Mo remembered a controversy when "Dr. Clark got orange jumpsuits from the sheriff 's department, and he had students who wrote graffiti on the walls to wear them and clean up the school grounds."

He communicated with the superintendent and asked for approval to renovate the school and hired additional painters, electricians, janitors, and other handymen to assist with the renovations. As a result, they installed new windows, made the necessary repairs, and cleaned-up EHS (Clark and Picard, 1989). *Ms. De-Mo* recalls,

> He called me in once and told me I was to take charge of school beautification. Each week I had to submit a new project. I had murals painted inside the building, had hanging plants and artificial plants on the small shelves built on corridor walls, and I suggested the fountain for the main hall (seen in the movie), mirrored tiles for the same small alcove in our main hallway.

> One week I had orange and blue ghosts spray-painted on the metal trash cans found inside and outside the building, but then I was stuck. I dreaded telling him I had no more ideas, but I finally did. He laughed and said he was waiting for me to tell him that because I had thought of so many.

Dr. Clark was determined to search for students who had an artistic ability to assist in redecorating the school. One of the informants, T. Bird, remembers, "Dr. Clark got the graffiti artists together, and he told them if you guys are going to do graffiti, let's just do something nice. Let's do something that represents us."

(Photo Courtesy of EHS Yearbook, 1986)

As a result, the students created an attractive mural of the mascot that was located in the entryway of the school near the principal's office and trophy case area. Another informant, *Kid Fresh*, recalls, "The whole trophy area in the center was always preserved, for some reason. Nobody ever messed with that. It didn't get graffitied up. That was almost like a sacred area or something.

(EHS Trophy Case – Photo Courtesy EHS Yearbook, 1893)

But before Dr. Clark, it was grimy." The EHS's mascot was a ghost. It was believed that EHS was built over a graveyard hence the appropriate name (EHS Ghost).

Informant *Cheeks* stated that "On the inside, we had murals on the wall. We had a *Beautiful* walkway with trophies, pictures actually of sports scenery so that everybody would know that this is the school of the Ghosts of EHS."

There were several insightful and inspirational paintings, posters murals, and drawings that placated the entryway of the school. Dr. Clark believed that his pursuit of finding students with the artistic ability generated magnificent results; the school ended up with a *Beautiful* mural and additional nice-looking works of art.

(Sonji Barbour & Vaughn McKoy - Class of 1986 – Most Athletic - Standing in front of a mural created by students – Photo Courtesy of EHS Yearbook, 1986)

Dr. Clark believed that students had energy; they had intelligence, which will all go to waste if the inner-city mindset was not broken. Dr. Clark believed that their energy just needed to be redirected with some guidance (Clark and Picard, 1989).

(Photo Courtesy of EHS Yearbook)

Supporting and Encouraging the Five Percenter Students to Learn More than the Lessons

In Clark and Picard (1989), Dr. Clark described the Five-Percenter situation as being "under the direction of the deadbeat gurus who organized and incited them, [it] was an insidious contagion to the minds and souls of poor Black youths seeking self-importance, adventure and panaceas" (Clark and Picard, 1989, p. 109).

> *Reggie* recollects, If you were serious, you had to actually study these Five Percenter lessons. And if you got caught not knowing your lessons, there was a serious chance that you could get beat up by other Five-Percenters, and they didn't play! The fact that you were a Five Percenter and you didn't know the lessons by a certain time, people were actually getting into fights. It was a serious thing.

> *John* stated, just like anything that starts out good, there's always a few bad seeds…growing up in a rough city like Paterson, and we started selling drugs, snatching pocketbooks, and stealing cars.

Dr. Clark described them as a "holier-than-thou bunch," that was to lead some of their people (ten percent) out of modern-day bondage and unto salvation. Although Dr. Clark may have personally felt this way about the group, he continued to endorse a strategy to connect with them. *Kid Fresh* shares his memory,

> I always go back to the story when Dr. Clark announced over the school intercom, and he spoke to them [Five-Percenters], specifically and pretty much said if you guys could learn these lessons from what they were calling "the lessons" the students were learning the Five Percenter lessons, then he would call them by their Five Percenter names.

Dr. Clark challenged them to learn their EHS lessons in addition to learning the lessons being taught by the leaders of this organization. If the students showed improvements in their classes, he agreed to call them by their Five Percenter names and practically legitimized what they were involved in. *T-Bird* thought Dr. Clark's way of relating to the Five-Percenters was innovative. In the interview he said,

> See at that time, and I just thought that method I thought it was incredible because most people who weren't Five-Percenters were rebelling against it. As time went on, it became more popular as most people were joining the Five Percenter, just because it was popular. And it almost became somewhat like a gang in my eyes, and from what I've seen that some people were using it to their advantage as to be part of a clique.

Dilligaf discussed that he was a great student at Eastside and was and is a member of the Five Percenter Nation and that "Dr. Clark loved him because his academics were excellent."

As a result, many of the students who participated in this way of life continued to learn their lessons as well as the lessons being taught in school. They felt respected by Dr. Clark and in turn, continued to respect themselves and respect education.

Lessons/Accountability/Intimidation of Teachers

(Teachers meeting with Dr. Clark in the gymnasium - Courtesy of EHS Yearbook, 1985)

Dr. Clark's interactions with his administrators and teachers were not always desirable. All informants described their perceptions and beliefs about the interactions between Dr. Clark, the administrators, and teachers. *Ms. Florence Jones* stated that Dr. Clark "was grossly obnoxious toward staff. He bullied teachers to a point. That's why many transferred."

She also felt that he did not want to have a relationship with staff members. Some of the informants indicated that it depended upon who the teachers were, and if the teachers subscribed to Dr. Clark's philosophies, his care, and concern for the students, discipline, and rules of order.

Mr. "B" believed that Dr. Clark held teachers and administrators accountable and wanted them to be concerned about the well-being and family life of the students at Eastside. *Mr. "B"* remembers that Dr. Clark uses to characterize the "teachers and administrators who stampeded out of Eastside once the bell rang on payday" as simply "getting a paycheck and hitting the highway."

According to *Ms. Smiley*, Dr. Clark would "yell and have hissy fits and jump up and down, threaten teachers with their jobs and their livelihood, if they did not do what he wanted. If he didn't like you, he got rid of you."

Some teachers were treated very well; however, some teachers were disrespected by Dr. Clark. It depended upon how Dr. Clark perceived them. *Coach Rosser* stated that he "thought Dr. Clark treated teachers and other administrators in a disrespectful manner" and described his relationship with Dr. Clark as *not* good and stated that, "I respected him, but I did not agree with him."

Coach "O" shared his philosophy about how he thought Joe Clark worked with teachers and staff; he purported that

> Dr. Clark always treated you fairly. Unless he realized that you were not going to be a positive influence on the students. Dr. Clark wanted all staff to work extremely hard, not only in the academic areas but also in the social development of each child. Dr. Clark wanted you to make a direct impact on their lives.

If you were a staff member who was going through the motions in the classroom, he would transfer you. Dr. Clark would document informal and formal observations and collect enough information to validate his rationale for the transfer. In time, Dr. Clark did create a positive working environment for approximately 250 staff members at Eastside High School.

Dr. Clark believed that to achieve victory in restoring order to EHS, he could not reveal to the teachers the total scope of his plans, and he did not go into detail on how he planned to succeed (Clark and Picard, 1989) According to *Mr. 13*, Dr. Clark "held teachers and administrators accountable for their actions." In regard to Joe Clark's leadership, he thought it was "puzzling when dealing with staff."

If he [Clark] respected you, he treated you with respect, if not look out!" He left it to the teachers to discern bits and pieces because he felt if he told them too much of the plan the critics among them, "especially the less visionary ones would start whacking away at the details, and the results of the entire plan could have been weakened" (Clark and Picard, 1989, p. 36).

Ms. Florence Jones stated that she believed Dr. Clark was "a bully toward staff. He was always yelling and screaming at some staff members. He was disappointing." *Flash* stated, "I think that he needed to put the teachers and students in shape. We needed that. I don't think it could have worked any other way."

Instead of telling his teachers how he was planning to create a new EHS, he just did it, and he left many teachers perplexed as to what his plans were. About halfway through his first year as principal, Dr. Clark had assembly meetings for his teachers and talked to them to provide additional opportunities to become more acquainted with him.

According to *Mr. Will*, Dr. Clark "treated the teachers and administrators fairly, with honesty and respect." He stated that it was a "pleasure and an honor" to work with Dr. Clark. *Kid Fresh* shared his memories about the school environment two years prior to Dr. Clark's arrival, which might have helped Dr. Clark justify his actions towards teachers.

> I think in the classroom, the teachers, for the most part, were decent, but then again, you know the class was either you waited for the class, or you tried to catch up with the class I have no real complaints about the teachers and what they taught us. I did learn lots of stuff in high school.

> Okay so, the difference was in the first two years…it was still a lot of clowning around going on in class…there were a lot of distractions in the class; a lot of disciplinary stuff that had to happen in class, and you have to sit there and wait for it to stop or try to get away from it, trying not to get in trouble with it…And you really felt like you were working hard to do the work, and a lot of people weren't!

> Students were getting passed on and got promoted and passed the class, and you know they didn't do crap! as a student, you would be kind of discouraged by that. There were fights in the classrooms, it was people getting tossed out, and it was a lot of back talking in class.

Ms. Florence Jones described Eastside High School as "chaotic" prior to Joe Clark and that "the previous principal was a non-factor." She described the academic and teaching environment as "teachers survive... no one thrived."

In Clark and Picard (1989), Dr. Clark discussed the transformations that happened in the preceding six months (before his arrival) with the teachers, and how, "the threats and verbal and physical abuse against teachers ended" [after his arrival] (p. 55). He discussed how "vandalism against their property and the school had ceased as well as sexual assaults" (p. 55). He talked about how the "chaos in the halls between classes, and the disruptive wildness of hoodlums in the corridors that used to be an everyday occurrence vanished." He stated to the staff,

> Apparently, very few of you took me seriously when I told you I was going to be ubiquitous now; perhaps you know better. Your distrust is understandable as I suspect that most of you have never worked under a real principal before. Yes, you are being monitored, but you're also being supported in your labors. Do your jobs, obey the rules, and you will find me as your staunchest ally (Clark and Picard, 1989, p. 55).

Clark enforced a simple management ladder, where the teacher has recourse to the department head, the department head had to report to the appropriate vice-principal, and the vice principal had to report to him (Clark and Picard, 1989). He believed the ladder worked for three main reasons;

> (1) They [the teachers] must perform or be ousted; (2) an ardent principal who keeps everyone on his toes, and (3) the added condition that anyone along that chain which does not feel the problem is being fairly or adequately addressed can directly go to him, (Clark and Picard, 1989, p. 41).

He told his staff that he wanted them to be "accessible and out patrolling the hallways" (p.41). And that he wanted them to be at least half as visible as he was. He also told his teachers that there would be no more of the "teachers failing to help a student in need because of administrative indifference" (p. 41).

Dr. Clark told teachers that they could possibly be transferred and/or fired if they did not agree with his rules. Dr. Clark "enforced a strict dress policy for teachers and administrators to dress professionally or be sent home if they did not comply" (Dr. Clark and Picard 1989, p.41). *Ms. De-Mo* remembered another controversy, and she stated that "Four male teachers refused to wear ties, and Dr. Clark wanted all males to wear ties and dress professionally. It was against their contract, and they refused. They wound up transferred." *T-Bird* shared his thoughts,

> I think he respected the teachers whom he knew were passionate about what they were doing. And didn't bite his tongue, so he didn't hesitate to call somebody out that he felt wasn't sincere about their work or wasn't passionate, or just wasn't getting things done. He treated teachers and administrators very similar to how he treated the students.
>
> The school was run like a military base sometimes. He was the general, and the teachers were the sergeants, and the students were the little officers. However, as you know, the sergeants still must listen to the general, and he definitely had them in tiptop shape. He was disrespectful at times because he didn't have a problem putting people out. So, you know, I think that he was disrespectful to those people and definitely respectful of those who were passionate. The ones, who were being disrespectful to us [the students], didn't stay around too long. He wanted to make sure the teachers were teaching and feeling what they were doing and doing it from the heart and not just going through the motions, especially for those teachers who were there for a long time. He was trying to implement change in them, just like a change in us.

Ms. Annette shared her experiences with Dr. Clark; she mentioned that Dr. Clark treated teachers and other administrators in such a way that "he seemed to respect those who stood up for themselves and those who were committed to their jobs. For those he did not like, he tried to get them to quit or transfer." She stated that she did have a "positive working relationship with Joe Clark." She worked well with him, and he was "supportive of her endeavors and was concerned about her professional growth."

Walk to the Right! Creating Order Out of Chaos

(Mr. Korenda, teacher - holding his "Keep Right" sign - Photo Courtesy of EHS Yearbook, 1987)

"Walk to the right!" was another one of Dr. Clark's strategies of utilizing and enforcing strong discipline in a chaotic environment in the hallways, by making students walk to the right. The student informants discussed the rule of having to walk to the right, where students moved forward, walked, and divided into two streamlines by walking toward the right side of the hallway or stairwell, which allowed order and direction with less chaos in the corridors and stairwells. With a high population of over 3000 students attending EHS in 1982, Dr. Clark used this as one method to create order. Informant *Kid Fresh* recalls his first day back to school

> when I walked in the door, he [Dr. Clark] was standing right there at the door with a bullhorn. The new school year, I was coming back as a junior. "All right, people let's move expeditiously." "Move to the right!" He was in the hallway, and you know we didn't even know where we're going. I was asking myself where my homeroom is. I mean, what are the hall rules this year? Who is this guy?

Dr. Clark stated that prior to his arrival, students at EHS had rarely ever seen their principal out and about unless it was something pertaining to misbehavior. Dr. Clark implemented his "Walk to the Right!" strategy to set the tone of firm order and calm that would last for the rest of the year (Clark and Picard, 1989). Informant T. Bird remembered,

> Well, yeah, yes, we had to "Walk to the Right!" of the corridor. And yes, I remember that, which was cool because you know, you had a high population. It would keep some of the tension down people bumping into each other. You know all that going back and forth to class definitely created some tension, and I guess that is some of the tension they were trying to get rid of it. Yeah, it made sense.

Dr. Clark ordered the teachers to stand in the middle of the hallway and stand at their posts until the bell rang. Dr. Clark stood in the entryway wielding his bullhorn and shouting, "Walk to the Right!" and the students moved forward, walked, and divided into two lines by walking to the right. The teachers were involved and formed the line of division, while some of them could not believe what they witnessed with their own eyes (Clark and Picard, 1989). *Karimah*, described her experience,

> Walk on the right side of the hallway. Dr. Clark would be out there with his bullhorn to make sure everybody was walking on the right side of the hallway. To me, that was the most orderly fashion, I mean. I can't think of a way not to do that because the high school was so overpopulated at that time, and in order to be organized and not run into people, it was the best thing that really could have happened. As a matter of fact, any time the bell rang, the teachers would be right outside the door standing in the middle of the hallway serving as a divider.

It has been twenty-nine years since the introduction of Dr. Clark's walk to the right strategy, and although it's no longer being implemented,

Ms. Smiley stated that,

> Staying to the right was a good practice…now when you walk down the hall, you got twenty kids walking across instead of in a straight line. It's rather difficult to walk down the hall on either side when you have so many students coming at you in one direction.

I asked *Moody* (current principal of operations at Eastside) what happened to the strategy of students walking to the right, and he explained

> It was a mandatory thing back then. It just became we were acculturated under Dr. Clark's administration. When the new principal came in, the focus changed somewhat. It was still Eastside High School; it wasn't that you had to "Walk to the Right!" You just naturally walked to the right. That was not an expectation.

> The expectations changed and if I had to say now looking back, the expectation probably went… if the superintendent was smart the expectation probably went to focus on those things that were academic in nature, and that we're going to help improve the test scores, and the focus was no longer on the cultural/discipline aspects of the school. That was already established. Dr. Clark put that in place, you would be a fool to reverse that, but now let's focus on what's happening in these classrooms. Let's look at our math scores. So that became the focus of the entire school.

Weeding Out the Miscreants and Thugs: How Dr. Clark Kept the Drug Dealers Out of the School

Within the first six weeks of Dr. Clark's tenure, he intensely studied the records of the student body and watched how the students interacted with one another. Within those six weeks, he believed he had a good idea on which students he needed to keep a watchful eye. He identified which students were students in name only, meaning that they did not have a sufficient number of credits that would allow them to graduate in a timely manner (Clark and Picard, 1989).

John stated, "I am not saying Dr. Clark was wrong for what he did or the methods he used, but we knew we were going to get kicked out soon, so we were even more defiant because we knew we were getting kicked out!"

Dilligaf believed that Dr. Clark, "did what he had to do, he really didn't kick anybody out. He got rid of the people who did not belong." *Dilligaf* further explained that "everybody knew they weren't supposed to be in the damn school causing confusion, getting in trouble, hustling and hanging out. It was the transaction spot for drugs." *Moody* stated that "some of those students that Dr. Clark got rid of may have really needed to be out of here!" He further explained

> They were really cancer to the building, possibly. So talking was over for them. I'm talking about seniors who were in the school for four years with ten credits. No! What are you talking about? This kid can't turn his situation around here within this time frame; he needs to go to an adult program.

Most of the informants indicated that they were thankful that the students who were troublesome, violent, and failing classes were expelled by Dr. Clark. This allowed the other students the opportunity to gain an education without distractions and violence. *Anthony* stated, "What I will give him the greatest credit for is making and creating an environment conducive for learning, and that was his big thing. He was getting rid of the people who weren't making the school conducive to learning."

The participants also described how Dr. Clark believed that the best way to keep the drugs out of the school was to keep them from getting in by locking and chaining the thirty-eight doors and stationing the security guards outside of the building. Dr. Clark engaged some of the teachers as patrollers of the hallways. Dr. Clark asked the following question,

> What can be done about the young who see no value in education and, consequently, learn nothing, who attack and denigrate the authority, consort with criminals, take drugs, get pregnant, on welfare, drop out, remain unemployed, and sink deeper into drugs and crime? (Clark and Picard, 1989, p.24)

Dr. Clark answered his own question by having all students who were fifth-year seniors were, failing classes, had high truancy records, and students without enough credits to graduate in a timely fashion expelled. Several students pleaded with Dr. Clark and asked if they could come back to school to get an education. Some of the informants talked about how they pleaded with Dr. Clark by utilizing personal experiences and inquired if they could come back to school to get an education.

As a result, they could attend classes and receive instruction. For example, *Dilligaf* was on the verge of being expelled for missing twenty-one days but appealed to Dr. Clark and was allowed to attend school with the agreement that he would not miss any more days of school regardless of any situation that may arise. *Reggie* was another student, who had to plead his case to continue his education at Eastside. *Reggie* was a fifth-year senior on the threshold of being kicked out of Eastside. He, along with his mother, had a meeting with Dr. Clark and was allowed to continue and graduate with the class of 1986. *Karimah* recalls,

> The strategies that he used were no-nonsense, he didn't take it, and if you threatened somebody, you would be kicked out. He used all kinds of ways to weed out everybody who wasn't there for education. If he knew you were disrupting his high school, you were out of there. That was his strategy of weeding out the good from the bad.

Those students who were serious and showed promise and tenacity were allowed back into EHS to receive an education either willingly by Dr. Clark or by the Paterson Board of Education, forcing Dr. Clark to reinstate those students he kicked out. According to *Kid Fresh*;

> You knew this. He was coming in order to straighten that stuff out! When the whole kids got kicked out because they didn't have the credits thing happened, they just didn't have juniors and seniors had zero credits, and they got kicked out! I thought the fact that they were

around and didn't have any credits, and they were the ones doing nothing but making my life more complicated. I felt like I could breathe and do my thing now that they were gone. I think it was far beyond anything else he could have done. I mean, you know. You can't—you can't have zero credits!

However, for those students who did not show potential, Dr. Clark made an appeal to the Board of Education to set up alternative schools for those students whom he considered to be social deviants and for those with learning disabilities. *Moody* stated,

> If I'm not mistaken, there might have been one alternative school, but the capacity was very limited, it wasn't an alternative school, to be honest with you. I think it was held at Public School Number 22. It had one teacher, and they would send students with discipline problems over there. So, it's not like it was a true alternative school; it was an area, more like a holding ground.

The Board of Education did not establish alternative schools, and as a result, Dr. Clark had to reinstate most of the 300 students whom he put out. Consequently, there were some students who were weeded out of EHS, one way or another (Clark and Picard, 1989). *Flash* stated;

> That was the part that he was showing everybody that he was in charge. I remember—the controversy with him being a disciplinarian, and I remember the controversy about the suspension, the large student group suspensions. He had to bring them back, and I just looked at that like him, you know just— just being a trendsetter and seeing things just a bit differently. So, I think that was a good thing. What he did for the school was to create an environment where you could actually succeed if you put your mind to it. He created that environment where at least—I want to say that academically, the school was sound.

By creating a strict visitation and identification card policy, Dr. Clark was able to keep drug dealers and those who might want to cause harm to the students out of EHS. Clark believed that "every worker, delivery person, student, teacher, and the security guard had to wear an identification tag to help keep the negative element out" of EHS (Clark and Picard, 1989, p. 53).

Reggie stated that "Before Dr. Clark, it was unorganized, teachers didn't care about students, and they showed examples of not caring about the students. Anybody could come in EHS, and just you know, walk the halls, and it was like a zoo." Dr. Clark believed that this practice of identification was a key part of his system (Clark and Picard, 1989). Dr. Clark stated that "every person who attempted to come into EHS had to show their identification card or had to go to the principal's office to get a visitor's pass" (Clark and Picard, 1989, p. 53). Dr. Clark made it clear that the

> Laminated photo ID cards had to be worn at all times, which also served as collateral for a hall or lavatory pass or for the use of certain equipment. This system made the administrator's monitoring duties much easier because they could easily identify people who did not belong in the school. This helped keep drug dealers out of EHS (Clark and Picard, 1989, p. 53).

The specifics included "replacing the ineffective security guards with effective ones, repairing the door locks and replacing the fence, and by keeping an eye on the students who would normally open up the door for drug pushers to get in." (Clark and Picard, 1989, p. 51). According to Clark and Picard (1989), he "stationed security guards outside of the building to serve as a perimeter defense, and he incorporated some of the teachers as patrollers of the hallways." (p. 51) *Pinky* stated that,

> I was scared to walk home sometimes because the school was located right in "da hood." One side to exit was Park Ave, whereas a lot of African American drug dealers and the like hung-out and on the Market street side is where the Dominicans, Hispanics, Latino and Latina's hung-out. EHS had an environment that was very interesting. It was very interesting because outside the gates, you saw people who wanted to be in EHS but probably most likely for the wrong reasons,

and they couldn't get in.

Dr. Clark believed that "the best way to keep the drugs out of the school was to keep them from getting in; by making the school a fortress that pushers could not penetrate" (Clark and Picard 1989, p. 51)

Dr. Clark also made use of a history teacher whom he appointed as his special assistant for discipline. This teacher used to play professional football for the New York Giants. According to Clark and Picard (1989), he was "big, fearless and dedicated to the well-being of his students, and had the reputation of the only person who can stand up to the hoods who were outside of the school" (p. 52). When *Ms. Smiley* was asked what she thought about Mr. Joe Clark locking and chaining the doors, she stated, "He did it so that the kids couldn't go to the doors and let their friends in and wreak havoc in the school." She also stated that he did it to "keep the bad element out. And you keep the kids who were supposed to be getting their education in." *Ruth* shared her thoughts about Dr. Clark striving to keep those he classified as the miscreants and thugs out of Eastside.

> I think when he tried to implement safety at the school like locking the doors. People coming into the school, strangers come to the school, you know, people walking in the school without permission. I mean, they didn't have a security guard at every entry. I guess he put in a work order for them to have better locks on the doors to protect us. And they [Paterson Board of Education] wouldn't do it, and so he chained us in, and they got an attitude, and if you try to implement any policies in the schools, they gave him a hard time.

Creating Community: Garnering Support for Reform

Clark was invited to several churches in Paterson, New Jersey, and was given the opportunity to speak to a number of parents of the children who attended EHS. Clark stated that the first thing that he did to reach out to the community was to formally introduce himself and his program at neighborhood churches (Clark and Picard, 1989).

Ms. De-Mo stated that he knew how to build public support among other things, "he went to a different church each Sunday," and "he bought coats for those who had none. He bought gym uniforms for those who needed them, additionally. He linked families up with social agencies to help get food, heat, etc."

Karimah stated, "Clark made a positive impact on EHS. He set the tone for real education in an urban environment that had previously forgotten the true essence of education and how important it is, especially for the African American community." Each week Dr. Clark would attend a different church service with the help of concerned ministers and would be given an opportunity to address the congregation. The motivational messages he shared with the parents stated that,

> If you persist, you will survive if you work hard and do not give up, though the obstacles are many, and the road is hard and long. You can advance. You can succeed. Your life will have meaning, even joy." High regard for education is the surest and the most decent way to advance (Clark and Picard, 1989 p. 71).

Dr. Clark shared his belief with the community that it is through discipline and hard work that a person truly overcomes and achieves. He spoke about his two decades of educational experience and how EHS needed their cooperation in order to carry out his reforms. He explained that he needed their support and the opportunity to extend to their children the opportunities for true education. *Pinky* shared,

> Dr. Clark would ask me how I was doing and if I needed help with anything, and if I needed anything to let him know. I loved Dr. Clark. Dr. Clark was like the dad I never had. I appreciated him. Dr. Clark helped my mother financially when it was time to purchase my school uniform because she did not have the money.

He promised to turn the school around and thus turn the students' lives around. Furthermore, he promised to give each youth a chance he or she deserves to be successful (Clark and Picard, 1989). According to Clark and Picard (1989), from the beginning of his appointment, EHS had been encouraging parental and community involvement and school programs and projects such as anti-drug seminars, career day, clubs, choirs and assemblies covering a wide variety of subjects, and all sorts of fundraising opportunities. Dr. Clark organized the Home School Council that used to be called the Parents Teachers Association and made sure that the Hispanic parents' voices and their particular concerns would not be lost in the majority. As a result, he organized a parental council solely for Hispanics (Clark and Picard, 1989). *Ruth* stated that "He would always send little notes and items home to my mother. My mother admired him. I thought that more parents should have come to more board meetings and spoke up on his behalf." *T-Bird* stated that,

> My parents loved him. They thought he was a little rough because he was throwing a lot of kids out of school, but after a while, they came to realize that what he was doing was something that people at EHS had never seen before. My parents loved him.

The Bullhorn - He's Everywhere!

(Photos Courtesy of EHS Yearbook, 1985)

While being very visible, Dr. Clark discovered many things that were taking place at EHS. He made time to observe and evaluate what was happening on a daily basis. Dr. Clark believed that in order "to be a successful principal, one must be a benevolent Big Brother" (Clark and Picard, 1989, p. 64) and should be "all-knowing and ubiquitous" (p. 64).

As stated by Dr. Clark, as a result, he was never in his office for more than a few minutes, and he believed that the principal's office was not a place where education happened. According to *Ruth*,

I mean, you always saw him. I mean, he did not just sit in his office.

He had that bullhorn. He walked around the school. He went into a class. He wanted to see what the teacher was doing. Seeing what you were doing so, he was always around. He was just always around. He was involved, not just in the administrative part but the day-to-day hands-on contact with the students and the teachers too. I really felt safe; I felt safer at Eastside and more respected than I did at Paterson Catholic High School.

According to Clark and Picard (1989), Clark was "always on the prowl in the corridors, in the classrooms, the gym, and on the stairs; everywhere" (p. 64). By roving the school he discovered who the kids were and by having conversations with them, he learned what they were thinking; he learned who the good and bad teachers were; what nuances could develop into serious problems; what difficulties the teachers were facing; he knew the status of what was going on in the school.

T-Bird stated, "Dr. Clark was always in the hallways and always in the classrooms. He wasn't someone who would just sit at his desk." Dr. Clark believed that his "constant physical presence was also a reminder of his disciplinary code" (Clark and Picard, 1989, p. 64). *Ms. De-Mo* stated, "I liked it. He was omnipresent, always in classes, the halls, and the lunchroom." Dr. Clark made sure that the security guards were in the right places and making sure students were in the classrooms, and learning was taking place (Clark and Picard, 1989).

Dr. Clark believed that the bullhorn became his trademark. He carried it at all times and incorporated this device for conveying and magnifying his voice of authority that helped regulate students walking along the hallways. Utilizing the bullhorn as well as the public address system gave the illusion of him being everywhere, and he could communicate with everyone in the school at the same time (Clark and Picard, 1989). According to *Cheeks*,

You always saw him. He did not just sit in his office. He had that bullhorn, and he walked around the school. He always went into the classrooms because he wanted to see what the teacher was doing, and he wanted to see what you were doing.

Utilizing and Enforcing Strong Discipline

Dr. Clark was very diligent about order and discipline, and advised students, parents, teachers, administrators, and staff to study the rules because they were going to be enforced without any exception. Coach "O," stated that "when Joe Clark became principal, he wanted all coaches to teach there in order to control their athletes and to help with overall discipline."

Throughout the interviews, enforcing the rules and discipline were discussed heavily by all of my informants. All of the informants could recite most of the ten-day suspension rules and could remember that Dr. Clark was very serious about giving a student a ten-day suspension if any of the rules were broken. As a result, most students would think twice about not obeying the rules because if the student had too many ten-day suspensions, they could then quickly be expelled. According to *Flash,*

> Here's a man who is in charge of everybody! He used military training! The big one is "no excuses!" and he was in your face. He recognized that we were falling behind academically; he tried to do everything he could within his level of power. His predominant strategies were discipline, the teachers, and having a close relationship with his students.

Prior to school opening, Dr. Clark created a new suspension policy that included: ten days of suspension for fighting, assault on a teacher (verbal or physical), selling of drugs or alcohol, disruption in the cafeteria, and vandalism, graffiti, theft, gambling, defiance of authority, or carrying weapons. (Clark and Picard, 1989 p. 53) *Reggie* shared a story about a fight he had.

This guy basically called me out. We had words, and I thought that was the end of it. However, as I was going into the classroom, he punched me from behind, and a fight began to break out, and he got the thrust of it. He got a beat down! He got the worst of the fight. And we both got suspended for ten days. *Beautiful* described how she got suspended for fifteen days.

I said Jennifer, go ahead now and leave me alone! I don't want to have to hurt you! So here she goes, stepping on the back of my shoes! She proceeds to get her stuff from the girl who is holding her stuff, grabs her coat, and swings her coat around hard and fast, and her coat hits me on the side of the face!

I snapped! and I reached in my pocketbook (I had a Home Economics class, so I kept my shears in my pocketbook), so I grabbed my shears, my scissors and I turned around, and I proceeded to jab them into her arm! Then I tried to get her again! But she had on a sweater. We proceeded just to fight! I remember Mr. Brown. Do you remember Mr. Brown? He comes out of nowhere, and he grabs me! I don't know what or how I did it, but I got away from that big man! And we started fighting again! I mean, we are continuously fighting!

We were by the trophy case and continued fighting! Somebody broke it up! I don't know who it was, but by then I had already snapped and blacked out! It took me a long while to come back down to earth. I cut somebody! I don't know whom I punched, but all I heard was 'Ooooooohhhhh!!!' then I do recall, do you remember Mr. Schwartz, the history teacher? It was him! I punched! I punched him in the eye by mistake! I got suspended for fifteen days!

Although most students agreed with Dr. Clark's strategies, there were some students who were not very fond of how he executed his strategies. *Anthony* found value in Dr. Clark's strong desire to keep the students safe at school. However, he felt that Dr. Clark was too aggressive and an attention seeker. *Anthony* shared his thoughts.

The only negative thing is I think he was just out there too much as far as the discipline and some of the tactics that were used were used just to get attention. I think my mom was pleased because she heard a rumor that it was a very violent place, and I didn't go there and get stabbed or killed. She was happy about that.

John believed that

his methods were unconventional by carrying the bullhorn and the bat around, which may have worked for some of the lame students who feared him, but those things did not work for my crew. His methods actually pushed us more over the edge and caused us to be more disruptive; it gave us a reason to be more disruptive.

Every informant described Dr. Clark's reverence for order and discipline. Dr. Clark as a father figure and role model and his three strikes and you're out philosophy. Dr. Clark was a father figure and a role model to several students who did not have a father in the home or a positive male figure in their lives. Many of the students were raised by single mothers, and sometimes that made it very difficult for some students to experience and appreciate firm discipline from a man. *Pinky* stated,

Dr. Clark was the father I never had at home. He was someone I truly respected and asked for guidance and confided in if I ever had a problem. There were many trials and tribulations that I went through as a child, being the baby girl of six kids, growing up without knowing who my father was, not having the financial support or guidance from my father. Dr. Clark, in my eyes, was my father figure.

Because of the instability that was found in some homes of single parents, EHS became an environment that was stable for some students. The data showed that many of Dr. Clark's students revered him as a father, a strong male figure, and role model, and one who cared about them personally and educationally. Dr. Clark believed that it was very important for him to connect with students and to know them personally, and often times, he found himself assisting families financially out of his own pocket.

Cheeks shared her memory

> Dr. Clark actually went to one of the young lady houses, which got
> pregnant, a classmate of mine that went to school with me in Public
> School Number 6. She was only in the eighth grade. Dr. Clark had
> gone to her house because her mom had put her out, and he went to
> seek and get them some help because her mom was poor, and the
> mom couldn't do anything, and she didn't know what else to do. For
> the most part, he got the family some help and got her mother a job
> and things of that nature to make it better for them.

Being a Father Figure and Role Model

According to Clark and Picard (1989), "Every student must have
someone he or she can turn to; at least one door must always be open."
EHS provided that help for students, even "when the parent was
unresponsive." "EHS had become the home a lot of these kids never had."
"Reaching out to students on an individual basis can and does cause a
change in their lives" (p.51).

Dr. Clark recognized this when he hit a dead end while seeking support
from a parent and then appealed to an older brother or sister to assist a
student. He realized that taking on the job at EHS meant that he would
serve as a surrogate father to a few thousand kids, and it was a major part
of the job (Clark and Picard, 1989). *Karimah* stated,

> Dr. Clark was like a father figure. He was very adamant about having
> respect for you and demanding respect for yourself from others. You
> just had that feeling that he was more so like a father than a principal.
> Thank you for being a leader, a father figure, a role model, and
> everything positive in a young lady's life that she needed at that time.

Dr. Clark knew he had to be there for the students when they reached
out to him because "the father doesn't let his kids go down" (Clark and
Picard, 1989, p. 84). Dr. Clark helped voluminous numbers of students
who were suicidal, confused, depressed, abused physically and sexually,

addicted to drugs, prostitutes, financially distraught, homeless, and pregnant as a teen. Dr. Clark provided referral services for them as well as utilizing his own personal finances to help students and their families (Clark and Picard, 1989).

One of Dr. Clark's philosophies that he shared with his students was that he always wanted them to do better, and he did not want them to fail regardless of the circumstances. *Dilligaf* stated that Dr. Clark "taught me so much by letting me see that father figure; that with somebody who can instill positivity in me, and that can-do attitude, and that's how he inspired me, and that's how he changed me."

Dr. Clark believed in tough love. He believed in giving student's discipline but also being genuinely affectionate. Coach "O," stated that Dr. Clark used "tough love, honest love in creating a self-worth environment for each student." However, he held students accountable for their actions and encouraged them to continue to fight for their education; listen to God; listen to their parents; go after what you want in life; don't ever let anybody stop you; don't wait for something to come to you go for it! *Pinky* shared her thoughts.

> He taught me that I did not have to lower my standards for boys, and he taught me that education was important; he taught me that God was significant; he taught me that discipline was very vital. He taught me that if I wanted something, I could go after it, and no one can stop me. And I thank him for that!

Flash believed that having assemblies on a regular basis, "the pep talks, the daily messages, the daily poetry or talks, pick me ups, pep rallies," was a way of "recognizing that the kids instead of just needing to pick me ups, but they needed inspiration on a regular basis, to get them to stay in school or come to school and do what they had to do." *Flash* believed that it was more of "a gift to inspire them on a regular basis, and a lot of us didn't have that father like treatment or someone who would say it the way that he would on a regular basis." Dr. Clark's overall strategy was to "make things right, to make things relevant, to make things work for the majority of the students."

Creating a Strong School Spirit by Utilizing the Alma Mater

ALMA MATER

Fair Eastside, by thy side we'll stand and always praise thy name.

To ever lend our hearts and hands to help increase thy fame.

The honor of old Eastside High brings forth our loyalty.

So cheer for dear old Eastside High! Lead on to victory!

So cheer for dear old Eastside High! Lead on to victory!

FAIR EASTSIDE

(Dr. Clark & students singing the Alma Mater at a football game - Photos Courtesy of
EHS Yearbook, 1989)

Every student informant described how they had to recite the alma
mater in public, alone or in a group, in English as well as Spanish. They
described how singing the school song after sports events (win or lose)
instilled pride and a sense of camaraderie among the students.

All informants could recite the alma mater twenty-five-plus years later.
All the informants shared their experiences in regard to singing the alma
mater and discussed how they felt that it was something that created high
school spirit that was beyond measure because it was one thing that we all
had to do regardless of who you were at EHS, and that included teachers
and administrators and staff. *T-Bird* recalls

> I can remember seeing him in the hallway, oh my God, oh man, don't
> get me started! (Excited) I can remember singing the alma mater so
> many times! I remember being called out in the cafeteria! I remember
> one particular time. He pulled me on stage to play my trumpet, and

right before I started to play, he said, wait, sing the alma mater for us before you play. I had to sing the alma mater on stage, and this was when I was a sophomore, and I had to sing it in front of the seniors. I will never forget that.

According to Clark and Picard (1989), "school spirit is not merely symbols, rituals or traditions. It is the spirit of effort, attainment, aspiration, and enthusiasm" (p. 166). Clark stated

It is the spirit of camaraderie, understanding of common needs, desires, and mutual respect for individual differences. It is the building of self-esteem, the fostering of sanity, and it is the awakening of brotherhood and sisterhood and the conquering of prejudice and hate (p. 166).

Dr. Clark believed that, "school spirit is the necessary companion to school discipline and that neither can exist without the other" (p.166). The alma mater was a tool that created an atmosphere that was high spirited and brought a lot of joy to our hearts and minds. Dr. Clark wanted all students to learn how to sing the song in English and in Spanish, and that allowed students to be on one accord, and it helped the Hispanic students feel just as important as the African American students who were the majority at that time. *Pinky* recalls,

Yes, I had to sing the alma mater, and we had to learn it in Spanish too. We sang the alma mater at all of our sporting events, assemblies. It didn't matter if we won or lost, and we had to sing the alma mater before going home. That song instilled a lot of pride in our classmates. We had a good time, and there was always something to do at EHS! There was a lot of school spirit, and I was one of many students who really had pride in EHS. I loved my school!

Ruth reminisces, "I had to sing the alma mater. It was in a group because you know he would call you out. He brought a sense of pride and high school spirit." Ms. Anjenett Ray, who was the Teacher Assistant to the principal, English teacher, and gospel choir director, is responsible for changing the alma mater to its famous gospel rendition that is recited by fans of the *Lean on Me* movie.

Anjanette Ray is at the organ in the auditorium.

Anjenett Ray
English

(Anjenett Ray – Photos Courtesy of EHS Yearbook, 1986)

CHAPTER 10

Emerging Themes from Teachers and Administrators

This chapter includes the eleven emerging themes that were developed from the thorough analysis of the data from the teacher and administrator (including Mr. Joe Clark) interview transcriptions.

The themes were: (1) Impact and contributions, (2) Not so positive memories, (3) Relationship with Dr. Clark, (4) Controversies, (5) Leadership style, (6) Student interactions, (7) Teacher and administrator interactions, (8) Perceptions of Dr. Clark, (9) Support and availability, (10) Expressions of gratitude, and (11) The *Lean on Me* movie. Each theme will be discussed in the above-listed order.

Impact and Contributions

When interviewed, teacher and administrator informants described what impact working at EHS had on their lives. These are some direct quotes from the teacher and administrator participants. I believe it is significant to acknowledge all the informants' thoughts and views regarding this theme because it articulates the impact that Dr. Clark had on the lives of his former teachers and administrators, which ultimately answers one of the questions that governs this phenomenological case study.

> Mr. *"B"* - I can truthfully say that my experience with Joe Clark changed my thinking about high schools and some of the tactics he used. Some of the things that he implemented, I still use today, to get the kids to know that, I am their friend and to trust me, and at the same time reiterate to them that, you've got to do your part. You've got to be the best student that you can be! And when you do your part, you will get the respect of being a student, and I can show you because I am an administrator, or I am a teacher.
>
> A lot of a lot of teachers probably walked away with that attitude because kids started looking at them differently, especially when they

saw them at the football games and basketball games. Giving them a little extra attention after school became a viable part of students seeing teachers in another light.

Coach "O" - Every day had a purpose. He made each day a day to improve a student's life. In hindsight, he truly groomed me and helped me develop my leadership qualities. My self-confidence improved tremendously. Absolutely, Dr. Clark had an impact on my life. His genuine love for his students and his ability to transform the dynamics of the school were impressive.

Coach Rosser - Yes, Dr. Clark had an impact; he taught me how *not* to treat students and their families.

Ms. Annette – Yes, I learned enough from him about teaching and administration.

Ms. De-Mo - I became an administrator because of his encouragement.

Ms. Florence Jones - I closely observed him for seven years. I learned from many mistakes, not from his successes. I learned what *not* to do.

Ms. Smiley - If anything, it was more annoying to affect my life. Every place I go, if somebody finds out that I'm a teacher, teaching at Eastside High in Paterson, they reflect back to what they saw in the movie, think it's gospel, and think how bad Eastside High School is and how could I teach there?

Not so Positive Memories of Eastside High School

When interviewed, teacher and administrator informants described some, not so positive memories that occurred while working at Eastside High School. These are some direct quotes from the teacher and administrator informants. I believe it is significant to acknowledge the informants' thoughts and views regarding their not so positive memories to gain additional insight into their experiences at Eastside High School. It is important to note that all of these comments refer to situations that occurred prior to Dr. Clark being assigned to Eastside High School.

Mr. 13 - Some of the student violence was unsettling.

Mr. Will - The tragic death of one of my students.
Ms. Annette - Adults were dating students, fighting amongst students, negativity amongst a few staff members.

Ms. De-Mo - Being physically assaulted by a student and seeing a security guard stabbed in the abdomen, learning of other attacks on colleagues, reading the negative press day after day in the news, TV cameras, and trucks all over the streets as we exited the school. English classes were generally 32-34 students, but I remember one with forty-seven students! I had kids sitting on radiators, sharing desks. Good teachers taught others "got by," and a few were disgraces to the profession.

Ms. Florence Jones - Gang violence, drugs, and poverty. The previous principal was a non-factor. He lasted three years. Teachers survived, no one thrived.

Ms. Smiley – I was physically assaulted by the same student twice. I was rammed and shoved in the hallway when I went to question a student about his hall pass as he came out of the bathroom. Well, they suspended him. He got arrested. And after he got let out of jail a month later, the same idiotic student assaulted me a second time. And he went to jail and stayed in jail for four months over the summertime. And when I went to the court hearing, his aunt apologized and told me that he was high on drugs.

Relationship with Dr. Clark

When interviewed, teacher and administrator informants described the type of relationship they had with Dr. Clark while working at Eastside

High School. These are some of their direct quotes; I believe it is noteworthy to acknowledge the participants' thoughts and views to gain additional insight into their experiences at Eastside High School.

Coach "O" - Mutual respect. He supported my coaching and my overall concern for the students at Eastside High School, and of course, my desire to become an administrator. He was respected by most students, staff, and parents. He put in a lot of energy into transforming the school.

Coach Rosser - Not good. It was difficult. I respected him, but I did not agree with him. I felt that he was media-oriented.

Mr. Will - I supported him from when he first stepped into the building.

Ms. Annette - I worked well with Joe Clark. He was supportive of my endeavors and concern about my professional growth. He made life fun, unpredictable, exciting, professionally friendly.

Ms. De-Mo - I loved him. I liked him because he knew who taught, who really cared about the students, and he cleaned house with the teachers.

Ms. Florence Jones - He wanted no relationships with staff; only students.

Controversies at Eastside High School

When interviewed, teacher and administrator informants described some controversies that occurred while working at EHS. These are some direct quotes from the participants. I believe it is momentous to acknowledge the participants' thoughts and views regarding the controversies to gain additional insight into their experiences at Eastside High School.

Coach "O"- The most famous one was locking and chaining the outside doors that lead into the school (safety issue). He did what he had to do. However, it was a safety issue.

Coach Rosser - Too many to recall, but all controversies were really blown up by the media. Many were teen issues that were turned into media issues.

Mr. 13 - The denial of due process and the theatrics at times were trying. I learned from them. Dr. Clark was placed in a unique situation, and he made the most of it.

Ms. Annette - Yes, one involved the "Virgin Club" put together by Dr. Clark.

Ms. De-Mo - Lots of controversies. Four male teachers refused to wear ties, Dr. Clark wanted all males to wear ties and dress professionally. It was against the contract, and they refused. They wound up transferred. Some parents protested that their kids were dropped and hanging on the streets. He told the parents to get jobs themselves! There were controversies when Dr. Clark got orange jumpsuits from the sheriff, and he had students who wrote graffiti wear them and clean up the school grounds.

Ms. Florence Jones - Transferring 125 teachers during the 1982 to 1983 school year was a travesty. He also dismissed fifty students for lacking credits and offered no educational options.

Ms. Smiley - His big thing was running around with the bat and keeping fire departments and anybody else he could keep out of the building, he always had the doors chain locked, which was a huge fire hazard.

Dr. Clark's Leadership Style

When interviewed, teacher and administrator informants described an incident or example of Dr. Clark's leadership or strategies that encouraged or discouraged them as an employee at EHS. These are some direct quotes from some of the participants.

Mr. "B"- Dr. Clark's leadership style was kind of like a General Patton type thing. Clark said, I'll lead, but you got to be by my side. So I went with him. I mean (laughs) we escorted people to the door, students as well as staff. I can't say brute force because he wasn't brute force. I was the brute! It was unique! It was unique because he addressed everything. He addressed students, administration; teachers; the community; they all were part of his management style.

Coach "O" - Very strong leadership, which was also reflective of his personality. His leadership was effective, though at times controversial. Mr. Joe Clark's leadership style had a direct effect on me developing my leadership style.
Coach Rosser - He was a good leader with poor strategies and tactics.

Mr. Will - His leadership skills were excellent. Too bad, he could not use them to run the district — he [Dr. Clark] thought/discussed everything out before acting. Absolutely strong!

Ms. Annette - Strong. He was a good disciplinarian. He led with wisdom. He knew what he was up against. He was a strategist.

Ms. De-Mo – Dr. Clark's leadership was very strong. I liked it. He was omnipresent - always in classes, the halls, and the lunchroom. He delegated the office work to vice principals. He knew about the families of staff members, Dr. Clark was able to inspire others, setting standards and holding all to them - including him. Also, not sitting in an office but getting into classes. He was available to students and staff members. He was able to get others to work collaboratively.
Ms. Florence Jones – Dr. Clark's leadership was immoral. Leadership is not a position in life. It is the behavior. His style of leadership was one of intimidation. He typically "shot from the hip." He bullied his way through his tenure. Dr. Clark was a self-serving leader. He placed his own needs first. Once he was on the front cover of *Time Magazine* in 1988, it was all about him.

Ms. Smiley - The Black Hitler (laughs) He was off the hook. He was a yeller and a screamer. He acted out terribly, and he tried ruling with a firm hand. And so he reminded me of my mother. I think it was more of flying by the seat of his pants. I could say his leadership was strong because he made people fearful. Just because you made people fearful to do what you want doesn't make you a strong leader. You could be a very weak person, and that's just how you compensate for it.

Student Interactions

When interviewed, teacher and administrator informants described their perception and beliefs about the interactions between Dr. Clark and the students. These are some direct quotes from some of the participants:

Mr. "B" - The students loved him because Dr. Clark gave them support; and identity; he gave them a good feeling of being in high school; he spoke to them—he knew so many kids by their first names. Dr. Clark made them feel like they were a part of humanity, and they belonged in school, telling them, "you are going to be treated like students, not just a paycheck for people."

Coach "O" - He lived by the three F's he was friendly. He was fair, and he was firm if need be. He gave them the confidence that they can overcome most situations, and yet he gave them the tough love approach if needed. He made each student feel important in their own special way. I know of two situations where he took money out of his own wallet and gave it to students. Tough love, honest love, creating a self-worth environment for each student. He gave them a sense of pride and most students felt important.

Coach Rosser - Personal appeal.

Mr. 13 - He used student-centered approaches.

Mr. Will - He treated all students as individuals. He always approached students with a positive attitude.

Ms. Annette - Tough love.

Ms. De-Mo - Personalization. He knew about students and their families. He helped connect them with scholarships, with financial aid, and so on. He bought coats for those who had none. He bought gym uniforms for those who needed them. He linked families up with social service agencies to help get food, heat, etc. I also remember him giving me his personal credit card to buy an iron for a young lady who was being made fun of and beaten up because she came to school in wrinkled clothes. He did a lot of those things but never sought public recognition.

Ms. Florence Jones - He had a great working relationship with students. If he did anything well, it was his relationship with students. He prided himself on knowing the names of all the students. The students loved him. Developing interpersonal relationships with students was his expertise. He was great at the students.

Ms. Smiley - I think when you are young, you're impressionable, and somebody has the persona that how great they are when you're not quite ready to stand up and say I know who I am. Clark gave a little bit of structure into their life, and they bought into his bravado. Because he wasn't all that great, but he tried. And that's what an impressionable young mind would remember.

Administrator and Teacher Interactions

When interviewed, teacher and administrator informants described their perception and beliefs about the interactions between Dr. Clark, administrators, and teachers. These are some direct quotes from some of the participants.

Mr. "B" described Dr. Clark's initial strategy with teachers, staff, and administrators during the first assembly when he met his staff for the first time. He called them out in regard to their negative behaviors and let them know that the negative behavior will not be tolerated any longer.

Coach "O" - Demanding teachers and administrators to work hard and help students maximize their potential. Most of the time, fair -- but if he knew that you were not an effective teacher or leader, he would transfer you.

Coach Rosser - In a disrespectful manner. It was difficult.

Mr. 13 - If he respected you, he treated you with respect, if not lookout.

Mr. Will - He treated everyone fairly, with honesty and respect.
Ms. Annette - He seemed to respect those who stood up for themselves and those who were committed to their jobs; harassed those he did not like, probably to get them to quit or transfer.

Ms. De-Mo - He had little respect for central office administrators. Dr. Clark felt that they were part of the problem. People either got on board or got out of the way!

Ms. Florence Jones – Dr. Clark was grossly obnoxious toward staff. He bullied teachers to a point. That's why many transferred. He was always yelling and screaming at some staff members. Dr. Clark was a bully toward staff. Staff disliked him.

Ms. Smiley - Some he liked; some he respected; some he obviously did not like; the ones he did not like. He did not respect and would attempt to make examples of them.

Perceptions of Dr. Clark

When interviewed, teacher and administrator informants evaluated Dr. Clark's style as a principal. They discussed their perceptions and beliefs and whether they agreed or disagreed; it was a topic of discussion in every interview. They described Dr. Clark as a man who had control of his school, teachers, students, administrators, and staff. He treated some teachers in a disrespectful manner. He held everyone accountable for their actions. These are direct quotes from some of the participants:

Coach "O" - Joe Clark did change the culture at Eastside. His leadership skills made both the students and staffs feel wanted and cared for. Yes, I am sure that he wasn't always perfect, but he was right for the school, and his style of leadership made the school a better place.

Coach Rosser – Treated teachers in a disrespectful manner. It was difficult.

Mr. 13 - Joe Clark is an interesting study of human relationships. He lost sight of his dream when the school became secondary to personal fortune and recognition. Dr. Clark was committed to making the school better.

Mr. Will - He was the BEST!!!

Ms. Annette - I think he was a good school manager who was needed at that time.

Ms. De-Mo - Things were so bad. I wasn't sure if he could clean up the school, but he did! It was an adventure every day. I knew I was safe, and so did other teachers, so it made it easy to teach without worrying about outsiders coming in or fights taking place.

Ms. Florence Jones - Prior to Dr. Clark, the school culture was chaotic. Clark improved the atmosphere tremendously and immediately.
Ms. Smiley – Dr. Clark was a good principal. He tried! He tried to make a difference. He tried. This means he did the best of his ability with sincerity in his heart, and you can't fault him for that.

Support and Availability

When interviewed, teacher and administrator informants described forms of support and availability from Dr. Clark. These are some direct quotes from some of the participants:

Coach Rosser – N/A

Mr. 13 - Dr. Clark encouraged me to pursue a principal's position. I am grateful for the guidance and opportunity he afforded me.

Mr. Will - It was a pleasure and an honor to work with Dr. Clark.

Ms. Annette - Fun, it was fun to work with Dr. Clark.

Ms. De-Mo - What I have said to him, you were right. I was administrative material! He recommended that I go into administration; he pushed me into going to graduate school for a degree in administration/supervision.

Ms. Smiley - Once, he wrote me a very nice letter because he thought I did something outstanding.

Expressions of Gratitude and Appreciation

When interviewed, teacher and administrator informants were given the opportunity to say some lasting words to Dr. Clark in response to the question, "If you could say something to Dr. Clark right now, what would you like to say?" These are some direct quotes from all the participants. I believe it is significant to acknowledge all the participants' thoughts and views regarding this theme because it articulates the impact/impression that Dr. Clark had on his former employees' lives.

Coach "O" - A big thank you.

Coach Rosser - Enjoy your retirement.

Mr. 13 - Thank you, what a ride!

Mr. Will - You were the best administrator Paterson Public School

System has ever had. Too bad you weren't assigned to the position of the superintendent. If you were, the district would probably be in better shape than it is today.

Ms. Annette - Thanks for your encouragement and support. Thanks for caring about students.

Ms. De-Mo - I thanked him because I had been ready to leave Paterson to teach elsewhere just to get away from the turmoil in the school. I didn't want to go. I loved my students and the school itself, but it was out of control.

Ms. Florence Jones – N/A

Ms. Smiley - Joe, I know you did your best, but I don't think it worked out as well as you had hoped. I would ask him to have a drink, and we would sit down, and I would tell him I think he was a Black Hitler, hypothetically.

CHAPTER 11

Unsung Heroes

It takes a village to raise children in a community, and Eastside was blessed to have the following three dedicated men Reverend Michael McDuffie, Mr. Alonzo Moody, and Mr. William Peter Nelson, who assisted Dr. Clark in his efforts to educate and nurture the young adults of Paterson, New Jersey. I believe that Dr. Clark did not do everything by himself. There are many unsung heroes who assisted Dr. Clark in meeting the needs of the students at Eastside High School. I would like to honor three men who assisted Dr. Clark and played a very integral role in the success of many students.

Reverend Michael D. McDuffie – Class of 1981

(Photos Courtesy of Mike McDuffie & Jaycen Moody)

Michael D. McDuffie was born on July 29, 1963, in Paterson, New Jersey. He is the 2nd eldest of four sons born to Deacons Isaac and Ruby McDuffie, also of Paterson, New Jersey. He received his education through the Paterson public school system and its institutions of higher learning, namely P.S. #21, Eastside High School, and The Passaic County Community College. Little did he know that his education was going to be significantly enhanced by a divine encounter. He then came to know Jesus Christ as His Lord and Savior at the age of 18. Michael had been predestined to become a servant of the Lord. Many ventures would soon aid him in his Christian growth.

He served as an aide for Youth For Christ, with Ron Hutchcraft Ministries. He is a former member of Redeeming Love Christian Center in Nanuet, New York, where he had been sent to further his Christian education under the pastoral leadership of the late Pastor Clinton Utterbach and his wife, Pastor Sarah. He remained there from 1981 to 1987. In 1986, he came under the pastoral leadership of the late Rev. Frederick H. LaGarde, who was the senior pastor of the Community Baptist Church of Love, Paterson, New Jersey. Michael became a licensed minister of the Gospel under his leadership in 1988. He then became the outreach pastor of the Agape Force Outreach Ministry and was the overseer of its alcohol and drug programs. Pastor LaGarde later ordained him in 1993.

In 1995, God called Rev. McDuffie to serve in yet a much higher capacity. He was given a vision in which he was to raise up mighty churches, businesses, and schools. He became the founder and Chief Executive Officer of "Kingdom of Might Theocratic Ministries, Inc."

Since that time, he has also become the Senior Pastor and Head Elder of the "Mighty Sons of God Fellowship Church," one of the manifestations of that vision, which was established in 1997. He is also the head instructor of S.I.T.U. (School of Intensified Training & Understanding) a bible-based training institution, which he has also established.

Rev. McDuffie has many other accomplishments and appointments to add to his credits, such as being appointed as "Chair Person of the Paterson Housing Authority." Rev. McDuffie also serves his community as an Instructional Assistant Teacher in the public school system and is a counselor for "YCS" (Youth Counseling Services). He is also the President of the Paterson Pastors Workshop. In addition to being a pastor, teacher and anointed prophet of God, he is also an author, whose literary, ministerial works has and continues to bless those who have had the opportunity and privilege to read them.

Pastor Michael McDuffie played an integral part in the lives of many students at EHS by introducing them to God and Jesus Christ. He provided assistance to those students who were in need of help and guidance; spiritually, emotionally, financially, and socially. He helped many students become successful in spite of their poverty-stricken circumstances. I believe that without Michael McDuffie's leadership, many students may have fallen by the wayside. I benefited from his guidance, as well.

Michael McDuffie graduated from Eastside High School in 1981 when Mr. Klein was the principal. Upon graduation, he was very involved in Campus Life, which was a Christian outreach organization at Passaic County Community College.

According to Pastor Mike, Dr. Clark attended the Community Baptist Church of Love every Sunday and heard Michael preach several times, and that's how they met. He stated that Dr. Clark was a Christian man and was "very bold with it too! Not to say that Dr. Clark was right with everything that he did, but he was a Christian man."

He stated that he, Ms. Vera Ames and Rev. Frederick H. LaGarde Sr., accompanied Dr. Clark on a regular basis and "laid hands on him" and made it a practice to pray with and for Dr. Clark. They walked with Dr. Clark in the hallways of Eastside High School and were there during the first five years of his tenure and were a support system during the controversies.

He also mentioned that there were other pastors who were very supportive of and prayed for Dr. Clark, that included Bishop Donnie Hillard, Pastor Bustor Soariezs, and Dr. Dean Trulear. They realized that Dr. Clark's method of doing things was unorthodox, and with nationwide attention, it was challenging to balance fame and all of the press that Dr. Clark was receiving.

He shared that they ministered and prayed for Dr. Frank Napier as well. He stated that "there was a lot of praying and spiritual things going on behind the scenes at Eastside during that time that the press never knew about."

He stated that Dr. Clark had his enemies too, that included some of the clergies who did not like his methods. He said that he defended him and declared to the other clergy that "God is using him" and asked them to pray for him. He said that he "doesn't think that Dr. Clark truly knows how much they served as his protectors and prayed for him behind the scenes and strived to help him become more effective in his principalship."

Pastor Mike volunteers as the chaplain for the Passaic County Sheriff's Department; serves as the director for the (IAAM) initiative program Infiltrate; Adopt a school; Adopt a block; Made discipline one's - this program will teach churches how to adopt schools as well as the 12 blocks around their church so that the members can come out of their churches and out of their houses and bring their ministries to the streets and be able to reach people. This would create a community that works together.

This program can allow community members the opportunity to connect with local businesses to create jobs and lessen violence. "This would be a major mobilization!" This initiative is connected to the Paterson Pastors Workshop Clergy on Fire, where he was elected president for the past four years of the 60+-year-old organization that was established by Dr. A. M. Tyler and some of the clergy backed in the 60s when Dr. Martin Luther King Jr. pilgrimage to Paterson.

This diverse (Black, Hispanic, and White) mixture of approximately 70 spiritual leaders meets on a monthly basis to strategize on how to protect their schools and their community. They are striving to lessen the violence around the schools and in the city. They are networking with security, police officers, and the sheriff's department. "There has been an abundance of violence in the city of Paterson, especially in the school districts."

They are establishing their own faith-based spiritual connections called "Pray at the Stop Sign," whereas they are teaching students to use their constitutional right to pray together on their way to school. They are asking students leave their homes at least 30 minutes earlier and to stop at the nearest stop sign and pray that evil stops before they get to school. This program will begin in February 2014. For the past 15 years he worked as a childcare worker for YCS (Youth Consulting Services), which is an orphanage that helps mentally challenged children. It is the second-largest nonprofit agency in the state of New Jersey. He works at that Kilbarken site that is located in Paterson. He is also the director and founder of a play titled the *Wisdom of Oz*, which is an urban remix of the *Wizard of Oz*. This project allowed them to raise funds for public schools.

(Courtesy of Mike McDuffie)

Pastor Mike is the Founder and Champion of Pillar College (formerly Somerset Christian College that is currently based at Passaic County Community College) which is a four-year accredited college that opened up in November 2013 to assist students in getting their bachelor's degree in counseling, psychology, family counseling, business administration, and biblical studies.

His three brothers Ronald, Derek, and Ivan, and his son attended Eastside. His younger brother Derek attended Eastside under the leadership of Dr. Clark, and his youngest brother Ivan was an extra in the *Lean on Me* movie

He believes that God called him to the ministry right after high school in 1981 and thus began his spiritual journey. While his brothers went away to college, he decided to stay local near his parents and attended Passaic County Community College for a few semesters. He was heavily involved in a spiritual organization called Campus Life, which was an organization that was birthed out of another evangelistic group called Youth Guidance, which was under the auspices of Rev. Billy Graham. It was an organization that ministered to young people and helped guide them in the right direction. They believed that the school district would take care of the mind, and campus life would take care of the inner personal spirit.

Dr. Clark was the first principal that allowed him to have an office in Eastside. He provided counseling and other services to help the students. Clark allowed him to teach an afterschool class titled "What's all this stuff about Jesus Christ?" He also stated that Dr. Clark made announcements with his bullhorn that "Minister McDuffie will have Bible study after school and those of you who are interested should attend."

He stated that a large number of students who are now in prominent positions of authority and power attended those classes. He described this as yet "another bold move by Dr. Clark to get the church involved with the morality issues of the school." The after-school class was then changed to a powerful Thursday night Campus Life experience, and it was a catalyst for him to provide additional outreach services for the community that involved softball, basketball, and baseball teams.

The Campus Life experiences led him to create an organization called "Crash Crew," which was "a group of young men that he took off the streets and coached them in basketball and baseball and lead them to the Lord and help them out emotionally." He believes that "this story will someday become a movie because some of these men who have come from severe poverty-stricken areas are now married with families and are pastors and professional businessmen."

The Campus Life meetings were also held at Faith Chapel Church located on Broadway in Paterson. He stated that Dr. Clark played a pivotal role in providing a space for many of the youth revivals, and many students were led to Jesus Christ.

He believes that his training and experiences from Campus Life garnered his current position as pastor and founder of Mighty Sons of God Fellowship Church, located in Paterson. He believes that Dr. Clark and Pastor Fred LaGarde Sr. were his role models for learning how to operate and use authority. He believes that "these experiences helped develop him as the pastor he is today."

When asked about the challenges he faced he stated,

Wow! When you deal with urban youth, our youth from the city of Paterson; it can't be just about Bible study; it can't be just about

Scripture, you have to take a holistic approach. You have to figure out how to take from Peter to pay Paul; some of these kids' parents were hooked on crack and we had to find them a rehab; some couldn't eat; you've got to find them food; you've got to find them clothing; you've got to find them apartments; some of the fathers were alcoholics some of the students got caught selling drugs, and we had to go to court with them; we had to put our money together to make things happen!

He spoke about the Agape Force Outreach group that was established in 1988 that held Tuesday night meetings at the Church of Love. This group became his small ministerial group that helped provide these services and programs for these groups of students who were in trouble, had emotional problems, and setbacks. These students came from all around New Jersey, New York, the Poconos, and Connecticut. He stated,

This small group of students was divinely called by God to do something that I have never seen done before. This was all a God thing! This group of students became lawyers, doctors, pastors only eternity will tell the lives that were touched by the students in this group.

McDuffie stated that during his time at Eastside, they were able to meet various famous people who came to visit. During the week of the premiere, there were several celebratory events planned that included a talent show, a Joe Clark basketball tournament – (The Paterson Joe Clark team VS the New York Giants football team), the premier and a church service on Sunday.

He, along with Vince Fusco and some of the people aforementioned, introduced the idea and were very instrumental in getting the world premiere of the movie *Lean on Me* to debut in Paterson at the Fabian theater.

Pastor Mike stated

> The Fabian theater was closed at that time, and it was dingy and nasty. We asked the owner to open up one of the theaters. We cleaned it up, put covers on the chairs, and prepared it for the premiere. The same small Agape Force ministry outreach group was the ones who were responsible for opening, cleaning, decorating, and inviting people to the theatre. We wrote and sent out letters to Dr. Julius Erving and other famous people and dignitaries. We had a Holy Ghost time!
>
> As the premier began, the Agape singers were standing in the hallway singing, and there were lights, cameras, and action as Dr. Clark walked on the red carpet into the theater. We had a band playing music as people were walking in and shaking hands. After the premiere, they traveled down the street, and dinner was served on the second floor at the Alexander Hamilton building, where Dr. Clark gave a speech and dignitaries were present.
>
> Although this was an exhilarating time, it was also one of the most significant disappointments I had ever had in my life because the Agape Force Outreach Teenage Ministry was *not* acknowledged for anything that they had done! They didn't call their names out! Nothing! And that was one of the most hurtful times my young folks were so hurt because they stayed up all night cleaning, sending out invitations, etc. And the students cleaned up the theater after the premiere.

I told them that if you do things for God, God will reward you later. The following students were members of the Agape Force Singers & Outreach Ministry from the Church of Love, Tamera Brown, Jamie Hendrix, Crystal Richardson, Helena Pierce, Gail Green, Ronnie Allen, Marvin Reed, Kevin Brown, Robert Nelson, Eric McKenzie, Coretta Scott, Andrea Bland, and Gregory Thomas.

After the premiere, the students still were not acknowledged for helping to provide services for these events. Pastor Mike explained to them that "one day, someone will acknowledge their hard work and dedication."

Joe Clark's movie grossed millions, and we received letters from all over the world from people who were happy with the work that Dr. Clark was doing at Eastside. Dr. Clark had become a famous star, and there were reporters following him when he came to church. Clark had his share of Judas's, people who were jealous of his notoriety. The clergy continued to pray for Dr. Clark and asked God for guidance and wisdom and for him to watch the things he said and did.

McDuffie went on to say that,

I think at times he became imbalanced because of the pressure of fame and I think it had an effect on him. I am not shocked by it, because who could handle that much fame and that much attention?

In the movie, they betrayed it as if the students improved their grades and passed the test, but that wasn't the real story. The credit we give Joe Clark, I feel, is forgetting the school set up so that it becomes a respectable institution and that the students are not wilding out and acting crazy!

Dr. Clark really did something that people did not expect. When he asked the students to leave, yes, that was true, and the controversy began. Dr. Clark had a way with words; he was a very smart man, and to watch him operate the way that he did was fantastic! He had something called the Virgin club were as he celebrated young women for practicing abstinence. He had a way of doing what he had to do!

I honestly think people were angry about the attention that Dr. Clark was getting. I think people wanted that same attention or may have been a little envious and jealous of him based on the perception at that time. When people start to see you rising in preeminence and begin to see you go further than they are, they tend to look for anything that you do wrong and magnify that.

Even if and when Dr. Clark went a little to the left or to the right, they magnified it. But they would not concentrate on the relationships he had with the students and how close he was with them. I must admit that some of Dr. Clark's methods were unorthodox, especially when he embarrassed some of the teachers in front of the students.

If given the opportunity, he would let Dr. Clark know that he and the other Clergy truly supported him and had his back! He would also ask why they did not give a shout out to the students of the Agape Force Outreach ministry. And he would also thank him for being Joe Clark and bringing notoriety to Eastside High School.

Pastor Mike McDuffie was featured in *Essence* Magazine. The photo was featured in the November 2011 issue of ESSENCE Magazine in an article entitled "My Comeback from a Setback," written by Tanisha A. Sykes. He was featured in the *Record* as the pastor who prayed for New Jersey Governor Chris Christie at a Paterson Board of Education meeting in 2013

He is happily married to Minister - Lady Jamie and is also the loving and caring Father of one daughter, Makiyah, and one son TaJuan, and one grandson, CaJuan.

(Courtesy of Essence Magazine & Peter Chin 2011)

(Praying for New Jersey Governor Chris Christie - Courtesy of Roger Grier, 2013)

Mr. Alonzo Moody

(Courtesy of EHS Yearbook, 1994)

"One who helps make a Difference" The following article is Courtesy of
the *Record* and the Eastside High School 1994 yearbook.

In 1994 Mr. Alonzo Moody was noted as the director of Paterson's
Youth Service Bureau, where he founded the Total Lifestyle and Support
Program for juvenile delinquents. Mr. Moody is also a state-appointed
member of the Paterson Schools Advisory Board; member of Passaic
County's Youth Commission and Child Placement Review Board;
member of the Board of Directors of the Paterson YMCA and the
County Boy Scouts; County president of the Black United Fund.

For 13 years, Moody and his wife, Kimaada, served as house parents
for Children's Haven, which involved raising nine foster children in
addition to their own while he worked a full-time job. He served as
Director of the Passaic County JINS (Juvenile in Need of Supervision)
facility as well as the County's shelter for Abandoned, Abused and
Neglected Children before heading the Paterson Youth Services Bureau.
Mr. Moody has been a supportive and committed member of Eastside
High School via the community for years. He is a positive role model for
our young people, and we commend him. To date, he and wife helped
fostered more than 100 children. Approximately 25-30 of the foster

children attended EHS, with 10 of them graduating along with his three biological children.

Mr. Moody shared with me that one of my informants, *Dilligaf*, was a member of a youth group consisting of some of the more aggressive youth of the infamous Alexander Hamilton Housing Development, also known as the Alabama Projects. This informant became the second juvenile to be ordered into the Total Lifestyle and Support Program, which is an alternative to incarceration program for juveniles. The purpose of this program is to reduce the number of commitments of Passaic County juveniles to the State Home for Boys and Girls.

This program was funded in 1985 with a grant from the Juvenile Justice Commission. At that time, Passaic County led the state in the number of commitments to the State Home for Boys and Girls the last 11 of 13 years despite being only the third-largest county in New Jersey.

Essex County is the largest county in New Jersey, and unfortunately, Passaic County was sending twice as many young adults to jail, and the vast majority of those juveniles were from Passaic City and Paterson. Mr. Moody had worked with the presiding juvenile court judge, the Honorable Carmen A. Ferrante, for years striving to figure out how to reduce the number of juvenile commitments from Passaic County.

During that time, Chief Justice Robert N. Wilentz of the New Jersey Supreme Court ordered the Presiding Juvenile Court Judge of each county to establish a Youth Commission, which was funded with monies set aside in the Chief Justice's own budget. Each commission was to elicit community proposals to reduce the number of commitments to the State Home for Boys and Girls. Moody seized this opportunity to submit a proposal based on the ideas he and Judge Ferrante had been discussing for years. That proposal was called the Total Lifestyle and Support Program (TLSP), and it is still in operation today. Although the grant was not large enough to hire the staff necessary for a comprehensive program, Moody utilized in-kind contributions from staff of other programs already under his direction.

The only eligibility requirement for participation in this program is that the juvenile must have a minimum two-year suspended sentence to the

State Home for Boys and Girls with no other options. This program was designed to work with the juvenile delinquents who were considered the **toughest of the tough**. This program was designed as a last chance-before incarceration program that does not tolerate lackadaisical attitudes or non-compliance with the stringent program rules.

Program participants had to attend the program for 11 hours a day, five days a week, and were monitored by staff that included unannounced home visits and telephone calls. The participants had a curfew of 8:00 PM each night, and if the participants did not abide by the rules and regulations, they would be bought back to Court, and the suspended sentence would then be imposed.

All participants had to be in attendance before 8:00 AM; according to Mr. Moody this program was very firm and had a strategic adherence to being on time; "at 8:01 they were late; at 8:02 the participants probation officer was called; at 8:03 the judge was called for a warrant and at 8:04 staff would begin the search for them and once found, they would be taken into custody and returned to court immediately.

He also stated that these participants who were late due to situations that were beyond their control, such as the bus being late, may not be terminated but still faced the consequence of one additional month for each minute late. If they were one minute late, they would have one month added to their sentence; if they were two minutes late, they would have two months added to their conviction and so on. In a nutshell, Mr. Moody did not play!

The program was designed to service 15 juveniles for 6 months at a time for a total of 30 minors per year. However, the average daily count was 38, with highs of more than 65. Between 175 and 247 juveniles were serviced yearly. He realized early on that the more acting-out juveniles crave structure, so the more the juvenile misbehaves, the more structured the program becomes. He learned that young people gravitate towards structure and guidance.

As mentioned above, the program is still in existence today, and it is still helping juvenile delinquents change their lives for the better. *Dilligaf,* the participant in this study, actually went back and worked for the program after he left the military.

Mr. Alonzo Moody shared with me that Dr. Frank Napier introduced him to Dr. Clark prior to Dr. Clark's appointment at EHS, and he stated that the students loved Dr. Clark because he was fair. Moody stated that he is continually talking to former students of Dr. Clark, who continues to love and respect him for how he treated and looked out for them. He could get in a student's face, yell at them, cuss at them, but yet, still hold them accountable. The students loved and respected him because they knew he was going to be fair about any given situation at that time."

He shared a story that stood out the most for him; he truly respected Dr. Clark's work ethic. He stated that Dr. Clark would usually be at work at 5:00 AM and would sometimes call him at 4:00 AM to discuss a student and how Mr. Moody can assist because a student was in trouble.

Mr. Moody respected and supported Dr. Clark because he understood what Dr. Clark was trying to do. The students respected and loved him, and Mr. Moody appreciated that because he knows that any adult who has earned the respect of young people is usually responsible for the positive development of these young people. Moody has worked with young people for over 40 years.

Mr. Moody graduated with the last class of Central High School, which became John F. Kennedy High School. Although he attended the rival of Eastside High school and was all RED and BLACK, his children grew up on the east side of Paterson, and they were ORANGE and BLUE through and through. He also shared that as parents, he and his wife realized that teachers at EHS held high standards for their students and stayed in constant contact with parents, and this factor increases the odds of their children becoming successful. This includes their foster children, as well. From 1977 through 1989, Mr. Moody and his wife were house parents of a group home for foster children. Approximately 30 of their foster children attended EHS, and about 10 of them graduated from Eastside along with their three biological sons.

(Courtesy of EHS Yearbook, 1994, Kwesi & Alonzo Moody)

Mr. Al Moody has three sons who attended, played football (each son received a full football scholarship to college), and graduated from Eastside High School. Zatiti Moody attended the University of Pittsburgh and is currently a principal at Eastside High School. Kwesi Moody attended Boston University and is a principal Dorchester Academy. According to Mr. Moody, this is the high school that President Barack Obama visited last year, and it is the only public high school in the country that is fully funded by private donations of Bill Gates. Malik Moody attended James Madison University and is a fireman in Paterson, New Jersey.

(Courtesy of EHS Yearbook, 1994)

As I further researched Mr. Alonzo Moody, I found the following tribute: On April 20, 1999, William James "Bill" Pascrell, Jr., the U.S. Representative for New Jersey's 9th congressional district provided a Tribute to Alonzo Moody,

> Mr. Speaker, I rise today to pay tribute to Mr. Alonzo Moody of Paterson New Jersey, an exceptional individual who has dedicated his life to public service. He will be honored this Thursday evening, April 8, 1999, by family, friends, and professionals for his outstanding contributions to the community.
>
> Mr. Speaker, Alonzo Moody, was born the sixth child to the late Allard Moody, Sr. and Mary Jane Moody. He has been married to his wife Sarah for 28 years and is the proud father of three sons; Malik Ali Angaza, Zatiti Kufaa, and Kwesi Tacuma.
>
> Alonzo earned a Bachelor of Arts degree in the field of Urban Planning from Ramapo College of New Jersey in 1976. He also attended Honolulu Business College from 1968-1969 in Hawaii, majoring in Systems Analysis. He has worked for the Department of Human Resources and the Paterson Youth Services Bureau for the past twenty-five years as Executive Director. His responsibilities include supervision and administration of programs, with direct accountability for their use in the community. He also coordinates all youth agency activities within the City of Paterson. Mr. Moody directs and supervises two youth agencies and fifteen staff members.
>
> On October 21, 1998, Mr. Moody was appointed and sworn in as Deputy Mayor of the City of Paterson by the Honorable Mayor Martin G. Barnes. As Deputy Mayor, he oversees issues involving youth, families, and recreation. In March of 1992, Mr. Moody became

Director of the Alexander Hamilton Development Resident Management Youth Program. He implemented homework study hours, a variety of recreational activities, counseling services, and other activities for the youth of the Alexander Hamilton Housing Development during the evening hours. Since 1991 Alonzo has been serving as a member of the Paterson Board of Education.

From 1977 until 1989, Alonzo and his wife Sarah have served as Children's Haven House Parents, providing a nurturing and supportive family environment for eight boys ages eight to fourteen placed by the Division of Youth and Family Services.

Alonzo served as an Assistant Basketball Coach at Passaic County Community College in 1979. From 1973 to 1980, he was an administrator for the Children's Shelter, Community Youth Worker Probation Counselor for Passaic County Probation Department, and Director of the Youth Summer Twilight Program for the Catholic Youth Organization. From 1966 until 1969 Mr. Moody also served in the United States Air Force as an Airman First Class.

Many community organizations have benefited from Mr. Moody's participation. He was a former member of the Paterson Task Force for Community Action, Inc., the Community Action Day Care Center, Inc. Board of Directors; and the Paterson YMCA Board of Directors. He currently serves on the Eastside High School's Home School Council, RISK, NJ Black United Fund; Passaic County Youth Commission; Municipal Drug Alliance; Village Initiative Executive Board, Children's Haven Board of Directors; and the Minority Concerns Committee.

Mr. Speaker, over the years, Mr. Moody has touched the lives of many people in his community. His warmth of spirit and caring nature has inspired an enormous amount of people. We are all gathered here tonight as a testament to Alonzo and to thank him for all that he has done for the well-being of his fellow man.

Mr. Speaker, please join me, our colleagues in the United States House of Representatives, Alonzo's family, friends, and colleagues, and the City of Paterson, New Jersey, in commending a truly great man (Capitol words, 2013).

Mr. William Peter Nelson, Jr.

(Courtesy of EHS Yearbook, 1989)   (Courtesy of EHS Yearbook, 1983)

The Marching 100 band was the most popular and sought after extra-curricular activity at Eastside amongst the students than any other sports, activities, or clubs within the school. The band was very popular and well-known for their spectacular music and dance performances in the school gym, the football field, colleges, and parades. They performed at MetLife Stadium (originally the Brendan Byrne Arena; formally the Continental Airlines Arena and the Izod Center) located in East Rutherford, NJ, every year and participated in marching band competitions. Participating in the band required a rigorous schedule such as practicing every weekday morning from 6:00 AM-8:00 AM, and school started at 8:35 AM. The hard practices and dedication validated the band to be compared to college/university bands.

The Band Director, Mr. Peter Nelson, had an established relationship with the Florida Agricultural Mechanical University (FAMU) Marching 100 Band. Every summer, the Eastside Drum Majors and other bandleaders would travel to Jacksonville, Florida, to learn and coordinate music and dance routines and returned to share that information with the EHS band. Mr. Nelson was very instrumental in helping Dr. Clark keep students in check and was a very strict disciplinarian and father figure to the band members as well. In a nutshell, Mr. Nelson did not play! He was and still is very well-loved and admired by band members.

(Courtesy of EHS Yearbook, 1985)

(Courtesy of EHS Yearbook, 1985, Pinky Miller second drummer on the left)

The band performed every Saturday during football season and demonstrated a triumphed remarkable professional music and dance performances that would make the crowd go wild, stand up and cheer.

(Courtesy of EHS Yearbook, 1985)

Participation in the band was a privilege. To be on the band or marching unit, every student had to try out; had to have at least a 2.0 GPA, and they had to be a well-behaved student; they had to listen and be able to take orders from their peers. The Marching 100 was well respected not only by those who attended Eastside High School but also to spectators and the community at large.

(Courtesy of EHS Yearbook, 1987)

William Peter Nelson Jr. attended Bonds Wilson High School in Charleston, South Carolina. After graduation, he furthered his studies at Allen University, where he received a BS degree in music. Mr. Nelson also studied music at (FAMU) and Grambling University.

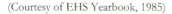

Smile Mr. Nelson, your on Candid Camera!

William Peter Nelson
B.S.

(Courtesy of EHS Yearbook, 1985)   (Courtesy of EHS Yearbook, 1986)

In 1974 Mr. Nelson was appointed as band director at Eastside High School. Upon assuming the responsibility as a band director, he inherited a band that consisted of 42 members and two drum majors who were Joseph McNeil and Donald Davis. Mr. Robert (Bobby) Wise was the assistant to Mr. Nelson for 14 years and was not on the Eastside High School payroll. Ms. Theresa Carter was the marching unit advisor. Mr. Dale "Skip" Van Rensalier worked as the very enthusiastic, crowd-rousing announcer for the band. Mr. Thomas page and Ms. Anita Odom also served as marching unit advisers.

Mr. Nelson left Eastside in 1989. Mr. Nelson is married to Selina H. Nelson and has been married for forty-five years; they have two children...Travis and Travelle. Mr. Nelson has a total of five grandchildren. Travis is married to Danelle and currently resides in New Jersey, and Travelle is married to Jaden and currently lives in New Jersey.

(Courtesy of EHS Yearbook, 1985)

Below is one example of Mr. Nelson's impact upon students as described by former student Donell Sellow: "Keep Climbing Until You Reach Your Dream" The best vantage point in most situations is typically on top! From there, the view is generally unobstructed, and the inhabitants are used to living in rarified air! While it can be a great place to watch a football game, it can be a great place to facilitate your life's work.

(Courtesy of EHS Yearbook, 1985)

High atop Hinchcliffe Stadium on a cold, blustery Thursday morning, my dad and I watched together for the first time a high school football game. It was as I know now the highly anticipated battle between the Eastside Ghosts and the Kennedy Knights High School Marching Bands. To paraphrase a line from a movie some years ago, "It's all about the marching band, baby!" and that it was!

(EHS Yearbook, 1985)

454

As a first-year elementary school musician still a couple of years before entering high school, I was impressed by Kennedy's performance. But the sights and sounds of the Eastside band indelibly left a mark on the heart forever! Not only was the music impressive, but to see the band dance while playing was defying, which was topped off by the final act; a rocket ship fast march from one end of the field to the other with fire extinguishers as the propellant!

(EHS Yearbook, 1985)

I don't know what others saw from the ground level, but from where I sat, I saw possibilities! My dad saw my face lit up with excitement as I told him my desire, and he said, "You can do anything that you put your mind to!"

At the very beginning of the summer break of 1975, I was now entering my freshman year of high school, and I, like many others awaited the receipt in the mail the confirmation of our desired curriculum for the school year. I choose the academic course of study with the junior band as an elective. The schedule had what I considered to be a mistake because it read senior band instead. Others, where I lived who also applied for junior band, had the same concern, so it had to have been an error. No error because, within days, we all received a letter to attend summer band camp for the opportunity to become one of the Marching 100!

(Courtesy of EHS Yearbook, 1985)

Band camp was grueling, and the upperclassmen were relentless! The expectations were   nothing short of perfection the first time out. I recall rehearsing the music in the band room and being allowed to carry our music onto the field, but that lasted no more than two days! We sounded horrible, and we were preparing for a halftime show in about a month, at least for those of us that would make it. It was so much to memorize the music, learn to dance while playing your instrument, learning how to march 8am to 5pm, and so much more that I enlisted the help of a neighbor just to get caught up. I had resigned myself to the fact that the learning curve was steep with my expectations adjusted accordingly, but there was absolutely no way was I giving up!

Cut Day! Chop Day! The dreaded "two-finger scissor" chop. You did not want to see that on any day! It was a steely, painfully permanent indication that your time had come to an end. Tears of anticipation were welling up not only for the freshman but upperclassmen, too! Becoming a part of the Marching 100 meant a lot to all of us. For some, it cost us money. For others, it was a long walk from differing parts of the city. And for some it meant doing what was necessary to negotiate whatever needed to be done! But for all of us who would make it, we had to put in the time on and off the field just to wear the Mighty Orange and Blue!

Mr. Nelson had set the standard so high, and his final speech of band camp was from the top of a ladder and straight to the point. "I wish I could use all of you, but I only have 100 uniforms. If your name wasn't selected, don't give up! Things happen, and you need to be ready to fill in. Keep coming to practice and keep learning the music and the dance routine. You never know what can happen!"

Those words penetrated my soul like a double-edged sword, hurting going in and coming out because just before those immortal words, I had been informed several times but finally confirmed by one of the trombone section upperclassmen that I had been cut! Too proud to cry and too tearful to keep my head down for fear that mist would freely fall, I did what I had to do.

I lifted my head up and cheered on my bandmates who were selected and had a dream fulfilled! But something happened from way up on high. Mr. Nelson looked down from his lofty position. Through the clearing, he saw a skinny kid as he paused from calling out the one hundred names. "What's your name, boy?" he would say. He should have known because I was taught by him to play the trombone and would play in various All-City bands in which he was the director, but I responded correctly. "Oh, yeah. Sallow!" not correct, but I understood, "What are you doing out there?"

Now I was embarrassed because for him to ask me that question must have meant my camp was so horrendous that I was obviously not one of those that should hang around! I held my head down and told him that he said we could hang around and learn the routine, and that was all I was trying to do.

Now I really wanted to cry, but he said to me, "Boy, I made a mistake. Get your horn and go get in line!" That was nearly 40 years ago. And the smile that was on my face then is the same smile that is on my face now!

(Courtesy of Eric Zimmerman)

From there I was the first underclassman to ever be selected for head drum major, managed my neighborhood baseball team, became a boot camp leader of 80 naval recruits and received honors for it, became one of the youngest head deacons managing nearly 80 deacons for a megachurch to managing a million-dollar budget for a government agency. All this I trace back to God, my dad, and Mr. Nelson.

Wintley Phipps, Grammy-nominated gospel artist and my pastor in the 90's singing a song that says, "Just keep on climbing until you reach your goal. All things are possible, so don't you give in. He'll move to your mountains. He believes in your dreams!" It doesn't matter the view from the bottom. Just keep on climbing and don't give up. It matters not what others say. It is always the Man at the Top who sees all clearly. He believes in your dreams!

Several of the original Marching 100 Band members honored Mr. Nelson with a portrait at the 2010 Band Reunion.

(Photo courtesy of Donell Sellow)

(Various Marching Band Drum Majors - Standing – Donell Sellow, Neal McKinley, Kevin Jackson, Denise Jackson, Reggie Mathews, Joseph McNeill, Zina VanRensalier, Skip VanRensalier Charles Primus, Samuel Colon, Keith Mays, DJcut Boddie – Seated – Mr. William Peter Nelson Jr. – Photo courtesy of Donell Sellow)

CHAPTER 12

Lean on Me Movie

The Warner Brothers' film "Lean On Me" began production in June, 1988. The movie depicts Principal Joe Clark's arrival at Eastside High School in 1982 and examines the transformation that has since taken place. As is evidenced from the following photographs, Eastside High School has truly become an urban mecca. Eastside has gone from disgrace to amazing grace — from shame to fame. Begin, now, your visual voyage of the old Eastside High School as portrayed in "Lean On Me."

THE REAL PRINCIPAL
LEAN ON ME

MR. JOE CLARK

THE MOVIE PRINCIPAL

MR. MORGAN FREEMAN

(Courtesy of EHS Yearbook, 1989)

(Courtesy of EHS Yearbook, 1989)

Please note that because the movie *Lean on Me* was a blockbuster hit [it grossed over 31 million] in the movies in the 1980s and 90s and can still be viewed on television, cable, the Internet and can be rented from your local DVD rental box, most viewers believe that they know and understand what was going on at EHS during that time period. However, please understand those movie makers can and will embellish and sensationalize the occurrences in movies just as some embellishments occurred in the *Lean on Me* movie. Please know that the participants in this study are speaking from their experiences, and this is their truth.

You can do it, but it's up to you.

She will take over when I'm not around!

(Courtesy of EHS Yearbook, 1989 Morgan Freeman & Robert Guillaume & Beverly Todd)

Some Embellishments in the Lean on Me Movie Include but are not limited to the following:

1. EHS being portrayed as a predominantly white high school in 1979 during the opening of the movie, it appeared that Dr. Clark was a teacher teaching predominantly white students at EHS. **Truth:** EHS was predominantly African American and Hispanic during that time.

2. Dr. Clark was the principal of a predominantly white elementary school. **Truth:** Dr. Clark was the principal of a predominantly African American elementary school [K-8th grade] that is located in a poverty-stricken area in Paterson, New Jersey. Public School Number 6 is located on Carroll Street. This elementary school had a negative reputation very similar to Eastside High School. Dr. Clark had the enormous challenge of reforming Public-School Number 6 very much in the same manner as he did at Eastside High School.

3. Thousands of students marched down to the Paterson jailhouse/courthouse to rally in support of Dr. Clark. **Truth:** The students did not march down to the courthouse, and Dr. Clark was not placed in jail. However, approximately 400 students marched down to the Paterson Board of Education and took over the board meeting in support of Dr. Clark. The Paterson police patrol cars escorted the students back to school.

4. Dr. Clark had an assembly and expelled/kicked all the miscreants and thugs out of the school in front of their classmates, and a large mêlée began on stage in the auditorium. **Truth:** Students were expelled, and there was an assembly of the 300 students, EHS Security guards, *Mr. "B"* and Mr. Joe Clark. All students were escorted from the auditorium to the exit door and had to leave the building.

Look at these fools.

(Courtesy of EHS Yearbook, 1989, Morgan Freeman)

The Impact of the Lean on Me Movie

When interviewed, teacher and administrator informants described what impact, if any, the making of the *Lean on Me* movie had on Eastside High School. These are some direct quotes from the participants. I believe it is essential to acknowledge all the participants' thoughts and views regarding this theme because it articulates the impact the movie had on his former teachers' and administrators' lives and provides the opportunity to gain additional insight about their experiences at Eastside High School.

Mr. "B" was adamant about letting me know that he was appalled by the *Lean on Me* movie and that, "by no means was the movie *Lean on Me* factual," because he felt that it was "not the image that Eastside High School should have been projected as." He did agree that there were "drug problems in the city," but he believed that "that was one of many problems in a city like Paterson." *John* stated that the

Lean on Me movie, didn't do it [the EHS story] justice! I was involved

464

in some major food fights in the cafeteria that were outrageous. The school was off the chain. It was wild! I think the movie watered down the violence, especially the race riots. A lot of things were kept from the teachers because they were in the classroom teaching, and they were not in those hidden spots where students hung out and sold drugs. The teachers did not have on-site experience because if the students saw a teacher or administrator coming, they would stop what they were doing, so of course, they didn't see what was going on!

Coach "O" - Still have it, and my children have watched it several times. The movie was on target!

Coach Rosser - A Hollywood version of things that were supposed to have happened. It presented our community negatively.

Mr. 13 - Hollywood at its best, I did not like the portrayals of our students. There were and still are so many great students at Eastside. *Mr. Will* - I watched the whole movie as it was being filmed. The movie was a little exaggerated. I thought it gave a clear perspective of what EHS was like pre-Joe Clark and during his administration.

Ms. Annette - The movie was mostly a Hollywood production that greatly exaggerated what Eastside was like prior to Joe Clark's arrival. It was good entertainment.

Ms. De-Mo - I worked as an extra and was in one large group scene. It is a great movie - gets you involved emotionally, and you root for Dr. Clark and the kids. A lot is true, but much is not. It is still a great money maker - always on, but the school, Dr. Clark, and the district made nothing from it, and it grossed millions! Yes, much was correct – the music teacher was told to exit, the coach who didn't stand for the alma mater, the boys singing in the bathroom, Clark overhearing, the fire doors chained, the arguments with the parent. But Dr. Clark was never jailed, and while students marched downtown, it was not for him, but changes regarding bilingual programs in the school.

I'm the boss, not you.

(Courtesy of EHS Yearbook, Morgan Freeman & John Ring)

Ms. Smiley - Probably the worst thing he ever did was to convince the board [Paterson Board of Education] to allow them to shoot the movie *Lean on me* in the school when school was in progress. Allowing actual students to star in the movie when they were supposed to be in class; they are not in class; they are participating in the film and failing their classes. That's absurd!

"So you're pregnant?"

(Courtesy of EHS Yearbook, 1989, Morgan Freeman & Karen Malina)

You'd better straighten up boy or kiss life good bye.

(Courtesy of EHS Yearbook, 1989, Morgan Freeman & Jermaine "Huggy" Hopkins)

The two main characters in the movie "Kenisha" and "Sam's" lives were based on several real-life student situations. Many students were teenage mothers and fathers, and several students were addicted to and sold drugs. An alumnus of EHS, Ms. Ashon Curvy Moreno, wrote the storyline for the character Kenisha. She was 16 years old, a new mother, and a junior attending EHs in 1987. She also had a concise speaking part in the movie "Dr. Clark! Dr. Clark!"

The Eastside "Song Birds"

I want the school's alma mater. Let's hear it.

(Courtesy of EHS Yearbook, 1989)

In the movie, while in the cafeteria, Dr. Clark pulls up a few boys and demands that they sing the school song to the entire cafeteria. After embarrassing themselves by not knowing the words, Dr. Clark warns them that they "better know the school song" or they would be suspended from school. While hanging in the bathroom, they get caught, and Dr. Clark again demands to hear the song, and that is when they amaze him with a five-part harmony of the alma mater that was taught to them by the new music teacher.

The 1989 Lean on Me Gala and Premier

In February 1989, The *Lean on Me* Gala and movie premiere held at the Paterson Fabian Theatre sparked local feuds and immediately ignited national news.

Welcome to the Fabian Theater.

Mr. Clark is in the spotlight.

(*Lean on Me* Premier & Gala - Courtesy of EHS Yearbook, 1989)

Love is blind!

The stars come out at night.

(*Lean on Me* Gala Karen Malina White - Riff and students Courtesy of EHS Yearbook, 1989)

Isn't she lovely?   I'm dressed to impress.

(*Lean on Me* Gala - Karen Malina White & Jermaine "Huggy" Hopkins - EHS Yearbook, 1989)

After the movie premiere, Dr. Clark appeared on The Arsenio Hall late-night talk show in Hollywood, California, to promote the *Lean on Me* movie.

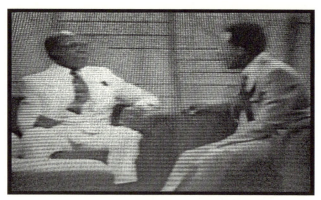

(Dr. Clark on the Arsenio Hall Show, 1989)

On February 15, 1989, while Dr. Clark was in California, a talent show produced by Eric Floyd, of the CavalCade Express All-Star variety show was presented to the junior and senior students and staff at Eastside. During the show, a performer named Wanda Dee was rapping and dancing seductively on stage, she had several male background dancers performing with who wore pants only. As part of the performance, she proceeded to snatch the pants off the men showing their G-string underwear, and the men were sexually gyrating on the stage showing their buttocks in front of hundreds of students. The crowd of students, teachers, and administrators began to yell and scream. (Some in protest and some in favor of the show). Some of the students wanted the show to continue. However, the administration closed the curtain, and the show abruptly ended.

This created a major uproar in the community. Many political leaders and city council members shared their dismay of what happened at Eastside during Dr. Clark's absence, and Dr. Clark was suspended for five days because of the incident. This situation generated additional apprehensions, and the Paterson Board of Education immediately called for Dr. Clark's resignation.

Dr. Clark believed that he was set up by members of his staff, council members, and the producer of the variety show because the group would not have performed that type of show if he was at the school. This "stripper show" caused another media frenzy and was broadcasted on the news and talk shows.

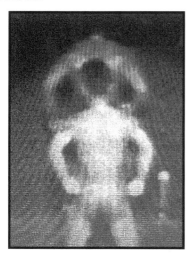 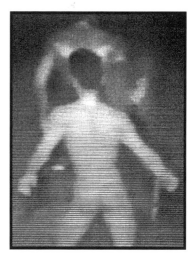

(Courtesy of Dr. Pinky Miller)

The producer, performing group, Paterson City Council members' students and staff members appeared on the "People Are Talking" talk show, hosted by Matt Lauer to discuss the event and the aftermath. Vera Ames, City Councilwoman, stated on the show that she was the only councilwoman who voted against Warner Bros' making the movie at Eastside. Mr. Floyd and Ms. Dee shared their opinions about the performance, and Mr. Floyd stated that Dr. Clark was well aware of the show. This incident was broadcasted on "A Current Affair" and several other local and national news shows.

After the suspension, Dr. Clark decided that he was going to take a six-month paid sabbatical and possibly was not going to return to Eastside, but was planning to write a book and possibly going to work with Mr. Dr. William Bennett in the White House under the Bush administration. Several students and teachers shared their discontent about Dr. Clark leaving, while others shared a sigh of relief. Dr. Clark underwent open-heart surgery in May of 1989 and gave up his position as principal two months later.

(Morgan Freeman & Joe Clark - Courtesy of EHS Yearbook, 1989)

Additional Information Regarding the Lean on Me Movie

According to Dr. Clark, Warner Bros. offered him a six-figure payment to own the rights to his life story to be portrayed in the movie *Lean on Me*. When speaking with Dr. Clark, he shared with me that he received a one-time payment for the rights of his story and that he does not receive any royalties from the movie. When asked, why did he take the lump sum and not the royalties, Dr. Clark told me that he didn't think he was doing anything special back then, he was just doing his job! I don't believe Dr. Clark truly understood nor currently understands the enormous impact (good, bad, or indifferent) he had on his students, teachers, administration, education, or the world.

The *Lean on Me* film opened at number one at the box office and grossed $31, 906,454.00. Unfortunately, neither Eastside High School nor the Paterson Board of Education received any of the 31+ million dollars that were generated from the movie back in 1989. The students who participated in the film as Extras were paid $50.00 for working at least 7 hours per day. The movie continues to play on television 25 years later and continues to generate revenue for Warner Bros.

Lean on Me 25th Anniversary - 2014

February 2014 marked the 25th Anniversary of the *Lean on Me* movie, and the alumni were very excited to celebrate our history. In October 2013, the following logo was created by alum Keith Williams Class of 1984 to assist in our efforts to raise funds and support the college education for the current students at Eastside High School. We understand the significance of furthering one's education and giving back to those who may be less fortunate.

(Logo created by alum Keith Williams C'84)

I wish Warner Bros. would have considered creating some type of educational college scholarship fund as a consistent way of being able to give back to the inner city, poverty-stricken children who helped them generate millions of dollars in 1989.

In hopes that Warner Bros. would join in our annual efforts to give back to the students at Eastside High School. I created a tax-deductible college scholarship fund for the current students at Eastside High School who are accepted into and enroll in college. Please help me give back by making a taxable donation toward the $10,000.00 annual scholarships by going to my web site Know-Our Story.com

In August 2011, after completing my dissertation, I spoke with Dr. Clark in regard to turning my original research into a book and produced a *Lean on Me Too* movie. Dr. Clark introduced me to Norman Twain, the producer of *Lean on Me*, and after reading my dissertation, he was very excited about the possibility. He shared my research with some of his colleagues and was informed that they did not believe there was a large enough audience interested in this endeavor.

Mr. Twain suggested I produce a documentary instead to garner interest. Norman Twain introduced me to the producer, Randy Simon. We began filming and interviewing alumni and administrators for the documentary at EHS during our C'86, 25th Reunion and tour in November 2011. We are in the developing and fundraising stages to produce the Know Our Story documentary.

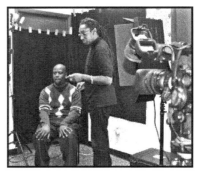

(Taping for the documentary, - Top – Greg Scott & Randy Simon, Co-Producer) (Bottom – Various Alumni - EHS, November 2011)

CHAPTER 13

Emerging Themes

A thorough analysis of the data from the interview transcriptions identified six emerging themes. These themes were created by way of recurring clusters of significant meaning statements that developed from the exploration of data from student participant interviews. (Creswell, 2007). The six themes that emerged were: (1) Support and availability, (2) A man of principals, (3) Leadership style, (4) Administration and teacher interactions, (5) Impact and contributions, and (6) Expression of gratitude. Each theme will be discussed in the above-listed order.

When interviewed, student informants described methods of support and availability that endorsed their perception and beliefs that Dr. Clark supported them and was readily available to them as a student at EHS. The situations they described explained the actions of Dr. Clark, taking the extra time and effort to get to know them personally, assist them, and provide support when necessary. These are some direct quotes from some of the participants:

Beautiful - He knew all the students by name.

Flash - He helped me get to the next level. He did meet my expectations. He helped me, and he paid out of his pocket for me to take the SAT courses so that I could get into the military academy. He took us out to dinner and paid for it out of his own pocket. He exceeded my expectations and my parents too. [Dr. Clark said] I will give you the environment, and you have to do it. You have to pick yourself up!

Kid Fresh - Dr. Clark's strategic approach to reach, engage, and connect with students was simple; he was there, in your face, helping you, guiding you, and leading by example. He knew all of his students by name, which made the connection more personable. You knew that when you spoke to him, you were speaking to someone who cared about your well-being. He also made himself available to you no matter what.

Moody - He was a celebrity. But he was still at the football games; he was at anything that had to do with students. And he was very supportive of students. He didn't tolerate the nonsense or the fighting. He wasn't dealing with that. But he was for students. Doing things unorthodox, outside of the box of what we would consider a principal like me coming out now. He was a student-centered principal and administrator. He was really into students while he was pretty hard on the staff.

Reggie - Dr. Clark had a way of making every student feel relevant and valuable. He wanted us to know that we had a special place and purpose within EHS. He often called students by their nicknames as a way of really connecting with us. He kept up with the latest slangs, trends, and made us feel as if he was going through the same daily challenges that we were.

T-Bird - Several times of pulling me out of my class to perform or something like that, and he would always come back and let me know I did an excellent job and said I had a good future ahead of me, and different good things like that, and he just let me know that whatever I needed that he would be there for me!

When interviewed, student informants evaluated Dr. Clark's style as a principal. They discussed their perceptions and beliefs and whether they agreed or disagreed with his style. It was a topic of discussion in every interview. They described Dr. Clark as a man who had control of the school, teachers, students, administrators, and staff. They described him as a no-nonsense type of man who would call you out and embarrass you if he thought it was necessary. He was a stringent man, and some of the former students believed he treated the school as if it were a military base. He held students, teachers, staff, and administrators are accountable. They also believed that he showed love and compassion for students who needed help. These are direct quotes from some of the participants:

Cheeks - He was a devoted and passionate educator. There are numerous success stories from other former students who will credit Dr. Clark for providing positive direction in their lives and contributing to their success.

Flash - He removed the chaos and brought order to the situation. He pushed the teachers to give more and to think differently. He set the standards.

Ruth - From my perspective, he did his job well. He did what he could to create a positive learning environment. He was involved, and not just in the administrative part, but the day-to-day hands-on contact with the students and the teachers. He made sure teachers were accountable, and he made sure that the students were responsible.

T-Bird - Yes, Dr. Clark was a good principal because he had control of his school, students, and faculty members. And you know he came there with a sincere passion for the students.

When interviewed, student informants described an incident or example of Dr. Clark's leadership style or strategies that encouraged them as a student, which endorsed their perception and beliefs about Dr. Clark's leadership style. They believed that his leadership style was autocratic, and most of them described Dr. Clark as being a good leader. They also described him as one who's willing to take a stand and lead, has the ability to capture the audience and make them believe the message he was striving to convey; although he was very boisterous while leading with a bat and bullhorn in his hands. These are some direct quotes from some of the participants:

Flash - The strategy was to encourage a safe environment, and he recognized a safe place for kids to come to school. His predominant strategies were discipline, [dealing with] the teachers, and having a close relationship with his students. I think he was an influential, dynamic leader. I think he had a vision, and I think that he was somebody you could follow, but you had to get in line. I think he was a born leader. He recognized achievement, and that was the military in him. I think it went to his head.

Karimah - Dr. Clark's leadership style at EHS was no-nonsense. He would put you on the spot to let you know that he did not approve of a particular behavior and would have you instantly correct that behavior.

Moody - If he was a weak leader, he would not have any success because the culture of the school was so strong and so dominant at the time.

Reggie - My definition of a good leader is someone who has the ability to capture an audience and who can make others believe in the message they are trying to convey.

Ruth - A leader is someone who lives what they can expect in you! I respect anyone who has a vision, which was trying to raise the expectations of minorities.

T-Bird - A good leader, someone willing to stand and take the lead while paving the way for those in need of inspiration, a person of purpose with the ability to guide those seeking direction. Yes, Dr. Clark possessed, definitely possessed these qualities!

Dr. Clark's Administrator and Teacher Interactions

When interviewed, student informants described their perception and beliefs about the interactions between Dr. Clark, administrators, and teachers. These are some direct quotes from some of the participants:

Beautiful - The teachers who bought into his way of running the school, they had no problems with him. I think it may have been hard for some of the teachers who were there or teaching at EHS prior to Dr. Clark coming to EHS. I think Dr. Clark respected the teachers who were doing their jobs.

Flash - It all depends upon who the teacher was and if the teachers bought into his philosophy. Some teachers were treated very well; some teachers were treated, in my opinion, sometimes disrespectful. I think that in that environment some of them needed to be disrespected. I don't think he purposely did it, and I think he had the mentality of a drill sergeant.

Ruth - Now (laughing), the only thing is that he would reprimand a teacher in front of the student. And I think that probably is what created the tension. He was very confrontational. I think he expected more out of them. He wanted them to give us their best. He wanted to make sure that he had teachers who were there, who were doing their jobs and wanted to be there.

T-Bird - I recall once when Dr. Clark had stopped me in the hallway and asked me to recite our alma mater. As I began to recite it, there was a lot of laughing going on from other students and one particular teacher. I knew the words. I got a little nervous and stumbled. Well, after I finished, Dr. Clark demanded that the teacher, who had been laughing to recite the Alma Mater.

He threatened to severely reprimand the teacher if he didn't recite it correctly. Well, the teacher also stumbled on a few words and needless to say. Dr. Clark let the entire school know about it over the PA system. While it seemed kind of petty, it reinforced his philosophy that we were all one within the school and trying to obtain one common goal. Teachers and staff were not to be excluded from that idea and had the same consequences as students when they fell short.

Impact and Contribution to Students' Lives

When interviewed, student informants described what impact, if any, attending EHS had on their lives. These are some direct quotes from student informants. I believe it is significant to acknowledge all the participants' thoughts and views regarding this theme because it articulates the impact that Dr. Clark had on his students' lives, that ultimately answers one of the questions that govern this phenomenological research study: What impact, if any, did former students, teachers and administrators perceive that Dr. Clark's leadership style as principal of EHS have on their lives?

Beautiful - Dr. Clark had a great impact on my life as a student at EHS.

Cheeks - Dr. Clark was a significant role model in my life, especially during my years in high-school. He had a way of making every student feel important and placed a lot of emphasis on being diligent. His influence continues to work through me, and I often hear his voice when [I'm] providing direction to my children. Yes, Dr. Clark prepared me for all that life has to offer.

Flash - You know when I graduated from college, one of the first people that I spoke to was him was Dr. Clark. And I told him, he probably doesn't even remember this, but I told him that I wanted to be a principal of a school, and he turned to me and said, 'don't be nuts, don't do it.' He said, don't do it; get your doctorate. You're too smart for that, don't do it. I picked the career with the highest level of potential. He definitely has influenced the way that I live my life. I remember that one saying that he used to say, 'If you're going to blame it on anybody, you can blame it on yourself,' and that is something that I tell my kids every day.

Karimah - My attending EHS has provided me the opportunity to learn and experience that it doesn't matter what kind of environment you're from as it relates to the goals you want to achieve in life. What matters is having people in your life that exude leadership and are there to teach you that you indeed can be all that you want to be if you possess certain qualities. Those qualities, of course, are education, patience, and understanding of yourself, of the world, and most importantly, of your immediate environment. For my future, it has taught me that education and learning never ends; it's an ongoing process, a life-long deed. Dr. Clark's impact on my life has made it possible for me to realize that our lives on earth are not only ours to live but also ours to give. Such as Dr. Clark had given so much of himself, has proven that it's so much better to give than to receive.

Kid Fresh - There is no question that Dr. Clark had an influence on my life. Both directly and indirectly, he created an environment that allowed me to be myself and to achieve more. If he hadn't come in, I am not sure what grades, attitude, or results I would have achieved in high school.

Moody - You have to first shock the culture and get the culture to the point where students were able to learn. And he did that. And he had an impact, as a powerful, African American male whom you can see, somebody who's African American who can take that leadership role and take control of the school. That was a significant impact on my life indirectly.

Pinky - As a student, the impact that Dr. Clark made on my life encouraged me to want to be a better student and a better person. He also made me realize that my journey through high school was there to shape me into the adult whom I would ultimately become.

Reggie - I learned that we mattered. It may sound corny, but we mattered. It had a profound impact. It shaped the decisions I made for my future. His positive influences were helpful, and its negative influences steered me in the direction of making something more of myself.

Ruth - My experience while attending EHS has impacted my life in unimaginable ways.

T-Bird - He showed me what discipline was about at an early age and respect and honor. He taught us to honor ourselves; there were a lot of times he made us think that people outside of Eastside thought low of us, and that was a way that was one of his tactics that he used to motivate us. To say things like; they think you can't do it, they think you can't achieve, and then you ask yourself those questions. I remember asking myself those questions and using them to motivate myself. I still ask myself those questions when I find myself in a situation. I have to say out loud that they think that I can't do this, and I say, "I can do this!" and I say it to my children as well...you don't know the impact that somebody has on your life, but you know, those little ways, those small reminders that still stick with you.

Expressions of Gratitude and Appreciation

When interviewed, student informants were given the opportunity to say some lasting words to Dr. Clark and were asked, "If you could say something to Dr. Clark right now, what would you like to say?" These are some direct quotes from all the participants. I believe it is significant to acknowledge all the participants' thoughts and views regarding this theme because it is an additional articulation of the impact that Dr. Clark had on his students' lives, which ultimately answers one of the questions that governs this phenomenological research study.

Anthony - I really don't have anything to say to him.

Beautiful - Thank you for all of your time and commitment to the school and the students of EHS, you left a significant imprint and impact on the lives of the students of EHS again, thank you.

Cheeks - I would thank him for his commitment to EHS and thank him for sticking it out through all the hard times and all the things that he was going through; going up against our justice system and thank him for sticking it out with us, and teaching us to do something to give back to others.

Flash - You have shown what it takes to be a true leader, and if I could be a small percentage of the person you are and the leadership that you've shown, and then I would have accomplished a great deal. I respect you as a man, as a leader, and as my former principal of EHS. You mean the world to me, and the world needs more leaders like you. I think that he did an outstanding job, and I am grateful for him for inspiring me with his words, especially with my kids and me. Follow your dreams.

Karimah - To Dr. Clark, I would like to say thank you for allowing me to grow as a person. Thank you for inspiring me, encouraging me, and for teaching me what it takes to survive in this world. Your strength and leadership have afforded me the opportunity to challenge the status quo and the nay-sayers who don't believe that inner-city youths are worth fighting for.

Kid Fresh - I would say thank you for doing what he did. Because he was able to polarize an entire nation with...he drew attention to the situation to the problem. I think for the period of time that he was there, he made a dramatic impact. I believe that. So I believe, in the end, Dr. Clark did a great job, and he had great results. And I think, probably saved a lot of lives too.

Pinky - I would let Dr. Clark know that he has inspired me to be a very independent, motivating, spiritual, educated, phenomenal woman. I appreciate him for his time, his effort, his tenacity, his big words, his love, his respect, his sacrifice, and, most of all, his heart.

Reggie - First, I would thank him for seeing something in me and taking the time out. You let me know that I had something special and that you knew that I would be able to make it in this world [and] at EHS.

Ruth - Thank you, and I love you! He gave me an opportunity to attend school. I met a lot of great people. If I would have stayed at Paterson Catholic, I don't think I would have the close friends that I now have as an adult. I believe he instilled pride in us too. He told us to keep our heads up to strive to be something in life, to contribute to society, and to have an impact on society.

T-Bird - I would say, thanks for the inspiration and sacrifices! Thank you for the willingness to provoke change and for the strength to see it through! Thanks for all the kind words and pats on the back! Thanks for being an essential part of my life! I would want to thank him for seeing something in me and taking the time out to get to know me. Thank you for letting me know that I had something special and that I would be able to make it in this world as a high school student.

CHAPTER 14

Discussion

This study was an attempt to give voice to thirteen alumni who attended and ten teachers and administrators who worked at Eastside. Understanding how Principal Clark's leadership style, methods, and strategies had an impact on the students and former employees can add to the literature that addresses topics that deal with success for African American students, large urban high schools, and the teachers and administrators who work in them.

A phenomenological case study inquiry approach was used to gain a better understanding of this phenomenon. Face-to-face and phone interviews were the methods performed to obtain information from the twenty-three participants who attended and worked at Eastside.

How do Dr. Clark's Former Students, Teachers, and Administrators Perceive his Leadership Style as Principal?

Based on the information gathered from the informants, Dr. Clark's leadership style was mainly a combination of autocratic, dogmatic, no-nonsense, charismatic, directive, situational, and paternalistic, with some aspects of servant leadership.

His methods were also described as harsh love-oriented, intimidating, immoral, and caring. How one experienced his style depended upon whether or not you were a student or staff member and whether or not he perceived you as helping or hindering his efforts. A large number of informants characterized him as a competent leader who took charge and showed great initiative and someone who was not afraid to take charge when faced with a demanding challenge.

In this regard, most of the informants indicated that Dr. Clark believed that they (staff and students) were all one unit within the school and were striving to obtain the common goal of student success. The informants also indicated that Dr. Clark respected his staff members whom he thought were doing their jobs well and reprimanded others (in public and in private) who did not follow his philosophy or procedures.

During the time period, Dr. Clark was principal; much of the literature talked about leadership as directing and controlling in order to achieve goals. Based on the thoughts about leadership during Dr. Clark's era, one might conclude that his leadership style was in line with the research of that period. Much of the thought regarding leadership continues to deal with the concept of management rather than or in combination with the concept of leadership. According to the participants, Dr. Clark did demonstrate good leadership through his efforts at empowering and building relationships with students and some staff.

It is clear from the interviews that Dr. Clark used his interpersonal influence. Even for those who thought his methods were counterproductive, they acknowledged his influence based on his interpersonal relationship with others. When asked if they thought Dr. Clark would have been successful if he had used a different leadership style, most of those interviewed indicated that based on the circumstances he faced and the need to make an immediate difference, his tactics and style were appropriate. This belief aligns with the concept of situational leadership.

The results from this study indicate that Dr. Clark viewed and regarded some of his staff members as falling into the category that McGregor (1985) described as Theory X; that is, people who avoided work, were lazy, lacked ambition, resisted change, preferred to be directed, had little capacity for creativity in solving organizational problems, and were deviously opportunistic.

Dr. Clark's distrust and lack of confidence in some of his staff members lead to tight control, close supervision, and substantial authoritarian responses. He also did not allow most of them the opportunity to assist in the decision-making processes. As a result, Dr. Clark was viewed as being a leader who was dictatorial, elitist, anti-democratic, and who acted independently of his staff members.

Furthermore, Dr. Clark was characterized as one who put the students' needs above the staff members. However, in the later years of his tenure, Dr. Clark is reported as treating people in a fashion that is more consistent with Theory Y, particularly with the teachers and other staff members whom he trusted along with the students whom he viewed as determined to stay in school and learn. Thus, he began to view those people as honest, hardworking, motivated, and committed to quality and productivity, as well as willing to take the initiative. There are data that indicated he began to share the organizational decisions that impacted the success and reform of Eastside.

Several informants thought that Dr. Clark became self-centered and only interested in his own movie and the writing of his book. According to some informants, he appeared as if he was not as involved as he used to be because it was about "the book," it was about "the movie," it was about the fact that "President Reagan called him" and they felt that "it went to his head." Instead of being the principal and making sure that Eastside was being taken care of, some saw him as beginning to celebrate all of the things that were happening.

I think that there were additional reasons for the change in his leadership style. I believe this shift also had to do with the fact that he had accomplished turning the school into a place where teaching and learning were the main foci because of his success in improving the behavioral and learning climate of the school. Additionally, a high number of staff members left EHS during his first four years, and as a result, he was able to hire the staff that he wanted, and there was less of a reason for him to conduct a Theory X based leadership style.

The results of the data revealed that Dr. Clark embraced charismatic leadership behaviors such as being dominant, self-confident, competent, having a strong sense of his own morals and values, being a role model, articulating his philosophical goals, having high expectations and exuding power. This charismatic style of leadership was demonstrated from the experiences that were elicited from the informant interviews. Further support was also demonstrated by the newspaper headlines, television talk shows, and news appearances, as well as the movie, Lean *on Me,* which most informants said was quite accurate.

Most of those who were interviewed indicated that he was a role model and someone who was looked up to as the principal and father-figure to the students. Moreover, most of the staff members who pursued school administration careers site Dr. Clark as a role model, although two informants described him as a role model of what *not* to do as a leader.

Dr. Clark also utilized the five different bases of power that included referent, expert, legitimate, reward, and coercive power. Dr. Clark's referent power was demonstrated by the reports from the students and parents who were fond of him, and who appreciated and respected him. Dr. Clark was perceived as competent in his role as principal, thus solidifying his expert power. He used legitimate power because he was hired as the principal and had the support of the superintendent. Dr. Clark used reward and coercive power, in that he used his authority to hire, fire, demote, promote, and suspend staff and students.

What Impact, if any, did Former Students, Teachers, and Administrators Perceive that Dr. Clark's Leadership Style as Principal of EHS has on their Lives?

According to the informants, Dr. Clark had a profound impact and contributed significantly (good, bad, or indifferent) to the lives of his students, teachers, and administrators. All of the participants expressed positive thoughts and feelings regarding the way Dr. Clark provided support and how he was readily available to students of EHS. He made an effort to get to know them personally and provided sustenance when necessary.

The results of my study indicated that Dr. Clark helped several students who had family problems. He acted as a referral agent to those single-parents who needed additional support by either helping families to move out of a housing project or assisting parents to find employment.

Additionally, Dr. Clark demonstrated accompanying valuable lessons to some informants, which consisted of "what *not* to do" as a leader and "how *not* to treat students and parents."

Dr. Clark was willing to take the lead while paving the way for those he thought was in need of his inspiration, guidance, and assistance in order to progress as a student or as an adult at EHS. This paving of the way included the influence Dr. Clark wanted to have on his students while they attended EHS and in life in general.

Dr. Clark's ability to establish and enforce strong discipline in a chaotic environment at Eastside was an essential factor that substantially impacted a noteworthy portion of students', teachers', and administrators' lives as scholars and employees. All of the participants in this study indicated that creating an environment that was conducive to learning was one of the most vital policies/strategies that Dr. Clark instituted that enabled them to succeed as students, teachers, and administrators.

According to many of the informants, getting rid of the students, Dr. Clark thought of as miscreants and thugs and keeping the drug dealers out of the school were two of the most significant and influential strategies Dr. Clark incorporated, as it allowed students the opportunity to learn and teachers to teach without constant interruptions and violence.

Removing the teachers, administrators, and staff members whom Dr. Clark thought were only working at Eastside to acquire a paycheck, was another occurrence that had a significant impact on the lives of the students and staff that remained. Dr. Clark utilized several strategies to clean up the outside and inside of EHS, which motivated students to respect and take care of themselves, their school environment, and to apply their talents in a positive way while at EHS and into the future.

Although his leadership style was intensely controversial, his students and most of his staff saw him as fighting for those who could not fight for themselves or who wanted things to be better at EHS. Based on the interviews, Dr. Clark opened doors for many people for whom doors may not otherwise have been opened. Dr. Clark assisted several thousand students in continuing their education by holding students accountable for their actions, for raising the bar, and not allowing students to make excuses for themselves.

CHAPTER 15

Conclusions

The study's first major conclusion addresses the question, how do the informants perceive Dr. Clark's leadership style?

The informants characterized him as a competent leader who took charge and showed great initiative when leading, and someone who was not afraid to stand up and take charge when a demanding challenge came along.

Most informants indicated that Dr. Clark believed that they were all one within the school and were striving to obtain one common goal. Administrators, teachers, and staff were not excluded from that idea and endured some of the same consequences as students when they did not do what he expected of them. The informants believed that Dr. Clark respected his staff members who were doing their jobs well and reprimanded others (in public and in private) who did not do their jobs or did not follow his philosophy or procedures.

The second major conclusion addressed the question, what impact, if any, did the informants perceive that Dr. Clark's had on their lives?

The majority (18 out of 23) of the participants expressed positive thoughts and feelings regarding Dr. Clark providing support and how he was readily available to the students of EHS. He provided guidance to them and made an effort to get to know them personally and assisted and provided sustenance when necessary.

The majority (18 out of 23) of the informants believed and perceived that Dr. Clark was a good principal and voiced their expressions of gratitude and appreciation and thanked Dr. Clark for inspiring, encouraging, teaching, supporting, and esteeming them.

The majority (18 out of 23) of the participants perceived that Dr. Clark's leadership style as principal of EHS had a meaningful impact on their lives. That impact included: making some of his students desire to be better persons; shaping them to be the positive adults they would ultimately become; helping them to realize that their lives on earth are not only theirs to live, but to also give to others; and teaching and demonstrating that it is better to give than to receive.

Dr. Clark taught the students that God was significant; education was substantial, that we do not have to settle for less, that the only person stopping us from being successful is ourselves. Most participants saw Dr. Clark as a person who was willing to stand and take the lead while paving the way for those in need of inspiration. Most saw him as a person of purpose with the ability to guide those seeking direction. He also encouraged several teachers to pursue administrative positions in education.

The third major conclusion of this case study is Dr. Clark's ability to establish and enforce strong discipline at Eastside

All participants in this study indicated that creating an environment that was conducive to learning was one of the *most vital* actions that Dr. Clark could have systematized in order for them to improve teaching and learning. Getting rid of the students whom Dr. Clark thought of as miscreants and thugs, and keeping the drug dealers out of the school were additional significant and influential strategies Dr. Clark utilized because it allowed students the opportunity to learn without constant interruptions and violence.

Also, as part of the student discipline process, students were required to walk to the right. While instructing students to walk to the right might seem trivial or simplistic, it was noteworthy because it was significant steps in being able to organize an overpopulated high school of more than 3000 students and keep them orderly while passing through the halls. This resulted in a decrease in pushing, shoving, and fighting in the corridors and stairwells. It was also a significant step in establishing a more caring climate and culture at EHS.

Dr. Clark encompassed several strategies to clean up the outside and inside of EHS, which motivated students to respect and take care of themselves, their school environment, and to embrace their talents in a positive way. Creating a healthy school spirit by utilizing the alma mater was very momentous because he created traditions that reinvigorated school spirit which aligned with the vision of learning, aspirations, enthusiasm, joy, optimism, camaraderie and mutual respect for individual differences as well as created a sense of unity and built self-esteem.

The results from the study showed that Dr. Clark exhibited several of the behaviors listed above in regard to personal and position power. Dr. Clark was understood to be a role model and someone whom students looked up to as the principal and a father figure. He was also shown to be a role model for several of his teachers, who later became administrators.

Dr. Clark used the five different bases of power that included referent, expert, legitimate, reward, and coercive power. He was able to use referent power because of the majority of the students and parents who were fond of him. He was able to use expert power because of the perception of many of his followers, who believed he was competent in his role as principal. He used legitimate power because he was hired as the principal of EHS, and he had the support of the superintendent. He used reward and coercive power as he hired, fired, transferred, promoted, and suspended staff and students as he deemed necessary. Reward and coercive power have been linked to transactional leadership.

CHAPTER 16

Concluding Comments

Based on the data that was revealed from the majority (18 out of 23) of the informants and from my own lived experience, Dr. Clark positively impacted the lives of many students who attended Paterson Eastside High School. Dr. Clark impacted the lives of many teachers and administrators at Eastside as well; however, the impact was determined by the relationship that each teacher or administrator had with him. The effect could have been positive, negative, or indifferent; the difference was based upon the way the staff member regarded Dr. Clark's leadership style and the professional or personal relationship they had with him.

African American school leaders can play a critical role in improving the conditions of schools and forming relationships with students that research says is important in effective schooling for African American and Latino students who reside and attend schools in urban poverty-stricken areas.

This study also afforded opportunities to reflect on Dr. Clark's leadership style from the lens of the people who experienced it. The voice of his students, teachers, and administrators spoke volumes about the strategies he developed that made an impact on their lives in addition to reforming EHS.

Dr. Clark is a man who believed that acquiring an excellent education is paramount. He also believed that education was a way to get out of poverty. He was known for saying that once education is obtained, no one can take it away from you. As a result, I, along with many of the students, informants endeavored to get as much education as we possibly could because no one can take that from us.

He told me that education was my ticket out of Paterson, New Jersey. I wanted to get away from the violence, the drugs, the gangs, and I wanted a better way of life. Based on the interviews, it is clear that the majority of the student informants believe the same as I believe.

Dr. Clark was a no-nonsense principal. He was a leader who did not allow his students to make use of excuses. Dr. Clark demonstrated that he wanted his students to do their best and never settle for less. Dr. Clark asked his students to trust that they would not have to be scared to go to high school and would be able to get a decent education that would allow them to go to college and to be successful.

Some educators would argue that Dr. Clark was an unusually strict principal and was too quick to give up on some high school children by throwing them out of EHS. Additionally, some educators would argue that they think Dr. Clark should have implemented a different alternative than kicking students out of school and giving upon them.

Furthermore, some would argue that no child should be left behind and that we should not give up on any children. I contend that we, as educators, should find a way to help assure that all children can get a quality education that would allow them to be successful citizens of this country and the world. However, based on the information gathered in this study, and given the conditions that existed at that time and the limited alternatives that were available, it could be reasonably argued that Dr. Clark's methods were appropriate for EHS.

Thirty-two years ago, there were no alternative schools or charter schools available in the Paterson area for high school students. At that time, there were no laws governing students' behavior that are as severe as they are today. There was also a lack of strict regulations that governed weapons in schools and designated drug-free zone areas. The student-teacher relationship was not as defined back then as it is today.

Through his actions and voice, Dr. Clark helped situate problems with secondary education at the forefront of the educational debate and brought additional light to the inequalities of obtaining a sound education in many urban areas. Dr. Clark provided information to the newspapers, television, and magazines regarding the impediments in urban education. Based on the data collected in the interviews, it is clear that he gave guidance to many teachers along the way.

I know that several of my classmates have become teachers and principals because of the impact Dr. Clark had on their lives. I believe that it takes a village to raise a child, and I learned that from Dr. Clark's example of being a principal. With his ability to stir up controversy and become noticed, he was able to build the desired community that was concerned about children's lives; and through his style and strategies, the village became more successful in raising its' children.

Although Dr. Clark took the brunt of the negative publicity and made many sacrifices, such as going through a divorce and having health problems during his tenure, he made a positive difference in the lives of most of those who attended and many of those who were employed at Eastside.

Some educators would argue that the students who did well at EHS would have done well regardless of Dr. Clark's presence because they had the gumption to work hard, notwithstanding the situations in which they may have found themselves. Additionally, some would argue that Dr. Clark focused positive energy only on the students whom he realized were go-getters and had the tenacity to succeed. I would suggest that they might be correct; however, there is one thing I know for sure, and that is, Dr. Clark made it possible for many students to succeed in an environment where their safety was no longer at risk and created an environment that was conducive to learning.

CHAPTER 17

What Happened to Dr. Clark once he Left EHS?

(Morgan Freeman & Dr. Clark - Courtesy EHS Yearbook, 1989)

Dr. Clark was on the lecture circuit for 25 years since the movie. Dr. Clark was nominated for the National Association of campus activities speaker of the year award in 1996, and he was one of the top five college lecturers.

In 1995 he took over the Essex County Detention Center housed in Newark, New Jersey, which he called "New Jersey's largest jail for youth when they said no one could run it, his heart began to" palpitate; with glee."

He said he knew it was the ultimate challenge. His beliefs were reaffirmed about our young people. "All incarcerated came from no homes, no mom or dad, struggling and embroiled with drugs, shootings, not going to school, no guidance. Most had the superb intellectual ability but had no chance in our society" (Amburn, 2012). Dr. Clark was released from that position due to putting 12 teens in handcuffs and leg irons at the Essex County Youth Detention Center.

Where is Dr. Clark Now?

Dr. Clark is in his early 80s now and currently resides in Gainesville, Florida, and has a 10-acre horse farm in Newberry, Florida. He has lived there for more than 20 years, and he has a beautiful landscape outside in front of the farmhouse that is surrounded by orange and blue rocks and other orange and blue novelties to resemble the Eastside High School colors.

He stated that he is addicted to horses, and he used to ride them for miles, and he used to grow vegetables in his garden. He is retired and shared that his wife Gloria has been a very supportive wife, "without her, I would have never been able to endure the pain inflicted on me by adversarial forces. She is a very good person, and I have been blessed."

(Dr. Clark & wife Gloria, 2012 - Senior Times Photo by TJ Morrissey/Lotus Studios)

Alumni Profiles

What Happened to the REAL Students from Eastside High School?

The following fifty-four alumni profiles are included to share some brief tangible information about the REAL students from Eastside High School. I believe it is vital to share that growing up in poverty-stricken circumstances do not dictate your future. I am delighted to share that talented people are doing extraordinary things that have come from Eastside High School in Paterson, New Jersey. I had the opportunity to listen to and retell these stories, while some alumni chose to tell their own histories, creating a diversity of experiences and voices.

1 – Mr. Gerard Booker – Class of 1985

(Photos Courtesy of EHS & Gerard Booker)

Gerard Booker is 46 years old and has two daughters, Keira and Tyshona. He has three grandchildren, Rayonne, Zyonna, and Jamire. He works at Passaic County Cerebral Palsy School for Handicapped Children as a Teacher's Aide and has been there for the past ten years. He has an Associate's Degree from Passaic Community College and a degree in Accounting from DeVry Institute. Gerard is a member of The Improved Benevolent Protective Order of Elks of the World (I.B.P.O. Elks of The World). My years at EHS were fascinating! I was a member of the EHS

MARCHING 100 band and the Dirty Dozen dance team.

I enjoyed my four years with my friends. I want to thank Mr. Joe Clark for keeping me out of trouble and making me the young man that I have become. A special shout out to the Class of 1985!

2 – Ms. Tomacinia Carter – Class of 1985

(Photos Courtesy of EHS & Tomacinia Carter)

Family Matters - The Whisper Out Loud Network (WOL) was inspired by the notion that family does matter. To that end, WOL proudly announces one of our newest shows, *Family Matters*. Through divine inspiration, the host Tomacinia Carter truly understands the importance of family. Tomacinia Carter or "T. Carter" was born in Paterson New Jersey grew up surrounded by her parents, four sisters and two brothers. She was raised to appreciate family and learned the value of family. T. Carter was born for this role, helping and inspiring others to care about the family while perfecting her own.

After graduating from Eastside High School, she went on to graduate from Phillips Business School. Later, Tomacinia earned countless certificates in various classes required for foster parent training, and numerous other programs specializing in assisting and caring for children with special needs/disabilities. Funny thing, she doesn't plan to stop learning, just as she doesn't plan to stop loving her family.

Tomacinia Battles & Beats Disability - Tomacinia was severely injured at the age of ten years old from a skating accident. Forced to have countless surgeries until well into adulthood (e.g., hip fusion surgery, surgery on her back, and femur) resulted in a lifetime of pain suffering and finally, total disability. After working for 16 years at the United Parcel Services, she was forced to retire early. Instead of being overwhelmed due to the problems associated with her own physical disability, her purpose came through rescuing children who needed love.

Family Matters & Tomacinia - Rescued Children - Tomacinia professed during her interview, "being a parent to my foster children and my biological son is my life's mission. And the only thing that matters is family." The mission of the WOL Network is to inspire change in listeners, communities, and families. *Family Matters* is Tomacinia Carter, and soon, the family will matter more to you.

The unique talk radio experience allows Tomacinia to use the show, *Family Matters* to develop her abilities further and help others discuss topics related to parenting. T. Carter's goal in every show is to help parents and families find real answers to family challenges. Tomacinia decided to become a foster parent after helping another foster parent with their children, recognizing a great need for help. Seeing the need and wanting to help, Tomacinia moved into action. Since then, Tomacinia has worked tirelessly to rescue foster children so that they would not have to suffer. Tomacinia has proved that disability doesn't mean "no ability." As a foster parent, she is also trained to provide care and attention to children with special needs or disabilities.

Family Matters - Today! - I am a business owner of a daycare. I teach my girls how to run the daycare as a successful business. The girls help me over the summer. As a parent, I am making sure that my girls understand and can appreciate all of life's possibilities. I don't want anything to stop them from accomplishing their dreams.

Family Matters The Future - Tomacinia plans to be a part of *Family Matters* for a long time. She plans to start a recreation center for all foster children. "I want to foster children to have a place where they have an outlet, and a lot of foster parents don't have the funds to send their children to various facilities. This would allow them to have activities in a learning center, right in their own communities." My legacy is my heart and expanding love!"

3 - Reverend William H. Cash – Class of 1986

(Photos Courtesy of EHS & Reverend William H. Cash)

Reverend William H. Cash is the Pastor and founder of Life-Changing Word Church International Incorporated located in Haledon, NJ. This ministry was established in April of 2006, along with his wife, Kim Maria Cash. The church's first worship service was held on April 16, 2006, Resurrection Sunday. With more than ten years in ministry, Pastor Cash is committed to encouraging hundreds to pursue a personal relationship with God and seeing lives changed by teaching the Word of God with clarity and understanding.

He enjoys working with young people by evangelizing to them through song and providing a practical perspective of the Word. He is a youth advocate and has dealt with many children who have cried out for help and needed guidance. Saving the youth is of great importance to

Pastor Cash because he realizes that by rooting them in the Word of God at a young age, they can reach their full potential and experience the abundant life God has in store for them.

God placed a sincere desire in Pastor Cash to see God's people taught the Word of God so practical that they can apply it to their daily lives and see change. Pastor Cash's educational background consists of attending Montclair State University in Montclair, New Jersey. He majored in Religion and minored in African American studies. He also has several certificates in Christian Training from Faith Fellowship Ministries in Sayreville, New Jersey, where the Pastor is David T. Demola.

Pastor Cash is married to Kim M. Cash and the father of Joshua and Jordyn Brianna. His family is one of the most substantial motivating factors in his life. He enjoys spreading the Word of God by educating, strengthening, and building people's self-image with the Word of God. He is saved and filled with the Holy Spirit and is committed to fulfilling the purpose of God for this generation. Pastor Cash has two other ministries. Life Changing Word Church International, Inc. Meeting Place: 522 West Broadway, Haledon, NJ 07508
Mailing Address: PO Box 9321, Paterson, NJ 07509 - Media Sites: www.lifechangingwordchurch.com and www.facebook.com/LCWCI www.facebook.com/WilliamHCashMinistries

4 - Ms. Tammy Cockfield - Class of 1985

(Photos Courtesy of EHS & Tammy Cockfield)

Tammy Cockfield graduated from Immaculate University Cum Laude with a Bachelor of Arts degree: dual major in Organizational Dynamics and Human Performance Management. She is a member of the Kappa Gamma Pi Honor Society, Delta Epsilon Sigma Honor Society, and Alpha Sigma Lambda Honor Society. Tammy has been employed with State Farm Insurance Corporation for 23 years and a Realtor with Century 21 for eight years. She has two children Shannon (27 years-old) and Justin (12 years old).

My experience at Eastside High School is one I wouldn't change for anything. I can honestly say I am proud to have been a Joe Clark student. He taught me to take pride not only in Eastside High School but also in myself. I've made some lifelong friends at Eastside High School.

5 - Ms. Ashon Curvy Moreno - Class of 1988

(Photos Courtesy of EHS & Ashon Curvy Moreno)

Once a Ghost! Always a Ghost!   Dr. Clark! Dr. Clark!

Yes, that was my only speaking role in the movie *Lean On Me*. Laughing to myself, no one knew I was writing a storyline for the film. It was a scary and exciting time in my life. I was a new mother, and only a junior attending Eastside High School in 1987, and I was writing a script for a movie. And they were paying me! A 16-year-old a lot of money for it! I hope I did Mr. Clark proudly!

Let's just say *Lean on Me*, was fiction, with a whole lot of truth wrapped around it. It is 2013, I am now 42, and happily married to a great man Anthony Moreno! I work in Special Education, and I love my job. I now have two kids, Tavon, my son, will be 28, and my Daughter Ashonta is 20. I still have the same best friend, Victoria Gurrant, more like a sister now. We are God Mothers to each other's daughters.

God and life have been good to me. I have attended two Class of 1988 reunions, and the "crew" is still the same, smart, funny, and loving parents. I have always been proud to say that I went to Eastside High School in Paterson, New Jersey! The look on people's faces is sometimes priceless! They say things like, "Wow, you turned out good!" **I tell them We all Did!!!**

6 – Ms. Maritza Davila – Class of 1989

(Maritza Davila & Steven Spielberg, 2019)

S T E V E N   S P I E L B E R G

It's 12:10AM, September 28, 2019, at Steiner Studios in the Brooklyn Navy Yards in the great city of New York, and we've just concluded filming our version of *West Side Story*. This has been a journey without precedence: a joyful, stunningly moving, endlessly surprising encounter with the story and score of one of the world's greatest musicals. My brilliantly talented, fiercely committed, generous and apparently inexhaustible cast and crew of hundreds have given our film everything they've got, and already I can say that the film we'll be releasing on December 18, 2020 owes everything to them, as does its immensely grateful director.

And while I'm on the subject of gratitude: On every day of the past four years during which we've been preparing, casting, imagining *West Side Story*, I and my team, cast and crew have been walking in the footsteps of four giants: Leonard Bernstein, Arthur Laurents, Jerome Robbins and Stephen Sondheim. For the light they've shed on the world, for Stephen Sondheim's insight, guidance and support, and for the openhearted support of the Bernstein, Laurents and Robbins estates, I owe more than I can possibly express.

We've filmed *West Side Story* all over New York, from Flatbush to Fort Tryon Park. The city lent us its beauty and its energy, and we drew deeply upon its grand, multicultural, multifaceted spirit. In addition, we spent three extraordinary weeks filming in Paterson, New Jersey. To the people of New York and Paterson, thanks not only for putting up with our trailers, tents, cranes and mid-street dance sequences; from the bottom of my heart, thanks for the warm welcomes we encountered everywhere, from pedestrians and policemen and neighborhoods and kids. We couldn't have made our musical without you.

Steven

(Letter from Steven Spielberg September 28, 2019)

Maritza was born and raised in Paterson, New Jersey. She is a very proud graduate of Eastside High School.

Maritza has 25 years of higher education experience and has been working with Passaic County children and nontraditional adults to help them earn a better future. As an undergraduate student, she assisted children from different public schools in Asbury Park and Long Branch in reading and writing. She was quoted in the Herald News in 1990 as "Doing the Right Thing."

Maritza earned her Bachelor of Arts in Communication from Monmouth University with a Concentration in Public Relations and Journalism and obtained her Master's Degree in Administrative Science from Farleigh Dickinson University in May 2005.

She is a Member of the New Jersey Education Association (NJEA), the

Passaic County School Counselors Association (PCSCA), the New Jersey Association for College Admissions Counseling (NJACAC), the Women Empowered Democratic Organization (WEDO), the former Chairwoman of Friends of Passaic County Parks, and the Democratic County Committee Member for her district.

At her leisure, she volunteers her time to work for the Democratic Party and has conducted citizenship drives for the Bengali community and many others. In June 2013, she was selected to serve as a New Jersey State Committee Woman for the Democratic Party.

In May 2014, she was elected as the 1st Latina Councilwoman at Large. Currently, she is the Council President Chair of the Paterson Municipal Council, a Member of the Economic Development Committee, the DPW Committee, Finance Committee, Street Naming Committee, Public Safety Committee, and a member of the Personnel Committee. In 2018, she co-developed and was on the board of SheCaucus, a nonprofit for the development of women.

7 – Ms. Deanna Michele De Vore – Class of 1987

(Photos Courtesy of EHS & Deanna Michele De Vore)

Deanna was born and raised in Paterson, New Jersey. She is the wife of Rodney De Vore and the mother of two children, Bryanna (18) and Jared (16). After high school she attended Bergan Institute and Passaic County Community College (PCCC) where she received her Associates degree in Science, She obtained a Bachelor of Science degree from William Paterson University, and Montclair State University, and presently attending Rutgers University of Medicine & Dentistry of New Jersey (UMDNJ) where she is pursuing her Ph.D. in Cell and Developmental Biology.

She taught at the Bergan Institute of Allied Health for 12 years and became a supervisor and currently serves as an adjunct Anatomy and Physiology professor at PCCC.

She has been an active member of Olivet Good Shepherd Church of Christ in Paterson, N.J. since the age of three. She has served in the roles of Minister of Music for 24 years, a Sunday School Teacher for ten years, Assistant Treasurer for two years, Ordained Minister for nine years, and Ordained Elder for a year. She has performed in various plays and musicals such as "Purlie," "Godspell," and "The Biography of Lorraine Hansberry" and has sung and soloed in a local school and community choirs. She also completed a musical voice over for an animated movie, and appeared on "Bobby Jones Gospel."

8 – Mr. Rodney De Vore – Class of 1987

(Photos Courtesy of EHS & Rodney De Vore)

Rodney De Vore is proud to be a lifelong resident of Paterson, New Jersey. He is a product of the Paterson Public School System as he attended PS # 10 and Eastside High School. Education was not his original choice of a career. While in high school, he desired to study law. However, while obtaining his undergraduate degree at William Paterson College, he began to substitute teaching at Eastside High School. That was when he fell in love with the idea of becoming an Educator and considered it as a career choice.

It was during these two years that he realized he had a passion for helping young people make a difference in their lives through education. He changed his major from Political Science to a double major in English and History and graduated with a degree in 1991.

He taught for a year at Eastside High School. Currently, he is employed at Passaic County Technical Institute and has in the past taught History, English, and Literature. He now serves as the Discipline Coordinator/Dean of Students with an enrollment over 3, 200 students. There are many duties under his job description, but his primary role is to maintain order, discipline, and safety throughout the school, which fosters the necessary environment and climate for students to learn efficiently.

During his tenure, he has also been a class advisor, worked on the African/American History Committee, Hispanic Heritage Committee, Teacher Mentoring Committee, Teacher of the Year Committee, as well as supports ALL student activities at PCTI.

He still makes use of his background in political science and is very involved in the politics and community of his beloved city of Paterson and State of New Jersey. He is the campaign manager and community liaison for Shavonda Sumpter, state assemblywoman of the NJ's 35th district.

He has been married to a wonderful woman, Deanna M. De Vore, for the past twenty-one years. And the desire and natural inclination to become an excellent educator were nurtured when he became the father of two amazing children, Bryanna and Jared. He knew he wanted to teach his children the necessary skills to succeed as well as have them be a blessing to others along the way.

As an active member and chapter president of the GREATEST fraternity, Alpha Phi Alpha Fraternity Inc., it has provided him the opportunity to work closely with young and talented teenagers throughout our city. Working with our Alpha Teens has given him the privilege to "pay it forward" and give back to our FUTURE LEADERS.

9 – Ms. Denise Durnell – Trigg – Class of 1986

(Photos Courtesy of EHS & Denise Durnell – Trigg)

Upon graduating from Eastside High School in 1986, I graduated from Rutgers University in 1990 with a B.S. in the Administration of Justice. I worked as a Criminal Investigator for the State of New Jersey. After being laid off because of the Afghanistan/Desert storm war, I become a Paralegal for a very successful local attorney. In 1993 I moved to Florid, where I became an eligibility specialist for the Health and Rehabilitation Services. I truly enjoyed working with the elderly and disabled who were in financial need.

I married Paul Trigg and began to have children soon after. I have three beautiful children. Our eldest daughter, Jordynne, is a freshman at Clemson University in Clemson, SC. She is studying to become a pediatric nurse practitioner. We have two elementary-aged children, as well. Paul, Jr. is seven-years-old, and Miya Joy is five-years-old. My husband, Paul, is a welder and a carpenter by trade. He is also the Supervisor at the Railroad. Also, for nearly 15 years, he has owned a Deck/Fencing company. Currently, I am the Marketing supervisor for Culvers Corporation.

Most importantly, Paul and I are blessed to be Pastors of our own church. I am still singing, and I am the Praise & Worship leader.

If it wasn't for the strong leadership of Mr. Joe Clark, I am genuinely unsure that many of us (children without a strong male presence in our homes) would have made it through school or the neighborhood or be able to go on to have a successful and fruitful life. May God bless him!

10 - Mr. Kenneth Eatman - Class of 1985

(Photos Courtesy of EHS & Kenneth Eatman)

Kenneth Eatman played football all four years at Eastside High School 1981, 1982, 1983, 1984 seasons and was selected to the All-Passaic County All-Star team in 1984. He was honored by the National Football Foundation and Hall of Fame of Passaic County as a Scholar-Athlete in 1985 for Football Performance, Academic Achievement, and School Leadership. He graduated in the top 10% of the class of 1985.

Kenneth attended Midland Lutheran College in Fremont, Nebraska 1985-1986, and experienced extensive playing time as a freshman running back. He left Midland after one year due to academic trouble and returned to Paterson. He sat out for almost two years but later returned to Midland in 1988. He excelled again in football, but this time as a defensive back and improved tremendously academically. However, he left Midland again, never to return.

Kenneth worked for three years at Bergen County Juvenile Correction Center in New Jersey.

He transferred to and graduated from Ramapo College of New Jersey in 1998 with a Bachelor of Arts degree in Psychology with an emphasis in research and statistics. He began teaching elementary school at Public School # 10 in Paterson in 1998 and currently teaches 8th-grade math at the same school.

Kenneth founded the Silk City Youth Football Team in 2006. Today the team has over 250 participants and is known as The Silk City Cardinals with six different teams ranging in ages from 5-14 years of age. The team serves the children of Paterson, New Jersey, and the surrounding areas providing mentorship, academic support, as well as team-building, and sportsmanship.

Kenneth is married to Rosa Maria Nunez-Eatman with three children ages 20, 12, and 5.

11 - Ms. Leslie Etheridge – Class of 1986

(Photos Courtesy of EHS & Leslie Etheridge)

Lesley Gist is a high school teacher in Wayne, New Jersey. The historian in her first became evident when she began research on the college paper, which would become The Gist of Freedom. She advocates for the recognition of the dynamics of multi-culturist collaborations in every talk she gives around the country.

Focused on the remarkable life of William Still and how he influenced the Underground Railroad and all he met along the way, her talks are committed to promoting social change brought about by people acting in good faith towards one another.

The Gist of Freedom is how Still Faith tells the story of William Still and Peter Gist. Their story is now a part of the National Park Service's National Underground Railroad Network to Freedom! The Still and Gist family legacies inspire us with a genuinely American Underground Railroad story of trial and triumph. In each of these me, the impossible becomes possible, and hope is fulfilled. Learn more by reading Lesley Gist-Etheridge's book The Gist of Freedom is Faith, and by visiting the following websites. - www.thegistoffreedom.com/Author.html www.undergroundrr.com/foundation/genealogy

12 - Mr. Eric Gass – Class of 1986

(Photos Courtesy of EHS & Eric Gass)

Eric was born Aug 6, 1968, he attended Paterson Public Schools # 4 and graduated in 1982. While at Eastside, I played baseball for four years and received Honorable Mention - All-County Team (1985 & 1986) and was inducted in the National Honor Society. Academically, I ranked 17th in the graduating class of 1986.

I attended Delaware State University and graduated in 1990 with a bachelor's degree in marketing. I played baseball all four years and received the following awards (All MEAC Team '89, Tournament MVP '89), and was inducted into Delaware State University's Athletic Hall of Fame in 2003.

I was very active in college and was a member of the Men's Council & was a class officer between 1989 and 1990. I was on the Dean's list in 1989 and 1990 with a cumulative GPA of 3.0.

I worked at Enterprise Rent a Car between 1990 and 1998 and left as a Location Manager. I worked at Bell Atlantic from 1999-2000 as an Account Executive/Yellow Pages advertising sale. Presently I have worked at The Hertz Corporation since 2000. I held the following positions: Business Development Representative, Business Development Manager, Regional Director/Off-Airport Operations, Sr. Account Manager, and currently, I work as the Director of Off-Airport Sales Strategies for North America. Growing up in Paterson, because of its diverse communities, has offered a tremendous exposure to various walks of life. My parents are initially from Sumter, South Carolina, and I was raised in a Christian home.

The church was a regular part of our lives and still is. My mother is a retired educator of 30 years. My father, who passed in 2001, was an Insurance Salesman/Broker. I have two siblings (brother/sister, I'm the youngest), and I have five nieces and nephews. I am the father of two beautiful daughters - Anaya Erica Gass (13) and Erin Danielle Gass (9). I created and lived by the following quote "Life is an unknown journey; it is impossible to be prepared for everything! But possible to handle anything!"

13 - Mr. Troy D. Gillispie – Class of 1986

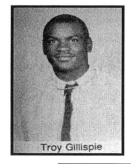  

(Courtesy of EHS & Troy D. Gillispie)

After high school, I attended Florida A&M University, South Carolina State College, Art Institute of Atlanta, Georgia, and the CDC University. Currently, I work as a Project Manager for the Centers for Disease Control and Prevention. I am the CEO & Founder of Let's Play Muzik Productions. I am also an Independent Marketing Specialist.

In the past, I served as a Reality Specialist for the Centers for Disease Control and Prevention; A Group Home Manager, Clayton County Department of Social Services; An Assistant Athletic Director, for the Boys and Girls Club of America and a Trumpet Instructor.

I enjoy spending quality time with family and friends, establishing financial stability, serving the community, traveling, and playing golf.

Favorite quote: "To laugh often and much; to win the respect of intelligent people and the affection of children...to leave the world a better place...to know even one life has breathed easier because you have lived. This is to have succeeded." (Ralph W. Emerson)

14– Mr. Winston Goode – Class of 1985

(Photos Courtesy of EHS & Winston Goode)

Winston Goode can be referred to as a performer, comedian, and just an all-around entertainer. He was born and raised in Paterson, New Jersey, from Jamaican born parents. His entertainment roots stemmed from being the permanent DJ (DJ Jahruff of Jahruff Entertainment) at either one of his family-owned night clubs & various clubs in North Jersey. This is where he mastered the ability to move crowds with his words and music choices. He also developed a keen ear for music and has dabbled a little in writing lyrics and music & scouting talented people.

Winston decided to get into professional comedy in January 2010 after performing onstage at Cozzy's Comedy Club in Newport News, Virginia. Since then, he has performed in the stage play "Amongst Thorns" written by Jessica B. Thomas in November 2010 and began a new venture as President and CEO of Just Jokes Media Entertainment in January 2011.

Although his family is vital to him, it is also the base of where his comedy lies. His family relationships and experiences have offered him limitless material to use. Winston is a devoted father and friend and has a dogged tenacity to complete any task or assignment he has an opportunity to take part in. He is an all-around funny guy with a loyal heart that can only draw people near to him for more than just business relationships but as real friends.

When not in pursuit of his entertainment career, you can often find Winston tinkering around under the hood of an automobile as he has a particular passion for cars, mainly European motor vehicles. He is an automotive technician by trade but, at this point, he translates his love of automobiles into more of a hobby.

Above all else, Winston is not only teachable, but he is willing to teach and share any of his talents with anyone willing to learn. So keep your eyes and ears open for this funny and talented individual whose name will undoubtedly become a household name shortly, because he is definitely on a quest to achieve GREATNESS!!!

15 - Ms. Coretta Goodwin-Smith – Class of 1986

(Photos Courtesy of EHS & Coretta Goodwin-Smith)

I am a proud graduate of the Class of 1986 from Eastside High School. Every time I view the movie, I see myself as the young lady that portrayed the pregnant teen, Dr. Clark worked with my mother so that I wouldn't miss out on school and he didn't want me to attend a school for pregnant girls. My son Chaz is now 29 years old and doing well. Dr. Clark taught us to face opposition head-on and deal with it. Dr. Clark made Eastside High School a safe haven.

After graduating from Eastside High School in 1986, I attended William Paterson University for two years. While working for Madonna Funeral Home in Passaic New Jersey and the LaGarde Family Funeral Home in Paterson, New Jersey, I realized that my education was not complete. At the age of 40, I decided to go back to school. I am currently attending the American Academy McAllister Institute of Funeral Services to get my Funeral Director's License.

Dr. Clark also taught us that hard work never hurt anyone, and because of his teachings, I have been able to work from home for a significant conference company for the past seven years allowing me to work, go to school, and be at home with my family.

16 - Tonya Ingram – Class of 1986

(Photos Courtesy of EHS & Tonya Ingram)

Tonya was previously employed with a New Jersey car dealership for the past ten years as an Assistant Finance Director. Currently, she works for AT&T as an International Care Manager.

She is the eldest of one sister and four brothers. She was born on August 15, 1968. Her best friends at Eastside were Veronica Daye, Amanda Geathers, Felicia Bullock, and Aicha Randolph. She was a member of the

Marching 100 band as a Dirty Dozen dancer and ran track for one year. Tonya has three children, and she loves her family.

17 - Ms. Shanell Irving – Class of 1985

(Photos Courtesy of Shanell Irving)

While growing up, I lived in the Riverview Tower project, also known as the Towers, and my school district was Kennedy High School. Although I was accepted to Passaic County Technical Institute and attended my freshman year, I loved what Dr. Clark stood for. I wrote him a letter asking him to attend Eastside High School, and I explained my reason. I wanted an education!

Dr. Clark called me himself and told me he accepted my offer and would be watching me and my grades to see if I was serious!!! During my sophomore year, Dr. Clark held to his word. Dr. Clark even knew my first real boyfriend and called us in his office to have "THE teen talk!!!" So that was the start of my great adventure at EHS!

I am a member of the class of 1986 but graduated in 1985 and went straight to Florida A&M University (FAMU), home of the incredible MARCHING 100 band. I didn't graduate from FAMU because my love for music was calling me; however, I attended FAMU for three unforgettable years.

I began working in the music industry, and that included writing songs for artists like Jaheim, Charlie Wilson, Destiny's Child, and Faith Evans, to name a few. I am partly responsible for helping to gain significant record deals for Trey Songz, Emily Kin, and Bayje and bringing MTV's America's next top pop group to Paterson, New Jersey, by putting together my own teen heartthrob group NJ5 and being Grammy-nominated for several projects.

I have two children, Joseph Moore Jr., and Emonie Brown, who attend William Paterson University (NJ) and Bloomfield College (NJ). I am very proud of my children, and I am a grandma!

I think I turned out pretty good, and regardless of what others may think of Dr. Clark, he was stern, and I wouldn't change a moment of him being part of my life growing up!

I am still making my music! I have a songwriter reality show coming to major TV in 2014 called The Writerz Rumble, and I am very focused on building better lives. Dr. Clark taught me not to give up, and FAILURE IS NOT AN OPTION!!! THANKS, DR. CLARK!!

Shanell Red #IBETHEPLUG Owner & CEO *Sesac

www.Phatthouseent.com and www.Thewriterzrumble.com

Grammy songwriter, singer, vocal producer, and artist developer.

*Manager artist-Project 2one5, Tokyo Roze, Symplicity, Sean Blaze,

International Nova *Songwriters & Producers- Jj (Jonathan Jennings),

Ringtone, Avery Segers (Hhbfm) & Michael Stokes Jr

IG- @Shanellred

FB- Shanell Red

Twitter-@SHAYREDBIGDRAWZ

18 - *Mr. Ainsworth Jackson – Class of 1986*

(Photos Courtesy of EHS & Ainsworth Jackson)

Mr. Jackson joined the United States Army Garrison, Japan (USAG-J) August 2008 to which he was appointed as a Logistics Management Specialist for the Directorate of Logistics within the Plans and Operations Division. Mr. Jackson was responsible for the preparation of the United States Army Japan (USARJ), and USAG-J's logistics support plans for mobilization, training base support, emergencies, and disaster relief.

Mr. Jackson assumed the duties of the Chief, Plans and Operations Division amidst debilitating personnel shortages later that year and was subsequently promoted into the position in 2009. Mr. Jackson's dedication to excellence was then rewarded with management directed reassignment to the Plans, Analysis and Integration Office (PAIO) as the Supervisor, Strategic Planning Specialist to mitigate significant personnel/capability shortfalls in July 2010.

Before his arrival in Japan, Mr. Jackson served as a Logistics Management Specialist for the Special Operations Command Europe (SOCEUR) in Stuttgart, Germany. Mr. Jackson's assignment with SOCEUR and his work on managing the organization's Joint Table of Distribution (JTA) and logistical support he provided to the theater Army, Navy, and Air Force Special Operation Forces (SOF) resulted in him being awarded the Joint Civilian Service Achievement Award.

Before joining government service, Mr. Jackson worked for the Department of Health and Human Services, Orange County Head Start, in Orlando, Florida, as a Quality Assurance Coordinator. Mr. Jackson's responsibility was to ensure all 22 geographically dispersed Head Start Centers were in compliance with 45 Code of Federal Regulation (CFR) and, most importantly, fostered children's intellectual, physical, social, and emotional growth so that they may reach their highest potential.

Mr. Jackson credits his success to the strong foundation he received while serving in the United States Army, which culminated after 20 faithful years of service. While on active duty, Mr. Jackson earned Associate of Arts Degrees from Lincoln Technical Institute and Barton County Community College and a Bachelor of Arts Degree from Upper Iowa University. He is currently in the process of completing a Master of Arts Degree in Education through the University of Oklahoma.

Mr. Jackson is married to his wife of 24 years, Mrs. Maria Jackson and his two sons attend the University of Florida, Ainsworth M. A. Jackson, Jr., and Adonis O. Jackson and he has one granddaughter Lorelai Cody Jackson.

19 – Dr. Michael V. Jackson - Class of 1985

(Photos Courtesy of EHS & Dr. Michael V. Jackson)

Dr. Rev. Michael V.R. Jackson is the son of Rev. John Louis Jackson and First Lady Rachel P. Jackson, formerly St. John's Missionary Baptist

Church in Paterson, New Jersey. Michael was called to the ministry at an early age, although he was told he was too young by the pastor of his father's church when his father became ill. Years later, Dr. Rev. Michael V.R. Jackson believes he was born into the ministry, and his father's mantle was passed onto him.

Education - Dr. Rev. Michael V.R. Jackson attended the Upward Bound program for college students in the 1980s and graduated from the famous Paterson, New Jersey Eastside High School in 1985. He went on to graduate from a private liberal college (Midland Lutheran) in Fremont, Nebraska with a Bachelor of Arts degree. in Journalism (1992) where he studied worldwide social and religious topics, e.g., Buddhism, Islam, Christianity, Judaism, and Hindu.

Professional Experience - Dr. Rev. Michael V.R. Jackson worked in the social services field with the youth and adults for several years as a Youth Treatment Specialist, Substitute Teacher, Church Summer Counselor, and Assistant Camp Director. He then focused on coaching middle and high school students and then moved on to collegiate sports teams. Also, he played and coached undefeated teams during the 1990s (Public School Six and the Paterson New Jersey Semi Pro Wolverines). He also worked for the Youth Advocate programs and Consultant programs in Newark and Hackensack, New Jersey, and attended and worked in different churches in Paterson and Teaneck, NJ (C.O.G.I.C).

While working in the nonprofit field, Dr. Rev. Michael V.R. Jackson worked with the County of Passaic by way of the Bridges to Success program at the Straight and Narrow social services organization in Paterson, New Jersey as a Program Coordinator and Employment Counselor/Job Developer, from 2000 to 2004. Dr. Rev. Michael V.R. Jackson moved to Ralston, Nebraska, in 2005 and worked at the Boystown Intensive Treatment Recovery Center and Midland Luther College in

Fremont, NE, as a Running Back Football Coach. After that, he went into Radio Marketing and Armed Personal/Private Security.

Ministry - Dr. Rev. Michael V.R. Jackson was called into the Ministry in the summer of 2008 in June. He was ordained by New Horizon Ministry by Rev. Michael and was granted an Honorary Doctorate from New Horizon Ministry in late 2008. He started his work at Peoples Mission Missionary Baptist Church in October 2008 as an Assistant Minister to Senior Pastor L. Bill Woods.

20 – Rev. Dr. Janeide A. Matthews-Chillis – Class of 1984

(Photos Courtesy of Rev. Dr. Janeide A. Matthews-Chillis)

Janeide A. Matthews-Chillis, Author, Entrepreneur, Mentor, Preacher, and Publisher. She received her call into ministry at an early age and finally surrendered her life to the Lord, took heed to the Masters' call, and made the decision to walk in her purpose. While recovering from a stroke in 2008, she started her very own Outreach Ministry. Through this experience and God's inspiration, she began her journey as a mentor, and author, later becoming a publisher of JMC Publishing Inc., helping others fulfill their dreams. She is a determined self-publisher and writer. Some of her books include "The ABC's of Brain Education," Fall to Rise Again, A

Minister's Sin, and many others, including her NEW Book "A Minister's Sin REVEALED, and Inspired to Inspire. All of her books can be found on Amazon.com, Barnes and Noble, and her website www.janeidechillis.com.

Janeide is the Founder of StepRite LLC, a corporation that provides event-planning, youth programs, missions, and outreach support. With God's grace and life's experiences, honed her innate quality of being a good listener, provider, and the ability to identify with people from all over. This indisputable quality is demonstrated throughout her unwavering commitment and service in her church and community. Janeide A. Chillis shared her gifts on many Boards and Associations, which included the Irvington Board of Directors under Wayne Smith, and Sandra Jones. NJ Notary, Kean Ministry, Christ Crusade, Food Bank of New Jersey (Hillside), Toys for Tots Foundation, YDP (Youth Development Program), Free Teens, USA, and Alpha Nu Omega, Inc.

Janeide embraces her journey of service to God's people while she continued education. She received her BA in Communications/Religion Studies & BS in Marketing from Kean University 2012, Master of Divinity 2015, and Sacred Theology Master's from Drew University 2016. She received an Honorary Doctor of Divinity from CICA Seminary and Theology School and her Chaplaincy in March 2016. Janeide then went further and received her Doctor of Ministry Degree from Drew University in May 2018.

Dr. Janeide A. Chillis has traveled to many countries, embracing the culture and learning about missions. Some of her mission adventures include, but not limited to, Africa (Ghana), Cuba, North Korea, South Korea, Jamaica, and the Dominican Republic, where she assisted in providing services for women and orphan children.

With God's direction, Dr. Janeide A. Chillis was able to embrace the call and concentrate on a vision by starting her very own Non-Profit 501c3 JMC Ministries, Inc. This step gives her the opportunity to help others and make an impact on the community, ministry, and other countries. Her ultimate goal within the Non-Profit is to help others become all they can be through spiritual leadership, mentoring, teaching, and inspiration, by the Grace of God.

21 - Minister Lady Jamie McDuffie – Class of 1984

(Photos Courtesy of EHS, Minister Lady Jamie McDuffie & Jaycen Moody)

Minister Lady Jamie McDuffie was born in the city of Paterson, New Jersey, on October 17, 1967. She is the eldest of three children born to James and Brenda Hendricks, also of Paterson, New Jersey. She received her elementary and high school education through the city's public school system. She chose to continue her education at Fairleigh Dickinson University, graduating with a Bachelor of Arts degree in Business Administration.

Jamie gave her life to the Lord in 1988 at the age of 21 at an Agape Force Outreach Service, which was held weekly at the Community Baptist Church of Love of Paterson, New Jersey. Little did she know that this would be where her future husband, the Reverend Michael D. McDuffie, would find her. Jamie has managed to remain steadfast and immovable in her walk with the Lord despite the many trials and tribulations she has had to endure over the years.

It became quite evident some years later that there was indeed a call on her life to minister the Gospel. Her Pastor and mentor recognized this gift at the time, the late Reverend Frederick H. LaGarde Sr., Founder Emeritus and Senior Pastor of the Community Baptist Church of Love of Paterson, New Jersey. She was licensed to minister the Gospel in 1995. She has fervently remained in God's service ever since, even though she had tried to escape the call many times.

She is well known throughout the community as a true woman of God. She has demonstrated the Kingdom of God to those around her in many ways. She was a former member of the "Agape Force Singers." In her spare time, she enjoys plays, jazz, and modeling for a Christian modeling ministry known as "Common Grace." Jamie is currently employed by the Paterson Public School System and has been for over ten years. Being the special lady that she is, she works with students with special needs at "Stars Academy."

In light of her busy schedule, she remains a loving and devoted wife and mother. She is married to Michael D. McDuffie, Pastor of the Mighty Sons of God Fellowship Church, of Paterson, New Jersey. She is the proud and devoted mother of two children, a son TaJuan and a daughter Makiyah Symphony McDuffie. She is also a proud grandmother of one grandson, CaJuan. Minister-Lady Jamie continually tries to exemplify every day of her life what it means to be a warrior on the battlefield of the Lord. We pray that God will continue to use this anointed, appointed, and full of wisdom mighty woman of God in a way that will suit His will and purpose for her life as it continues to magnify and glorify God.

22 – Mr. Eric McKenzie - Class of 1986

(Photos Courtesy of EHS & Eric McKenzie)

Eric B. McKenzie, at age 45, I must say that attending Eastside High School from 1982-1986 were the best years of my education while being under the guidance and leadership of Mr. Joe L. Clark. It was the most exciting and life-changing memoirs of my life; through his leadership, I learned to accept responsibility for my actions and deal with the consequences of my actions and decisions.

I owe a lot to Mr. William Peter Nelson, former Band Director, who was a father to many students at Eastside when our dads were at work or not involved in our lives.

I currently serve as a Deacon at my church. I am married to Lillian (Class of 88), and we have five children and two grandchildren. I am currently signed to Universal Music Group with the Hi-Lite Juniors of New Jersey, a gospel group that I have been a member since age nine. I love my family, and my life experiences have helped me become a better man and person today. If I had to do it all over again, I would start from my years in high school at Eastside High School.

23 - *Mr. Vaughn McKoy, JD, MBA – Class of 1986*

(Photos Courtesy of EHS & Mr. Vaughn McKoy)

Vaughn is well known in New York and New Jersey for his 25 years of leadership of corporations, communities, and people. His experience spans federal and state government, nonprofits, law firms, and corporations, where he earned a reputation as a business-savvy lawyer who is at home in the boardroom and the trenches. He has been recognized for his ability to influence, motivate, and organize to achieve goals, and has been recruited as a straight-shooter and a big-picture thinker.

Currently, Vaughn is the Business Administrator for New Jersey's third-largest city, where he was tapped by the new Mayor to help lead the city's transformation. Prior to this, Vaughn held various legal and business roles of increasing responsibility with New Jersey's largest utility company and completed his tenure there as Managing Director and Vice President where he led and oversaw the management of the law department for a company subsidiary. As an Assistant Attorney General and Director of Criminal Justice, Vaughn was one of state's top prosecutors after stints as an Assistant U.S. Attorney and a lawyer in private practice for several prominent firms. He is currently affiliated with Inglesino Webster Wyciskala and Taylor, LLC.

Vaughn is a part-time professional speaker, certified coach, author and mentor and the CEO and Founder of The McKoy Group, LLC, a consulting firm offer keynote speaking, workshops, seminars, and coaching. He is a TEDx Presenter and Certified John C. Maxwell Speaker, Coach, Trainer. Determined to give back to local communities, Vaughn is a long-time leader of nonprofits, serving as a board member for regional organizations, including Rutgers University, UNCF, The Boys and Girls Clubs of New Jersey, Mentor New York and the Global Foundation, Inc.

In 2012, Vaughn was named General State Regulatory Counsel for Public Service Enterprise Group, Inc., New Jersey's most significant energy holding company that he first joined in 2006. He's a chief representative to the Board of Public Utilities and other regulators across the region for both the parent company and its business units. Additionally, Vaughn is PSEG's lead counsel on legal, regulatory, and compliance issues, including practice before federal and state courts and regulatory agencies.

Before joining PSEG, Vaughn was one of New Jersey's top prosecutors, second only to the Attorney General, and first-in-command of the New Jersey Division of Criminal Justice. He's also been a federal prosecutor and a lawyer in private practice. He's a graduate of NYU's School of Business, Rutgers Law School, and Rutgers University—where he was a top scholar-athlete and played football all four years.

Determined to give back to local communities, Vaughn is a long-time leader of nonprofits, serving as a board member for 10 New Jersey and regional charities. His contributions to law, business, and communities have been recognized with dozens of awards.

Vaughn is routinely called upon to build and steer partnerships among diverse stakeholders. He does so by making use of productive and long-term personal networks with influential figures throughout New Jersey and the region, including political figures, regulatory and administrative officials, community advocates, and business leaders. He solidifies businesses "good corporate citizen" reputations by listening to and responding to the community perspective. By focusing on achieving business goals and by understanding obstacles, he develops scenarios that enable all stakeholders to win.

Vaughn is equally adept at building internal coalitions. He's successfully led corporate-wide, multidisciplinary initiatives involving: strategic planning with executives, division leaders, and other stakeholders; best practices and policies; employee training and re-training; and community outreach. Because of the breadth of his experience, Vaughn is sought out by executives to identify viewpoints of competing parties and constituents (including government agencies) and to create strategies to address those views, enable corporate growth, and protect business interests.

Leveraging experience and achievements in both business and law, Vaughn leads—and implements—corporate-wide strategy plans that account for changing need, markets, technology, and regulatory or legal landscapes, and that promote organizations' abilities to adapt and expand. As a business lawyer, Vaughn ensures legal strategies consistent with overall business objectives, including cost reduction and risk reduction. He's handled and overseen high-level litigation in federal and state courts and administrative agencies, as well as sophisticated workplace investigations.

In addition to being an award-winning businessman, Vaughn is an author and motivational speaker. In his honest and revealing autobiography, *Playing Up: One Man's Rise from Public Housing To Public Service Through Mentorship,* the former Rutgers University football standout leads the reader through the mind-set and strategies that put him on the path to success from inner-city Paterson, New Jersey, and Eastside High School to the United States Attorney's Office and beyond. *Playing Up* can be found on VaughnMckoy.com as well as on Amazon.com, Kindle, Nook, Barnes and Noble, and other fine booksellers.

24 - *Daryl L. Miller – Class of 1986*

(Photos Courtesy of EHS & Daryl Miller)

After graduation, Daryl attended Passaic County Community College, where he received his Associates degree in Business Administration. He furthered his education by attending Lyons Institute located in Hackensack, NJ, and received his diploma in Heating, Ventilation, Air – Conditioning and Refrigeration. He has worked in this field since 1988. He served as the Senior Engineer for CBRE Corporation and currently serves as a Project Director for URS Corporation.

Daryl believes that attending EHS under the guidance of Mr. Joe Clark taught him the significance of strict discipline and that education was his way out of poverty.

Mr. Miller has five children; Dominique Miller graduated from Atlanta Metropolitan College, Janay graduated from Georgia State University with a Bachelor's degree and the University of Georgia, earned a Master's degree in Social Work; Evonne graduated from Georgia State University with a Bachelors degree, Darylynn currently attends Georgia State University, and Olandha now attends high school.

25 – Dr. Olandha Pinky (Seldon) Miller – Class of 1986

(Photos Courtesy of EHS & Dr. Olandha Pinky Miller)

Dr. Olandha Pinky Miller attended Public School # 24, Eastside High School, and Montclair State University, where she received her Bachelor of Arts degree in Communication Studies and her Master of Arts degree in Counseling and School Guidance. She received her Doctor of Philosophy degree from Georgia State University in 2011.

Dr. Pinky Miller, the author of this book and the Executive Producer of the upcoming *Know Our Story* documentary *Know Our Story* LLC. Dr. Miller has over 18 years of experience working in higher education and has been employed by the following institutions: Montclair State University (NJ), Miami University (OH), The College of William & Mary (VA), Saint Peter's College (NJ), Clark Atlanta University (GA) Georgia State University (GA), The University of South Dakota (SD) and Allen University (SC). Dr. Miller has held several positions as a Hall Director/Academic Advisor, Area Coordinator, Assistant/Director of Residence Life & Housing, Assistant Dean of Students, and the Vice President of Student Affairs.

Dr. Miller loves working with students; she thrives on being able to help them in a time of crisis and help guide them toward becoming successful citizens. Dr. Miller currently serves as an exceptional education teacher in Georgia. She is a proud member of Alpha Kappa Alpha Sorority Incorporated. Dr. Miller has five God-fearing, intelligent children

26 – Dr. Lilisa Mimms – Class of 1987

Dr. Lilisa Mimms Councilwoman-At-Large "A Better Paterson"

(Photos courtesy Dr. Lilisa Mimms)

"The only team that matters is the one that WE are ALL on!"

Council-at-Large – Paterson City Council   lilisamimms@aol.com

A career in Human Resources, Customer Service, and Operations Management professional with over 20 years of experience enabling customer delight and supporting top and bottom-line business objectives at Fortune 100 companies.

Skills and Professional History

Strategic Planning	Management/ Administration
Team Development and Leadership	Operational Efficiency
Employee and Benefits Management	Leading and Negotiating

Professional and Political Experience Summary

Verizon, incorporated in New York Choice TV: 1999 - 2008

Paterson Board of Education: 2014 - 2017

State Paterson Planning Board Vice-Chair: 2016 - Present

Education and Training

D. M. Theology, The Christian University Paterson NJ, Summa Cum Laude (2009)

Master Certificate, George Washington University, New York, New York (2007)

Masters, Religion Education, Alpha Bible Institute, Nutley, New Jersey Summa Cum Laude (2008)

B. S., Marketing, University of Phoenix, Phoenix AZ (2004)

A. S., Marketing, Passaic County Community College, Paterson NJ (2000)

Professional Highlights - Verizon. Incorporated and New York Choice TV

Facilitated cross-functional teams that included Technology, Legal, Operations, and Information Technology to develop a cross benefit analysis (CBA) to rationalize key investments in producing over $141 million in savings over 15 years.

Developed key metrics and policies to increase team performance and drive behavior resulting in 11.8% sales increase

Developed company-wide curriculums, processes, and policies to enhance HR performance and alignment with strategic objectives.

Led large teams of 250 employees and consultants to deliver world-class customer experience and support.

Increased Net Promoter scores by 3%

Developed a tracking tool which reduced nonproductive dispatch by 5% within 3 months saving the company over $500,000

Pioneered sales initiatives that improve sales by 10% within a 90-day period

Identified and mentored subordinates who displayed talent and skills resulting in 20 employees being promoted in 5 years

Developed and executed strategies that increased employee retention cut costs, and supported revenue growth.

Paterson Board of Education

Gained 2 areas of local control (Fiscal Management and Personnel)

Introduced cost-benefit analysis

Recommended all school calendars Include school board meetings to increase parent participation

Requested comprehensive Special Education plan to be developed to ensure compliance

Introduced a Parent Survey form to track parents' concerns when they come to the board meeting so identify steps of resolution

Provided fiscal oversight of budget to ensure our children will receive a thorough and efficient education

Fought against a 2.8% tax increase for homeowners 2017 - 2018 budget

Requested 3 - 5-year financial plan

Fought for PS# 21 to become turnaround school which resulted in higher tests scores, teachers and every classroom an improvement in several performance metrics

Requested all school buses have one 1-800 numbers and an operator ID

Associations and Affiliations

Leadership Paterson, Cite New Jersey, WAVE, NAACP, Women's Ministry President, Domestic Violence Advocate, Christian Women's United for Church of Christ, Vice-Chair of Star of Hope Ministries

27 - Mr. Zatiti K. Moody – Class of 1993

(Photos Courtesy of EHS & Zatiti K. Moody)

Mr. Zatiti Moody formerly served as Principal of Operations at Eastside High School. Before this appointment, Mr. Moody was the sole Administrator at the Great Falls Academy, formerly known as the "Paterson Alternative High School" for nine years, where he instituted a highly effective and rigorously disciplined behavior modification program which promulgated his promotion to the historic Eastside High School.

(Various EHS Alum & Staff Members - Courtesy of Zatiti Moody)

Mr. Moody's passion for assisting in the restoration of young lives and inspiring, meaningful change was fostered early in life by his parents, Mr. and Mrs. Alonzo, and Sarah Moody. Both are longstanding community activists and humanitarians whose contributions to the Paterson community are immeasurable. They have led a tireless struggle to uplift their community as a whole and as such, were enlisted by the President of the Executive Board of Children's Haven to run a group home for abused, abandoned, and neglected boys. For thirteen years, Zatiti and his brothers Malik and Kwesi were reared among the over 200 foster children placed in the care of their parents. It was there that Zatiti forged his own identity through the plethora of trials and tribulations.

Mr. Moody is an exemplary role model and a product of the school system he now serves. He graduated from Eastside High School, where, as a senior, he demonstrated a strong aptitude for success academically and as a student-athlete. He graduated in the top 5% of his class, ranking #7 in a class of over 350 students. Not only did Moody excel academically but was a force to be reckoned with as a three-sport athlete, having gained national recognition as one of the top student-athletes in the country. This was no easy feat considering the apparent obstacles of living with wayward youth.

Moody was highly recruited by several colleges and universities but chose the University of Pittsburgh to further his academic and football interests. On the football field, he started as a defensive end three years in a row in the competitive Big East Conference. There, he gained national recognition in the Nation's Capital as one of the top student-athletes in the college ranks. He was one of thirty student-athletes to receive this prestigious National Award for Academic and Athletic Achievement from the National Association of Academic Advisors for Athletes (N4A).

Mr. Moody's academic abilities rivaled his athletic accomplishments. He was named to the Big East Academic All-American team when he graduated with a 3.8 GPA in the field of Social Work. Impressed with Mr. Moody's passion, accomplishments, and perspective, the University of Pittsburgh offered to absorb the costs associated with securing his Master's Degree in Social Work, in exchange for his accepting a position as an Academic Advisor to the athletic student body.

Mr. Moody completed his master's degree and certification as a Certified School Social Worker. He was highly recruited by the Pittsburgh Public Schools. However, Zatiti made the conscious decision to return to the city he loves to continue onto the path of community service like that of his phenomenal parents.

At the age of 23, Mr. Zatiti Moody accepted a School Social Worker position at the Great Falls Academy, where he excelled as a counselor and mentor to some of the city's most disaffected students. Mr. Moody quickly garnered the respect and attention of his Principal as well as the Superintendent of schools for his impact on the students and their families that he served. After only three years of working as a School Social Worker, the Superintendent appointed Mr. Moody to the position of Supervisor, where he functioned as the sole administrator of Great Falls Academy for nine years.

He is credited with the successful implementation of the Positive Peer Culture Behavior Modification model and is responsible for its replication throughout other school districts and agencies throughout the country.

In 2009, Mr. Moody was appointed as the Co-Principal of Eastside High School. In his first year returning to his alma mater, he instituted some of the tenets of the Positive Peer Culture Behavior Modification model and had an overwhelmingly positive impact on the culture of the school. The following year Mr. Moody was named as the Principal of Operations and continues to instill the core values of Positive Peer Culture to influence the newly established school culture that creates the environment for student success.

In addition to his meaningful work and contributions to the Paterson Public School system, Mr. Moody finds the time and energy to dedicate to various progressive community-based organizations such as; Vice President of the B.R.O.T.H.E.R.S. of Paterson (Brothers Reaching Out To Help Everyone Rebuild Self). Member of BAND (Ban Against Neighborhood Destruction). Former mentor of the Youth Advocate Program (YAP), former member of the Paterson Mayor's Task Force, former Consultant for the School-Based Youth Services Program, member of Black Men Talking (BMT), and Board Member for both the Mural Arts Program (Halls That Inspire) as well as the City of Paterson's Youth Services Bureau program (Total Lifestyle and Support Program).

Mr. Moody was featured on several media outlets, including Eyewitness News, FOX 5, MY 9 News, CBS News, and News 12 for the work that he has done in the community of Paterson as a High School administrator. Along with his efforts with the BROTHERS organization in their implementation of alternative educational strategies and techniques used to educate the public about the importance of voting and ending gun violence. Mr. Moody was also featured on Univision for the work that he has done with the schools during Hispanic Heritage Month.

Although Mr. Moody continues to be committed to his mission of creating an environment better than the one he inherited, he is most proud of the work that he does in his home, where he is a proud Husband and Father. Zatiti Moody resides in the City of Paterson with his lovely wife Dawn Moody and three children; Kiana Briggs 19, Khadija Moody 12, and Akil Moody 9.

28 - Diana "Dottie" Moore – Class of 1988

(Photos Courtesy of EHS & Diana Dottie Moore)

(Photos Courtesy of EHS & Diana Dottie Moore)

Diana is a very proud graduate of Eastside. She has lived a life that has battled through many tough circumstances. During her sophomore year, she became pregnant, and her mother abruptly and sadly passed away from cancer. Diana has a life story that encompasses child abuse, abandonment, drug abuse, and ultimately, the power to overcome obstacles with the help of her Lord and Savior Jesus Christ.

Diana attended Job Corps after high school. She worked as a school bus driver and worked for New Jersey Transit System for more than ten years. Diana has three children Dominique, Robert, and Destiny. She was blessed with her first granddaughter. Diana shared her motivational life story with various audiences.

Diana sadly yet graciously passed away in 2014 from her battle with breast cancer. She and Dr. Pinky Miller were in the process of writing her autobiography that will help change the lives of many. Her astonishing life story will be finished by Dr. Pinky Miller and available in 2020.

29 - *Terrie Moore – Class of 1986*

(Photos Courtesy of EHS & Terrie Moore)

I was born Teresa (pronounced Teressa) Darcelle Moore on February 19, 196, in Paterson, New Jersey. I am the youngest of five children. My parents, Lorenzo and Louise Moore, were hard workers who provided my siblings and me with the essential tools for life. They were both committed to raising their five children in a loving environment and teaching us that education was important. My father worked for the U.S. Postal Service, while my mother worked as a housekeeper.

I started my education in the Paterson public school system. I attended Public School #21 from kindergarten to eighth grade. I began playing the clarinet in the fourth grade. Three of my siblings played instruments (saxophone, flute, and trumpet). My parents encouraged us to play any instrument we wanted, but we had to be good at it. After graduating from grade school, I attended Eastside High School under the leadership of Mr. Joe Clark.

I developed a love for music at a very early age, but it was not until I attended a high school that my passion for music flourished. I was a member of the infamous Marching 100 band all four years of high school. I played clarinet and was one of the first people to receive the position of Section Leader as a freshman. Three of my siblings before me were also members of this prestigious group. Some of the best musicians were birthed from this magnificent band. I was honored to be a student of one of the best band directors in the world, Mr. William Peter Nelson.

During high school, I also developed a love for singing. I participated in several music showcases and talent shows. Singing became my passion, and in my later years, I would realize that it was also my calling. During my sophomore year in high school, I met and dated a handsome young man by the name of Dennis Smith. We dated for approximately one year but later realized that we were better as just friends. We kept in touch during the remainder of our high school years but lost contact shortly after graduation.

After graduating from Eastside, I attended Delaware State University, but the freedom proved to be too much for me to handle. I dropped out after one semester and went back home to Paterson to find employment. It was during this period that I met a loving and caring young man by the name of Stanley Brown. Stanley was four years my senior and was a friend of one of my siblings. I had known him for quite some time but never thought he and I would ever date. After dating for six months, I became pregnant.

In November of 1991, six months into my pregnancy, Stanley was shot and killed. I was pregnant and afraid. However, I knew that my strength was necessary for my unborn child, who was due to arrive in February of 1992.

On February 5, 1992, I gave birth to a beautiful baby boy. I named him Tevin Dante' Moore. In March of that same year, I gave my life to

Christ. This day would change my life forever. I knew I had the hard task of being a mom and a dad, but God would be with me.

In June of 1996, I reunited with my high school sweetheart, Dennis Smith. We began dating and were married a year later in August of 1997. Dennis, Tevin and I were a family, and I thank God for allowing Dennis to be a father to my son.

In 2001, we purchased a home in Tannersville, Pennsylvania. Our life was beautiful, and we felt complete. We had our faith, our family, and now our new home. In 2004 my husband's health began to deteriorate. He could no longer work, and he had to receive around the clock care. In April of 2006, Dennis passed away.

I was again a single parent and alone. However, I had faith in God that was unshakeable. I knew that God placed me where I was for a reason and that He would see me through any situation I was going through.

After Dennis' death, I needed to keep myself occupied. I joined a church and began singing with a group that would later travel the United States to spread the gospel of Jesus Christ. This was a humbling experience, and I learned a great deal about God's love and how he can use someone to uplift His kingdom. I knew that staying active would also minimize the grief I was experiencing with the loss of my husband.

I decided to pursue my education and go back to school. I enrolled at the University of Phoenix online and completed my Bachelor's degree in Business in 2012. I am currently an Accounting Supervisor for the largest beverage manufacturing company on the east coast.

Tevin is an accomplished musician and pursuing a career in music. I know that God has complete control over my life, and I am so blessed to have experienced everything that I have gone through. My love for God and my family has been my strength and the reason I am still standing.

30 - *Mr. Laron Lateef Moses – Class of 1984*

(Photos Courtesy of EHS & Laron Moses)

Laron was a freshman in 1980 and was supposed to graduate with the class of 1984. He was a sophomore in 1982 when Dr. Clark became principal and made tremendous changes in the school policies. As a result of the transformation, he was kicked out of Eastside High School before he could graduate due to missing more than 21 days of school (a new policy set by Dr. Clark).

Currently, Laron has an entrepreneurial spirit. He is self-employed, provides remodeling work for homes, and assists with income tax returns. He is a carpenter by trade and is a subcontractor that repairs houses. He started a few businesses, and he enjoys taking good care of his family.

31 - *Mr. Darren Napier – Class of 1986*

(Photos Courtesy of EHS & Darren Napier)

"THE PERILS OF DRUGS AND CRIMINAL ACTIVITY"

Darren K. Napier, 288994, was sentenced to 20 years with a ten-year bid for armed robbery. He was incarcerated on December 11, 1996 and Released on September 11, 2007.

Darren was born on January 8, 1969 and raised with both parents in the household. He is the son of a prominent educator, Dr. Frank Napier Jr., who was the first African American Superintendent of Schools in the city of Paterson, New Jersey. Darren excelled in High School as an athlete and received a football scholarship. He was scouted by several major universities, and later looked upon by many NFL teams, the Philadelphia Eagles being #1 on the list. Darren was side-lined by drugs and alcohol and left behind two daughters within the community.

While incarcerated during 1996–2000 in the Passaic County Jail, in Paterson, Darren became the Founder of and Outreach Ministry. Darren began sharing his testimony, by speaking to students in various schools and speaking to adults in the community about the dangers of using drugs, and how being involved in gangs could lead to criminal activities and causing incarceration.

While incarcerated during 2002-2002 in the Northern State Prison, Newark, New Jersey, Darren became a member of Northern State Prison, Drama Club, whereas he performed in plays and skits and offered alternative ways of deterring youth as well as adults from any criminal and drug activities within our cities.

While incarcerated during 2002-2004 in the Northern State Prison, Newark, New Jersey, Darren became a member of the Northern State Prison Outreach Program and Prisoners Speakers Forum. I am offering testimony, performing skits for youth affiliated programs, adults, teachers, prosecutors, senior citizens, Jewish Community, Prison Assessment Centers.

While incarcerated during 2004-2006 in the Northern State Prison, Newark, New Jersey, Darren became involved in the "Project Pride" program. Darren began traveling from within the compounds of prison to speak at schools and colleges promoting the responsibility of drug education, addressing children about the perils of crime and the harshness of incarceration.

2008-Present - Darren was released from jail and on track to give back to the community by assisting youth and law enforcers by sharing his life experiences. He is currently working as the Adult Basic Education Instructor at the Newark Comprehensive Center for Fathers.

Darren is married to Ebony Napier, and they have four children.

To book a speaking engagement, please contact Darren by email at darren.napier23@yahoo.com

32 - Dr. Alfreda (Lawrence) Paige – Class of 1987

(Photos Courtesy of EHS & Dr. Alfreda (Lawrence) Paige)

Alfreda was born in Paterson, New Jersey. Throughout my schooling, I attended Public School # 4 and Public School # 26. My grammar school tenure was shortened by a year because I was skipped from 3rd to 5th grade because of my high academic achievements. I graduated from Public School # 26 and entered Eastside High School in 1983, and I graduated in 1987.

All my years at Eastside were under the leadership of Mr. Joe Clark. It was a priceless experience that I will never forget. The words gingerly and expeditiously were not commonly used words for me. But Dr. Clark's daily word of the day tremendously increased my vocabulary. This is one of the reasons I am a lifelong learner in the field of education. Dr. Clark instilled in me that failure is not accepted. His determination to keep the students that wanted to learn in a "safe" environment inspired me throughout my life.

I was a member of the Eastside Marching 100 band. I was a member of the "Dirty Dozen" dance team during the football season. I was also a cheerleader for the basketball season. Although I was actively involved in extracurricular activities, due to life's challenges and influences in a low socioeconomic community, I still allowed myself to partake in negative influences. I was called to Dr. Clark's office regularly. Thanks to him, I was never suspended for the bad behavior that I exemplified while in high school. I perceived this as Dr. Clark gave me a chance because he saw greater in me than I saw in myself. Due to home and societal influences, I chose not to go to college right after graduation. Instead, I wanted to work to help my single mother with bills. I also wanted to be trendy and stay close to my friends.

After waking up from a bad dream and hearing the voice of Mr. Joe Clark yelling through his bull horn, "Alfreda! Are you staying out of trouble?" in the fall of 1993, I decided to go to college. I applied and was accepted to Morgan State University (MSU). I attended MSU for one year. After struggling every week to run home to see my boyfriend, who was known on the streets as a drug dealer, I decided to come closer to home. I transferred to Kean University in Union, New Jersey. I graduated in May 1997 with a Bachelor of Arts in Political Science.

Later, I earned my Master of Administrative Science in 2000 from Fairleigh Dickinson University in Teaneck, New Jersey. I was a teacher for ten years for the Paterson Public School System. After having children, I considered relocating to Georgia. But not having any immediate relatives that resided in Georgia, I prolonged my move for several years. I had also started pursuing my doctoral degree in education but was struggling to finish.

After standing at attention and listening to Mr. Joe Clark's speech at my high school 20th-year class reunion in 2007, all my goals were rejuvenated by his charge to my class. He was handing over the bull horn to us. Dr. Clark instructed us to take charge! In 2011, my husband, two daughters, and I relocated to Georgia. In 2012, I received my doctorate in Education (Ed.D.) in Administrator Leadership for Teaching and Learning from Walden University. As I continue to take charge, my next goal is to write my autobiography.

33 - Ms. Elena Payamps – Class of 1985

(Elena's two sets of Twin Daughters - Riding camels Courtesy of Elena Payamps)

(Elena's two sets of Twin Daughters - Courtesy of Elena Payamps)

(The Royal Palace in Dubai)

(Elena Payamps)

This is Elena H. Payamps, a proud graduate of the class of 1985 of Eastside High School. Thank you so much for giving me the opportunity to share our success stories and for having the chance to say "Thank You" to Mr. Joe Clark. He has been most appreciated and mentioned here in Dubai, United Arab Emirates (UAE).

I have shared my story with everyone here in Abu Dhabi and the students that I have educated over the 30 years I have been here.

Sometimes the students blame their parents, but Mr. Clark always said, "Don't blame your parents, blame yourself if you don't move forward in your life regarding your education." Everything I have accomplished in education, always comes back to what I have learned from Mr. Joe Clark and of course my beloved parents who were always there for support and encouragement.

I thank God for my life experiences at Eastside High School. I am the person I am today for those experiences in my life. Here in UAE, everything is given and provided. Education is free, and there is absolutely no reason for anyone not to go to school or university. The government really takes care of everyone's education here, and I have educated some of the royal family, and VIP students give me a lifetime opportunity of sharing my knowledge with them all.

I am a graduate of Daytona State College, University of Phoenix, and soon to complete a DBA/Ph.D. from Abu Dhabi University. I acquired a bachelor's degree and two master's degrees, one focusing on education and decided to go for a Ph.D. I was a Science major and worked towards a medical degree.

I worked as an intern in my medical field and assisted in surgeries at Barnett Hospital before I left New Jersey to marry my true love. After arriving here in the United Arab Emirates, God must have wanted me to teach, so I started to work in a newly established Scientific Private School that was designed for the royal family and very high-profile students. I followed their education until the University level. Out of the nine students, three of them are medical doctors; two are seeking their master's degrees in Engineering, one is a Marine Biologist, and one is in Public Health with a minor in Human Humanitarian. I enjoyed educating the students, so I left the surgical ward and went back to University to get a Master's in Education with a specialization in supervision and administration.

I have been working for the Royal family of the United Arab Emirates for over 30 years. I am presently working as an Academic Consultant/ Advisor, and I love my job. I have had success with the nine students mentioned above and continue to implement my educational philosophies in schools and universities here. When I share my story with students that I meet, they cannot believe that I have come so far to make a difference in their lives.

At the present time here in the UAE, I am developing projects for the implementation of Safety Awareness within the institutional structure, working closely with the American Heart Association. I am working with the United Nations Emirates Diving Association with a project that has been implemented for the past eleven years, and it is very close to my heart. This project includes taking the sons of the royal family out to clean and dive and clean the shores.

We work closely with the environmental agency of the UAE. Clean up Arabia involves people from all walks of life in actions that make a real difference. This project was developed for the purpose of helping to shape the people's consciousness concerning littering in our waters. This project generally aims to clean the marine environment from pollution.

I also follow educational scholarships that are offered to outstanding students by the children of the royal family. We have also done the first research competition in the country for undergraduates from Abu Dhabi University and all Universities in the country. Also, it was a privilege for me to be part of the volunteering team in Abu Dhabi for the Special Olympics 2019 alongside my daughters. Helping my girls be aware of students with determination and helping them to fulfill their dreams in their own ways. It was a lifetime opportunity for us, and it was also very special to me to be able to do this with my girls and all the athletes that took part. (Truly blessed)

Dr. Clark changed my life, and I love to share my knowledge with other students. I am a mother of two sets of twin girls. I love my work, I am direct and critical, and all those things. But at the end of the day, I go home to my husband and my diamonds (daughters), and that is pure bliss.

I remember having a conversation with Dr. Clark one day in his office, and I needed to know that I was unique and smart. He told me to believe in myself and give it the very best. I kept those words in my head and landed a job overseas straight after college. When I tell my friends and my students where I came from and what school I attended, they can't believe that I am so easy going but firm towards education and educating our future generation. I thank my beloved parents Lidia Gonell de Payamps and Rafai (Tofo) Payamps, for being the amazing parents that they were and for their encouragement that anything is possible no matter where you come from. Thank God, the Almighty! For always leading me in the right direction and making it possible for me to share my knowledge with all the students that I have educated.

Keeping humble and sharing my life with my daughters first and my students is a real blessing for me. Thank you, Dr. Clark, for your incredible motivation, encouragement and helping me to believe in myself! I ask God always to give me the patience I need to help, care, educate, and share what God has given me.

34 - Reverend Helena Pierce – Class of 1986

(Photos Courtesy of EHS & Helena Pierce)

Evangelist Helena Pierce, of Community Baptist Church of Englewood New Jersey, where the pastor is the Rev, Lester W. Taylor, was born a raised in Paterson, New Jersey, by her devoted parents, Walter and Ruthie Pierce. She is the mother of five children and the grandmother of three.

As a young lady, Evangelist Pierce attended Greater Holy Tabernacle Church in Elizabeth, New Jersey. It was there she devolved her love for the word of God and her joy of singing, under the teachings of Reverend Jessie Wooten. In 1992 she later joined St Paul fire baptized holiness church in New Rochelle New York, where she served faithfully for 20 years.

Evangelist Helena Pierce received her degree in business administration from Monroe College in New Rochelle, New York, and is now working on her degree in sociology. She is a published poet and author. Her first book is titled "***The Diary of a Church***," a story of her life and how God used the pain of the death of her three-year-old son, rape of her sister and depression, to be able to say "I made it all work together for the Good."

She was ordained in the fire baptized church and served as District Evangelist for the New York district for 15 years, and she has been licensed to preach the gospel for over twenty years.

She is a psalmist, and songwriter and her voice can be heard on recordings such as Pastor Franklin Brown and New Territory, and The Voices of St. Paul, *In control* The Garden State Choral Chapter *30th Reunion Project,* and Allen Memorial G.O.G.I.C *Deliberate Praise volume* 1 and other recordings.

Reverend Helena Jones is moving forward in her women's ministry, Founder of the Women *of God's Own Design. Women of G.O.D* are geared to helping women become proud of who they are by teaching the necessary steps of loving oneself, and the importance of a renewed mind. You will find her ministering in the streets of Paterson, New Jersey, to the addicts, the homeless, and helping women from all walks of life as she strives to be the masterpiece God intended her to be.

She follows the footsteps of her mother, the late Rev. Ruthie Pierce, who gave to the needy and the untouchables. She has ministered in prisons and shelters in the tri-state area. You will be encouraged and uplifted by the effective delivery of God's word, by his present time anointed vessel of God.

35 - Jennifer (Carrion) Reed – Class of 1986

(Photos Courtesy of EHS & - Jennifer (Carrion) Reed)

She was born and raised in Paterson, New Jersey. She attended Public School's number 15 and 21 before attending Eastside. She worked as an Assistant Sales Account Executive.

Before her current position, she was a Jr. Buyer. She enjoys her career. She has one son and a grandson and enjoys them tremendously. She appreciated her high school years and stayed in contact with several alumni.

36 – Riff – Class of 1988

I want the school's alma mater. Let's hear it.

(Photos Courtesy of EHS & Riff)

Riff is an R&B/Pop vocal group from Paterson, New Jersey, formed while its members were teenagers attending Paterson's Eastside High School. The ensemble began under the name The Playboys in the late 1980s, with style strongly influenced by doo-wop.

After singing in the 1989 film *Lean on Me* (which is based upon events occurring at Eastside High), the group changed its name to Riff and signed to SBK Records, releasing a self-titled album in 1991. The group scored several respectable hits, including three in the Billboard Hot 100. Their song "Family" appears on the Teenage Mutant Ninja Turtles soundtrack. Following the success of the album, the group appeared on The Arsenio Hall Show, The Tonight Show and Soul Train (just to name a few), and opened on tour for Vanilla Ice and LL Cool J. The group's second album, *To Whom It May Concern*, was released in 1993 and had two charting singles on the R&B charts.

Anthony "Chill" Fuller, Dwayne "Stylz" Jones and Michael "Nitty Green" Best went on to join the group Men of Vizion. In 2009, Riff reunited and started work on returning to the R&B industry with a new album, "25 Years Strong," which was released in December 2013.

37 – Ms. Janice Robinson – Class of 1985

(Photos Courtesy of EHS & Janice Robinson)

International singing sensation Janice Robinson, the daughter of the late, great Dr. Rev. J.J. Robinson, conquered the music industry as a singer, songwriter, choreographer, actress, and performer whose pen has written popular music's most inspirational tunes since the 1990s internationally.

After becoming a young scholar of vocal music at the iconic East Side High School in Paterson, New Jersey, under the leadership of famed principal Mr. Joe Louis Clark, Robinson's rise to fame began while she was a student at Adelphi University. Legendary producer Niles Rogers and singer Carole Davis, whom Robinson became her choreographer during the late1980s, discovered Janice. During her college years, a meeting with a family friend landed her a coveted spot as a back-up singer for Rick Wes during the sold-out world *Hangin' Tough* tour headlined by 1980's teen pop royalty The New Kids on the Block. Months after the tour, Robinson nabbed the lead singer role of the Euro---dance/pop group Snap! Who ultimately taped her first TV performance ever with the #1 international hit "The Power" on "Soul Train."

Garnering exposure in the music industry by working around the world's most popular acts allowed Robinson to shine in the forefront as she formed the Euro---dance/pop group Livin' Joy with Italian deejays Paolo and Gianni Visnadi in 1993. Serving as the lead singer, she penned and recorded the group's debut single "Dreamer," which debuted at #1 on the UK Singles and Billboard Hot Dance Club Play charts in 1995. "Dreamer" is now a global Euro---dance classic that has also charted well in Australia, Italy, and 24 other countries.

In 1998, Robinson pursued a solo career as an alternative rock/soul artist. Her demo landed in the hands of Grammy Award-winning/Golden Globe-winning entertainer Queen Latifah, Latifah's manager Shakim Compere, A&R veteran executive Larry Rudolph, and EMI publisher Evan Lamberg, who were all instrumental in her singing to Phil Quartararo President Warner Bros Music at that time. Quatarero felt like he discovered the female version of rock/soul singer/guitarist Lenny Kravitz. She immediately began working on her debut album *The Color Within Me* with an A-list selection of producers and musicians including Allen Sides, Ry Cooder, Waddy Waddy Wachtel, Steve Feronni, Jim Keltner, Siedah Garret & Richard Page. The LP caught the legendary rock 'n' roll singer Tina Turner's ear, which prompted her to handpick Robinson to open Turner's *Twenty-Four Seven Tour,* which also included pop music veteran Lionel Richie.

Simultaneously, Robinson was known in the music industry as the "writer with an honest pen" as she collaborated with artist/producer Wyclef Jean to write music for American singers Tevin Campbell, Taylor Dayn, and Kristine W. after striking a publishing deal with EMI thru Lamberg. Upon closing the *Twenty-Four Seven Tour* in 2001, Robinson took a break from recording to live in Europe, raise a family and continue honing her songwriting gift, as suggested by Turner.

In 2002, Robinson gave birth to daughter Kura while living in Paris. Robinson threw herself deeper into her songwriting craft that which began to take off tremendously in the international markets.

Throughout the 2000s, Robinson's songwriting became a high demand in the international markets for a diverse group of artists, including winners of Pop Idol in Belgium, Czech Republic, Poland, and Australia. She also scored hits for American artists V-Factory and former Disney TV star Ashley Tisdale. With more than 21 singles internationally to her credit, Robinson landed a new publishing deal with Warner Chappelle Music in 2007 for her lauded efforts. Robinson also collaborated with industry heavyweights David Morales, Junior Vasquez, Guy Roche, Rob Fusari, Mark Batson, Red One, Bryan Todd, Michael "Smidi" Smith, Lee Horrocks, David Frank, Jay---E Epperson, Stereo, Timo Maas, Stuart Brawley, and multiple top---charting songwriters Diane Warren. Robinson has also worked with former American Idol finalists Frenchie Davis, Nadia Turner, and David Hernandez as well as actress Tikka Sumpter.

In 2008, Robinson gave birth to her younger daughter Amaya. While she was beginning to enjoy the arrival of her new baby, Robinson's father, whom she cared for many years, passed away. Her father's passing inspired her to record an album of new material upcoming aptly titled album *The Preacher's Daughter* through her own label Dreamer Entertainment. The initial response from industry peers has been unanimous praise for her new album.

Robinson's craft has been hired for upcoming projects by globally renowned deejay/producer/remixer David Morales and American singer Deborah Cox. She is also releasing a new dance single "Every Breath," produced by DJ John Dahlback & Greg Cerrone, internationally through Big Beat/Atlantic Records. Robinson is also featured on Morales' new single "What Do You Believe" from his upcoming album *"Changes."*

Currently, Robinson is signed to Kobalt Music Publishing to administer her songs where Senior Vice President Al Butter Mclean drove to Robinson's home during an east coast snowstorm at 11:30 pm to present Kobalt Music to her in early 2011. "That meant a lot to me," beamed Robinson, who is recording her brand-new album *The Preacher's Daughter*, an inspirational concept album summarizing her life's journey. Throughout over 20 years in the music industry, Robinson's career has come full circle like a top-charting singer and songwriter.

Robinson is a devoted mother who cherishes her family. Robinson is an internationally known music artist who is influential in today's Euro---dance sound. Robinson is a "Dreamer" who realized a fantastic journey as a musician in an industry where many peers do not endure similar longevity in the music business. https://twitter.com/singsongmomma and http://www.facebook.com/janice.robinson.

SOLO DISCOGRAPHY

The Color Within Me (album: Warner Bros.); "Nothing I Would Change"; "Finally Taking Over"; "Dead End Girl"; "Afterlife"; "Search for Love"; "1664 Park Ave"; "Sleeping in the Playground"; "Color Within Me"; "Gracefully Gliding"; "It Really Don't Matter".

SINGLES & SONGWRITING CREDITS:

Dreamer" (Undiscovered/MCA); "Nothing I Would Change" (Warner Bros.) "The Gift" (Promo); "Dreamer: Remixed" (Promo); "Earthbeat" (Mercury/Manifesto); "I'm Free" (Dream Beat); "Children" (Planet4); John Dahlback& Greg Cerrone featuring Janice Robinson "Every Breath" (BigBeat/Atlantic) Frenchie Davis "Loves Got A Hold On Me"(Frenchie Davis); Deborah Cox "If It Wasn't For Love"(Decco/HoshG); Promise Land Featuring Sandy B "Never Be Lonely" (Subliminal) Abigail –"Let The Joy Rise" (Inherit); Ashley Tisdale – "Suddenly" (Warner); Brahim "So Into You" (SonyBMG); Brenda Radney - Forthcoming Album (Ten Man); David Morales (featuring Janice Robinson) - "I Make You Gaga" (ULTRA); "What Do You Believe" (ULTRA) Hania Stach –"Regroup"

(EMI); Kristine W –"Let Love Reign" (RCA) Leana – "Pack Yo Bags"; Livin' Joy- "Dreamer" (MCA/Universal) Lucas Prata – "Feel The Love Again" (Ultra) Lucas Prata & Reina – "Love Of My Life" (Ultra) Natalia – "Risin'" (Sony/BMG); Reina – "If I Close My Eyes"(Robbins); "On My Own" (Robbins); Rickie-Lee Coulter – "I Appreciate U" (Shock Records); "Melody of Life" (Shock Records) Sandrine – "The Story Of Us" (Sony/BMG); Taylor Dayne – "Crash" (Intention); "Whenever You Fall" (Neptune) Tevin Campbell – "Never Again" (Warner) – co-written with Wyclef Jean Laura Hildebrandt "My Life Again" (Red Wallet Records); Udo - "One Of A Kind"(SONY BMG); V-Factory – "These Are The Days"; "Pump It (Bring The Heat)"; Joe T. Vanelli (featuring Harembee) –"Sweetest Day Of May" (Positiva) Martina Schinderlova (winner of Czech Republic Idol) – "Stupam" (Ario)

TV APPEARANCES:

CNN, Showbiz Today, Access Hollywood, MTV News, Top of the Pops UK, Big Breakfast, Fully Loaded, Oxygen Network, Fox News, Charmed, WB Network.

38 – Mr. Andre Ruff – Class of 1986

(Photos Courtesy of EHS & Andre Ruff)

Andre attended Public School #24 during his 8th-grade year and was known as a dynamic basketball player and played on various local basketball teams. He wanted to be a professional basketball player in the

NBA.

He continued playing at EHS during his freshman year but was kicked off the team after arguing with one of the coaches. Andre believes his focused changed from basketball to the street life because instead of going to practice and staying off the mean streets of Paterson, he now had to protect himself in the streets while walking to and from school. Andre was a flashy dresser and always had the most popular items and wore gold chains.

Andre was unaware of the drug scene until he got into a fight on his way to school. The person who came to Andre's aid was a drug dealer, and they later became friends, and he was introduced to the drug dealer lifestyle.

Andre was a member of the class of 1986. However, he was incarcerated before it was time to graduate for dealing drugs. Being young and confused, he found himself running around with the wrong group of more youthful individuals who were involved in criminal mischief and wanted to be like them.

After being incarcerated several times (at least eight times), he realized that the criminal lifestyle was not the life he wanted to lead, and he realized that if he kept involving himself in negative behavior, he would end up in prison. Andre did not want a prison number.

As a result, Andre decided to pursue his education and attended a program through Passaic Community College to obtain his GED.

Andre began to work at a hospital as a cook and realized his intense desire for cooking. He was very driven, continued his education, and worked his way up to be a manager and a chef at various hospitals in New Jersey. He began to "break down barriers" and dispelled the myth that people can't realize their dreams and do something positive with their lives after incarceration.

Currently, he is working as the lead chef at Holly Name hospital in Teaneck, NJ. Andre always wanted to make his mark in the world and decided writing a book was his way to make his mark. Andre is the author of an urban fiction titled the *Night Club Lover,* which can be purchased on Amazon or his website. www.nightclublover.com.

Andre's experiences with Dr. Clark were something that he will never forget. Dr. Clark knew him by name and used to call his name out loud on the bullhorn and told him to "get to class!" Andre has three children; two boys ages 28, 26, one daughter who's 11 years old, and five grandchildren.

39 – Ms. Shwana Ruth-Bridges, ESQ – Class of 1986

(Photos Courtesy of EHS - Dr. Clark & Shwana Ruth-Bridges)

Too ghetto for the burbs & too burb for the ghetto. I'm where Hip Hop Meets Scripture Legally.

Shwana Ruth-Bridges is a top-notch Corporate and Entertainment Attorney and political blogger, who is known in the blog circle as the outspoken and often controversial "Attorney mom." Shwana is also the owner of Pink Cotton Entertainment, LLC, which is a company that provides top-notch entertainment that uplifts and inspires the American Black community. Her first pilot project under Pink Cotton Entertainment was Character Corner TV, which was showcased on Internetfabulous.tv. The archives for Character Corner TV and Radio can be viewed at www.pinkcottonent.com.

Shwana has a Bachelor of Arts Degree in English from Delaware State University and Juris Doctor from Seton Hall University School of Law. After completing her judicial clerkship with the late Honorable Stephen H. Womack, she opened her law practice in Clifton, New Jersey.

While watching a VH1 television special chronicling the financial troubles of R&B group TLC, Shwana became interested in entertainment law as it related to the royalties management process. Her opportunity came when Shwana was hired as an Attorney in the Royalties Department for Bertelsmann Music Group (BMG). In her position with BMG (now Sony BMG), Shwana was responsible for managing the royalties accounts for American Idol Seasons 1, 2 and 3 and such artists as Christina Aguilera, Kelly Clarkson, Dave Matthews, Heather Headley, Foo Fighters, Elvis Presley, Boyd Tinsley, Clay Aiken and other artist signed to RCA Music Group Record Label. This experience proved to be extremely valuable in enhancing her legal skills as an Entertainment Attorney and Legal Consultant.

More recently, Shwana had the esteemed pleasure of representing *N-Secure* movie Screenwriter Christie Taylor in a collection case whereby she was able to assist her with obtaining screenwriters payment through the Writer's Guild of America. Also, Shwana was one of two attorneys that represented *VH1 Basketball Wives* Tami Roman in a child support case against her ex-husband, former NBA Basketball Player Kenny Anderson.

In that case, Shwana was able to secure a six-figure settlement by going after his NBA pension account.

Shawna's ultimate goal is to become the next syndicated Conservative Radio Talk Show Host. She wants to be the new voice of common sense crying out in the wilderness of liberalism, lust, and corporate slavery. Shwana strongly believes that being a Black Conservative does not mean that one has to ignore the gray elephant of racism that is standing in the living room of America.

Shwana is a member of Alpha Kappa Alpha Sorority, Incorporated, and Corporate Counsel Women of Color. Shwana currently resides in Georgia with her husband and three children.

Areas of Practice: 18 years of legal experience in the areas of government, telecommunications, entertainment, transportation, and corporate law.

Contact: There is a $150 consultation fee per legal question. All consultation fees are non-refundable and must be paid before the consultation. Please send all inquiries to Bridgesesq@gmail.com.

40 - Mr. Wilson Santos – Class of 1989

(Photos Courtesy of EHS & Wilson Santos)

In 1987, Wilson Santos founded a Dominican gang at Eastside High School called "La Dominican Connection" (LDC) to unite the small population of Dominican students as a line of defense against other well organized, Puerto Rican, Black, and Jamaican gangs. In a short time, LDC's membership grew and expanded to three chapters at other local High Schools.

For the next two years, Wilson would be involved in many gang fights, some of which resulted in people being shot, stabbed, and brutally beaten. In one such drawn-out battle against a Puerto Rican gang from Market Street in Paterson, Joe Clark had to intervene to try and forge a truce. It took some time for a fragile peace to take root finally. After four turbulent and troubled years, Wilson managed to graduate from Eastside in 1989, the same year Dr. Clark left the school.

Upon graduating, Wilson enlisted in the Army as an only means of escaping an all too obvious fate that several of his friends were not so lucky in avoiding since some of them were eventually shot and killed, sent to jail or deported back to the Dominican Republic. After leaving the Army, Wilson returned to Paterson, where he worked odd jobs with no direction toward a concrete future.

In 1992, Wilson was fortunate to be accepted to the Educational Opportunity Fund program at Montclair State University – a decision that altered his life forever.

Since then, Wilson has earned both his Bachelor's and Master's degrees from Montclair State, where he studied English with a concentration in American Literature and an emphasis on Film Studies. He has taken film courses at New York University and studied Literature at Kingston University in England. He has written two original feature-length screenplays. The first, titled "Love & Ecstasy," was optioned to Swiss independent filmmaker, Tomi Streiff in 1996.

As a poet, Wilson's original spoken word dance projects have been released on various record labels, offering him international recognition as a DJ, Producer and spoken-word artist with performance bookings in

Belgium, Chile, Dominican Republic, England, Holland, and Puerto Rico, as well as in most major US cities.

Wilson is currently writing a memoir chronicling the last 25 years of his life, with the first chapter titled "*Lean on Me*," which details his four years at Eastside High School. He is also compiling fifteen years of his poetry into book form while pursuing a Ph.D. in American Literature. At present, Wilson teaches composition in the first-year writing program at Montclair State University. Aside from teaching at MSU, Wilson is a creative Graphic Designer and entrepreneur. He is the sole proprietor of the following two companies: http://d-signstudio.net/ OR http://revobaby.com/

41 – Mr. Gregory C. Scott – Class of 1986

(First Lady Michelle Obama & Greg Scott - Photos Courtesy of EHS & Gregory C. Scott)

In 2019, Gregory C. Scott is a proud dad, grandfather, nonprofit Chief Executive Officer, social entrepreneur, community leader, executive leadership coach, and leadership development strategist.

Mr. Scott currently serves as the President & CEO of Community Action Partnership of Orange County, a leading national network championing issues of poverty, self-sufficiency, financial stability, and community and economic development. He also has served as President and CEO of New Directions for Veterans and the Weingart Center, both in Los Angeles, California. Mr. Scott's leadership is pivotal in providing exceptional social justice programs and services that enable people to achieve economic security for themselves and their families. His efforts have led to substantial growth through the addition of quality programs, marketing, advocacy, media and public relations, branding, increased community partnerships, asset generation and fund development, strategic planning, board training and development, and the building of influential organizations; during very challenging US economic periods.

Mr. Scott has been honored with many accolades; among them are the Joining Forces award from Former First Lady Michelle Obama and Dr. Jill Biden (for a comprehensive national Veterans support initiative to mobilize all sectors of society to give our service members and their families the opportunities and support they have earned,) Ford Unsung Hero Award, Weingart Center Community Award, National Black MBA Association Community Hero Award, J.U.G.S. Los Angeles Community Leadership Award, Los Angeles County Board of Supervisors Community Leadership Award, and the Bank of America Builders Award.

A passionate visionary and change agent, Mr. Scott has demonstrated successful experience as an executive in both the private and nonprofit sectors. He leads his teams in producing world-class services, strong organizational development acumen, economical solutions to address challenging social issues affecting disenfranchised individuals and their families. Tackling topics such as diversity, poverty, financial stability, youth development and education, inadequate healthcare, social services and families, food, and hunger, acute case management, mental health and substance use counseling, affordable housing, and homelessness, to name a few. Mr. Scott has garnered both corporate and individual philanthropic support and is known as a thought-leader in the industry.

Mr. Scott's additional experience includes serving as Regional Vice President for Sylvan Learning Systems, Executive Director of the Neighborhood Youth Association, and National Director for AmeriCorps for YouthBuild USA.

Mr. Scott currently serves on the Board of Directors for the Anaheim Workforce Development Board, Holman Community Development Corporation, Southern California Edison Consumer Advisory Board, and the Southern California Counseling Center (SCCC). He held executive committee positions with the Los Angeles Center of Community Economic Development (Chair), the Breese Foundation Board of Directors (Vice-Chair), and on the Board of Directors for the Orange County YMCA Community Services Branch.

Before his move to the Los Angeles community, Mr. Scott was appointed by the Governor of Massachusetts to serve as Vice Chairman of the Board for the Massachusetts Service Alliance Commission, charged with allocating funds to public service organizations and Initiatives for national service. He was also a member of the National and Community Service Coalition and the National Youth Employment Coalition.

In 2014, Gregory C. Scott served as President and CEO of New Directions for Veterans (NDVets). Located in Los Angeles, NDVets is a growing and dynamic organization serving Veterans and their families. The agency is committed to positively impacting the lives of veterans – both men and women – who have served in the U.S. military.

He focused on producing solutions to the challenging social issues affecting disenfranchised individuals and their families in the areas of Veteran services, homelessness, education, workforce development, healthcare, mental health, low-income housing, and youth development.

Mr. Scott's commitment to organizational success has earned him numerous accolades and awards. He prides himself on leading by example and creating an "air of excellence" wherever he is. Before his appointment at NDVets, Mr. Scott served as President & CEO of the Weingart Center Association in downtown Los Angeles. He has also served as Regional Vice President of West Coast Operations for Sylvan Learning Systems; Executive Director of the Neighborhood Youth Association; Executive Director of the Susan G. Komen Breast Cancer Foundation of Orange County; and National Director for YouthBuild USA, the national headquarters and intermediary for the YouthBuild program.

Mr. Scott believes he was called to serve and support people and organizations with the same philosophy. His community service has included executive committee positions with the Los Angeles Center of Community Economic Development (Chair), the Bresee Foundation Board of Directors Vice-Chair), and membership on the Board of Directors for the Orange County YMCA Community Services Branch.

While serving with YouthBuild USA in Massachusetts, Mr. Scott was appointed by the Governor to serve as Vice Chairman of the Board for the Massachusetts Service Alliance Commission, charged with allocating funds to public service organizations and initiatives. He was also a member of the National and Community Service Coalition and the National Youth Employment Coalition.

Born and raised in Paterson, New Jersey, Mr. Scott is a proud graduate of the iconic Eastside High School featured in the famous movie, Lean on Me. He contributes a great deal of his leadership to former Principal, Joe Clark, and his experience at EHS, where he learned the essence of leadership, success, and vision for his future. He continues to hold on to those values today and has strong relationships with all of his former classmates.

Mr. Scott attained a Bachelor of Arts degree from William Paterson University and received his Master of Science degree in Community Economic Development from Southern New Hampshire University. He holds certificates from the Wells Fargo Executive Director Program, African American Board Leadership Institute, and the Executive Leadership Program at the Stanford University School of Business. A public speaker, Mr. Scott, has appeared on The Today Show and is often interviewed by both local and national media. He is also a contributor to the Huffington Post, as well as a professional network and internet marketer. internet marketer.

42 - Mr. Antoney Smith - Class of 1987

(Photos Courtesy of EHS & Antoney Smith)

It was the summer of 1983; I had never felt such heat as I disembarked my PAN AM flight from London, England. Recently divorced, my mother came to the US for a fresh start, and after a few years in the States, she asked my brother and me if we wanted to join her. Talk about culture shock. Growing up in London and Birmingham in the UK, I was accustomed to diverse communities. I had attended schools with Whites, Asians, and Blacks; the majority of Blacks were of Caribbean descent. My parents were both Jamaican immigrants who came to the UK in the late '60s.

I remember having a strange feeling about Paterson, but I could not put my finger on it. And then one day while shopping downtown, I realized that Paterson had almost no White people. I later came to realize that New Jersey was extremely segregated, and you had train tracks that divided races of people. Within my first month living in Paterson, I heard gunshots for the first time in my life, and I was almost robbed at knifepoint.

Upon entering Eastside High School, I noticed the vast differences between British and American school systems. In my previous school's discipline was paramount; one would never talk back or question a teacher. Corporal punishment was permissible; students stood up anytime a teacher entered the room. Boundaries were clear; students knew exactly what they could and could not get away with. Initially, discipline was truly lacking at Eastside.

The vast majority of kids wanted to learn; however, teachers spent most of their time dealing with disruptive students. I can honestly say that although some may not have liked his methods, Joe Clark changed the overall culture of Eastside and put the school on a path conducive to learning. He held both students and teachers accountable for their actions. His approach was similar to what I had in England, where discipline was an integral piece in the educational process.

Athletics also played an essential role for me while in school. Being an above-average soccer player in England, I initially tried out for the freshmen soccer team. I later quit the team because I felt the coach at the time was clueless about the game of soccer. At the recommendation of a classmate, I eventually joined the track and cross country teams. Here I found coaches who not only knew their sport but fostered relationships with their student-athletes.

Mr. Shipp and Mr. Boinstien both ran successful athletic programs and helped mold successful students. The track team became my second family; we were always together; if we were not at practice or a track meet, we were at each other's house. Looking back, it was probably these friendships that kept us off the streets; we each pushed one another to succeed.

Upon graduating high school in 1987, I enlisted in the Army and served three years in Landstuhl, Germany. While in Germany, I took advantage of the college assistance the Army provided and enrolled at the University of Maryland, Munich Campus. I also took advantage of CLEP's (College Level Exam Program), and by the time I was honorably discharged from the Army, I had completed over 60 college credits. Still unsure of what I would do once I got Stateside, it wasn't until Sgt. Nancy Ruffin told me I should continue my education.

She demanded and pushed me to apply to William Paterson University and even paid the $50 application fee. I subsequently went on to graduate with a Bachelor of Arts degree in Sociology and later completed my Master's degree in Rehabilitation Counseling at the University of Medicine and Dentistry of New Jersey.

Presently, I'm married with three beautiful children and currently work as a supervising counselor for the New Jersey Division of Vocational Rehabilitation. I have been working for the State of New Jersey for over 20 years.

43 – Ms. Paulette Steeves - Class of 1988

(Photos Courtesy of EHS & Paulette Steeves)

My name is Paulette Steeves, and I am a graduate of Eastside High School, Class of 1988. Back in high school, I was voted Most Athletic out of my graduating class. I relocated from New Jersey to Atlanta, Georgia, in 1995, where I completed my degree in Criminal Justice at Georgia State University. I am currently a divorced mother of two, who is a full-time Accounts Coordinator for a corporate company in Georgia.

I am an amateur competitive bodybuilder, currently working on becoming a pro. I also have a training business. The passion I had for health and fitness in high school has only continued to grow over the years, which is why I continue to make it a priority in my life. This year I will be crossing over from bodybuilding to Physique with the hopes of earning my pro card in Women Physique.

44 - Mr. Marc Stevens – Class of 1988

(Photos Courtesy of EHS & Marc Stevens)

A native of Paterson, New Jersey, Marc, involved himself in a variety of activities at EHS. He played baseball and basketball for four years, and he was a member of the Criterion, the school newspaper. He was a member of the school's concert choir and the boys' glee club. His love for the Mighty Ghosts remains as strong as it was when he was a student being guided and led by the magnanimous Mr. Joe Clark. He went on to attend and graduate from Delaware State University in 1992 and began his career in education at Public School # 6 in Paterson.

He married and moved to Baltimore, Maryland in 1998. He was married for 13 years, and from that union emerged three sons, Amani, Mekhi, and Jahsha. He currently is a high school English/Theatre teacher at Randallstown High School in Randallstown, Maryland. He is active within his community serving as an assistant boys' basketball coach and the head baseball coach at RHS. He also is a vibrant community actor and has been featured in over 40 theatrical productions while living in Maryland.

45 - Mr. Marvin Sykes – Class of 1987

(Photos Courtesy of EHS & Marvin Sykes)

Marvin was born and raised in Paterson, New Jersey. Growing up, Marvin had all the things a kid could want from a mother and grandmother. His passion as a young kid was playing baseball. Marvin dreamed of becoming a professional baseball player and moving his grandmother and mother into a big house. He also wanted to give his relatives a good life and wanted them to live like movie stars. As Marvin became older, his dream was the same, but because of the influences around him, the dream became smaller and smaller.

Hanging on the corner with friends became more of the regular routine for Marvin, but as his friends started to go to jail, Marvin opted for the military and joined the US Army.

Once he came back home after serving in the Army, Marvin had a little daughter. He knew he had to find a way to take care of her because he didn't want to be an absentee father.

In 1992 Marvin's grandmother overheard Marvin tell his friend the police department was taking applications. His grandmother told him to take the test, although that was the last thing on Marvin's mind. Nonetheless, he listened to her and took the test. Grandma passed away in June of 1993, and close to the first anniversary of her passing, the police department notified Marvin that he was hired if he still wanted the job. Marvin began his law enforcement career in August 1994.

Before becoming a police officer, the most money Marvin Sykes ever made was on tax returns. To receive $1,300 on a tax return was big money to Marvin before becoming a police officer. Once he started his law enforcement career, his bi-weekly pay was like receiving a tax return every two weeks. Marvin felt he made it with this good government job. Marvin started spending out of control over the years. It would prove to be costly later. To combat all his spending, Marvin took on numerous extra jobs and overtime at work to pay bills. Marvin realized he was still broke, but on a higher level. At this point, something had to be done because work was not cutting it alone.

Marvin was always an entrepreneur at heart and wanted his own business. But most companies required large down payments to invest. Marvin was introduced to network marketing direct sales. This is where you have an opportunity to build a business within a business. Over the years, Marvin tried six or seven different companies and failed at all of them. While he was trying various business debt was growing at an alarming rate.

Because Marvin was not used to credit or the salary of his job, he went through it pretty quickly. Marvin states, "I never really saved because I was going to get a pension when I retire." So in 2008, when all the credit card companies jacked up their interest rates, Marvin had more going out, then he had come in. The timing of the prices going up along with Marvin being upside down in his mortgage was crucial to the family's survival.

In June 2008, Marvin decided to try network marketing one more time. He walked into a Barnes and Noble and picked up a magazine and took it home. Once home, Marvin contacted the company representatives, and one of the leaders in the magazine called Marvin back. This gentleman mentored Marvin and taught him the business of network marketing.

Marvin was in foreclosure and facing bankruptcy at the time his mentor took over changing Marvin's life. Marvin's wife was skeptical about Marvin starting yet another business. She was supportive but didn't believe he would succeed. Marvin started to follow the process of the business plan. His business picked up. Many people were having success in the industry. Marvin began to rise in the company. Marvin made the National Director All-Stars team numerous times and was also a top 10 representative in the company. Success started to come based on a choice to succeed.

Marvin Sykes eventually hit the position of Senior Vice President in his current company. He received stock options in the company and went on an all-expenses-paid trip to Europe on a 6-day cruise from Spain to France & Italy. The BMW he received for hitting SVP is a dream come true. One of the biggest excitements Marvin had was taking his wife to the Dominican Republic for her birthday in December 2011. Mrs. Sykes has never been to a warm climate to celebrate her birthday in her life. We owe that to this opportunity.

While still working his full-time job as a police detective, Marvin started to work his business. Within three years Marvin was making more part-time with his company then he was making full time at his job in the police   department.

While in Italy, Mrs. Sykes told Marvin, "THANK YOU! Had you not fought for our family, life would still be just below normal, now we are above normal." Life has indeed changed for the Sykes Family. Now Marvin is waiting on those he can share his knowledge with to help them improve their situation. Marvin says, "GIVE ME 3 TO 5 YRS AND YOU WILL NOT RECOGNIZE YOUR LIFE FINANCIALLY". That is what Marvin's mentor Dwayne Johnson told him in June of 2008, and it came true. Connect with Marvin Sykes on twitter –

https://twitter.com/#!/MarvinSykes

Connect on Facebook

http://www.facebook.com/profile.php?cropsuccess&id=698368970

46 - Ms. Juanita Thomas-Boyd – Class of 1986

(Photos Courtesy of EHS & Juanita Thomas-Boyd)

Juanita M. Thomas was born on February 6, 1968, and was raised in Paterson, New Jersey. She attended Public School #8 from Kindergarten - 8th grade. She graduated from Eastside in 1986 and is a member of Mr. Joe Clark's first graduating class.

Juanita had many goals, dreams, and admirations as a young child. Many people thought that she wouldn't achieve much success; however, she went against the odds to achieve success. She obtained several Professional Memberships such as The National Mathematical Society (2011) and Delta Pi Kappa (2004).

About Juanita's Math Lessons - Juanita's math lessons were founded in September 2001 by Mrs. Juanita; she began individual math tutoring sessions for elementary, high school, and college students in her home. She had a passion for helping students succeed in math. Her clients grew, and she couldn't find quality tutors, so she expanded her lessons to DVD tutorials by topics. The DVD's are like having a live tutor in your home.

Juanita's math lessons are family-owned and operated in Paterson, NJ. Since opening in 2001, we've treated every customer like they were a part of our family. Other companies may offer similar services, but our services come with a personal touch.

Juanita Thomas-Boyd, Owner - Founder of Juanita's Math Lessons: Prof. Juanita Thomas-Boyd has an extensive Educational Background in Mathematics. She attended Montclair State University and received a BS in Applied Mathematics in 1999. She also attended Seton Hall University in 2002. She received an Information Technology Certificate. She has an extensive teaching background; she taught at William Paterson University (2001), Paterson Catholic Regional High School (1999-2004), and she taught at several daycare centers.

She is currently a Substitute Teacher for the Paterson Public School District, and she is currently serving as a part-time adjunct professor of Mathematics at Passaic County Community College since 2002. Her recognitions include Who's Who Among American Teachers (2004-2007), and she was also featured in *New Jersey Education Now* magazine (April Edition, 2012) Juanita's contact information www.juanitamathlesson.com or thomasjuanita@hotmail.com.

47 – Ms. Vivian Thorpe – Class of 1986

(Photos Courtesy of EHS & Vivian Thorpe)

Hi, my name is Vivian Thorpe. I am a graduate of the famous Eastside High school class of 1986. I was a part of the Marching 100 band and experienced the Mr. Joe Clark era. I will never forget the memories we created as a class. After graduation, I worked odd jobs until I found my dream job. Two years later, I began working for the state of New Jersey at North Jersey Developmental Center (NJDC) my occupation consist of being a physical education teacher for the mentally challenged. I have been working at NJDC for the past 25 years. I love helping the mentally challenged because it allows me to assist people who cannot support themselves and achieve goals that the individual nor families thought they could ever reach.

In the past, there have been newspaper articles written about me for training the consumers at the center. The greatest reward from working at NJDC sees the smiles on their faces. Throughout my life, I've experienced many ups and downs from being homeless twice to being a single parent with two great children. I have one son and one daughter. My son's name is Eric Thorpe, and he graduated from Montclair State University with a bachelor's degree in Psychology. And my daughters' name is Jessica Thomas, and she is currently a sophomore at Rutgers University, going for her bachelor's degree in Criminal Justice.

Some of my fondest memories of being an Eastside ghost is when Mr. Nelson used to make us get up at 5:00 in the morning to practice for the band and still had to go to all my classes afterward. Being in the Marching 100 band, we use to go from state to state for band competitions and to learn new band routines from Florida A&M. I remember going on the camping trips with our (back then) drama teacher, Dan Martin. In closing, I would like to thank Mr. Joe Clark for being one of the best principals because he was caring and would go to the end of the world for his students and provided things for us as students when a lot of our parents could not. SO HARD TO BE A MIGHTTTYYY GHOOOOSSSSTTTT! CLASS OF 86'

48 - *Reverend Janel D. Tinsley-York - Class of 1987*

(Photos Courtesy of EHS & Reverend Janel D. Tinsley-York)

Reverend Janel D. Tinsley (York) was born and raised in Paterson, New Jersey, where she received her elementary and high school education. She attended EHS from 1983 - 1987 and believes that it was an excellent experience and lots of fun. Getting up early for band practice and then on to the halls of the school to hear Dr. Clark was very rewarding. Principal

Joe Clark was like none other his stern ways were just what was needed, and I am so glad to have been under his leadership.

She attended Christian Bible Institute and New York Theological Seminary and is currently enrolled in Liberty Baptist Seminary, Lynchburg, Virginia. She was licensed to preach on February 22, 1998, and Ordained on August 16, 2009, by the North Jersey District Missionary Baptist Association, Rev. Dr. Lester Taylor, Moderator.

Rev. Janel serves on the ministerial staff at Trinity Baptist Church Hackensack, NJ, under the leadership of Pastor Jonathan B. Whitfield. Rev. Janel has labored in several capacities, to name a few, Youth Director, Singles Ministry, Director of Praise Dance Ministry, and Advisor for the Youth Choir, Director of Christian Education, and the Church Administrator, and teacher of the Teens at Youth church. She now facilitates the Young Adult Ministry and teaches Youth Bible Studies.

She has also taught in the "True Love Waits" program, which is a program held in Paterson, New Jersey that teaches abstinence, which is held at Second Baptist Church and Canaan Baptist Church. She received the "Religious Award" from the NAACP Passaic chapter in 2006.

Rev. Janel has a passion for Ministry, but her ministerial duties are not the only ones that keep her busy, she is the proud mom of two beautiful children Ashley (22) and Rajon (14)

All of that is fine, but what's most important is that she is SAVED, SANCTIFIED, and FILLED WITH THE HOLY GHOST, and she is not ashamed of the Gospel of Jesus Christ. *"Humble yourselves therefore under the mighty hand of God, that he may exalt you in due time" 1 Peter 5:6*

49 - Mr. Timothy M. Tobias, MSW – Class of 1986

(Photos Courtesy of EHS & Timothy M. Tobias)

Timothy was born and raised in Paterson, New Jersey. In my sophomore year, I joined the EHS Marching 100 band drum squad and enjoyed every minute of it. Shy and timid during my adolescence, I was courageous enough to sing in various talent shows gaining popularity amongst my peers. As a result of a love of music, my senior year was very memorable.

I broke out of my shell, developing many close relationships, and was selected to be a part of the EHS Class of '86 graduation entertainment troupe. My four years at EHS were the best of my life; it allowed me the opportunity to build a foundation of strength, togetherness, support, and hope that would later be translated into the tools and life skills necessary to overcome any obstacle placed in my way.

After overcoming many adversities, I decided to further my education in 2005; I successfully obtained an Associate of Arts in Liberal Arts at the Borough of Manhattan Community College (BMCC) in 2007. Upon receiving my AA, I enrolled at New York City College of Technology (NYCCT) -CUNY, where I obtained a Bachelor of Science in Human Services, graduating in 2011 with honors. In May of 2013, I graduated with my Master's in Social Work from The Silberman School of Social Work at

Hunter College

As a recent graduate of The Silberman School of Social Work at Hunter College, my passion and interest focus on conducting scholarly research that reflects the psychological and sociocultural challenges among Black and Latino Lesbian Gay Bisexual and Transgender (LGBT) Youth. And developing a community-based organization geared toward providing preventative services to help improve the quality of life among Black and Latino inner-city youth. I currently reside in Brooklyn, New York. In my spare time, I enjoy reading, fitness, playing basketball, singing, and spending time with family.

"Those who say it can't be done are usually distracted by others doing it."
James Baldwin

50 - Darnell Van Rensalier – Class of 1987

(Courtesy of EHS Yearbook 1987, Darnell VanRensalier & LaVonne Bobongi Wall)

Darnell VanRensalier, born to Skip and Darlene; raised in Paterson, New Jersey. I attended Public Schools #'s 13 and 24, then EHS. Played youth basketball for Father English and Riverside Vets, then-freshman year at Eastside, as well as ran cross country freshman year also. Joined the famed Marching 100 band sophomore year as a trumpet player, as well as the Jazz and concert bands. I was a section leader and outstanding musician senior year. I graduated in 87 and went on to attend Howard University. I have played in Marching and jazz bands. Pledged Alpha Phi Alpha fraternity in the spring of 1990, then formed a singing group called Shai with 2 fraternity Brothers and another best friend, who would eventually sign a record deal in 1992 with MCA records and release the #1 hit single "If I Ever Fall In Love" and multi-platinum album under the same title. Shai sang for President Bill Clinton's inauguration and was awarded the NAACP Image award in 1993. Moved to LA with the group, started mentoring gang youth, and in 2013 started S.O.S. ("Sounds of the Streets") music mentoring program to provide inner-city youth leadership and guidance as well as focus on creative and musical expression, and positive Self Identity building strategies. Positive role models include my father, mother, grandmother, uncles, aunts, elders in the Paterson community like Mr. Nelson, Mr. Smith, Mr. Moore, Mr. and Mrs. Talley, Rev Richardson, Coach Kelly, Ms. Odom, Ms. Weeks, Mr. Page, Mr. Moody, and so many more.

Darnell is a member of the R&B singing group Shai. Shai, originally named Beta (after the majority of the members' Alpha Phi Alpha Fraternity Inc. chapter - The "Bloody" Betas), was formed at Howard University in Washington, D.C. Three of its four members, Marc Gay, founding member Carl Martin, and Darnell Van Rensalier, belonged to the same fraternity, Alpha Phi Alpha, and along with good friend Garfield A. Bright, decided to take a chance at turning their hobby of singing at talent shows into a career.

While still in DC, Carl met a DJ from radio station WPGC at a softball game and passed a demo tape of "If I Ever Fall in Love" to him. That same week, the DJ played it on the air. Other radio stations soon followed suit. Record labels began calling them, and they signed with Gasoline Alley. Shai began quickly putting together their debut album, which was recorded in three weeks. Carl E. Martin wrote the single "If I Ever Fall in Love" on a long ride back from his home in Louisiana to Washington, D. C. It was written about his ex-girlfriend Camille, who also attended Howard University.

"If I Ever Fall in Love" was released as the first single and peaked at #2 in the U.S. The next two releases from the double-platinum album, "Comforter" and "Baby I'm Yours," each peaked at #10. The group's next album release was "Right Back At Cha," a remix album of sorts that primarily consisted of new versions of their previous hits, with a couple of new songs as well. A completely reworked version of their last hit, "Baby I'm Yours," simply titled "Yours," was released as a single and peaked at #63.

Shai returned in 1994 with "The Place Where You Belong," from the Beverly Hills Cop III soundtrack. It was the group's final Top 40 single. In late 1995, their follow-up album Blackface was released (#42 Pop, #15 R&B). It featured their final R&B Top 20 single "Come With Me" (#43 Pop). The group's last chart appearance was the follow-up single, 1996's #89 single "I Don't Wanna Be Alone" (the remix of which featured Jay-Z).

Although they have continued to record, the 1999 album "Destiny" was recorded without Carl Martin (who had left the group after Blackface's release), and their 2004 studio album "Back From The Mystery System" ... The "Love Cycle" was recorded with new member Erik Willis.

In 2008 Garfield A. Bright and Darnell Van Rensalier released their duet album "Worldwide" as D-n-G of Shai on the Fight 4 Mu (ALIVE) label in Germany. Marc Gay and replacement member Erik Willis had left the group and are now replaced by Riff & Men Of Vizion member Dwayne Jones.

Members - Darnell Van Rensalier, Garfield A. Bright, Dwayne Jones, and George Spencer III. **Former members** - Carl Martin, Marc Gay, and Erik Willis

Albums & EPs - 1992: If I Ever Fall In Love (3x Platinum); 1993: Right Back At Cha; 1994: End Of The Road (unreleased); 1995: Blackface (Platinum); 1999: Destiny; 2004: Back From The Mystery System: The Love Cycle; 2007: Love Cycle: Back From The Mystery System (re-release of the 2004 album); 2008: Worldwide (as D-n-G of Shai)

51 – Mr. Nathaniel Waithe – Class of 1986

(Photos Courtesy of EHS & Nathaniel Waithe)

I came to Paterson, New Jersey, in the summer of 1983 from Guyana, South America. I started attending Eastside High School as a sophomore in the fall of 1983 in the second year of the Mr. Joe Clark era. My sisters Dawne and Leonie were already attending Eastside, along with three of my first cousins. Our family had over twenty students who attended Eastside dating back to 1971.

Eastside was very different from the strict British influenced, uniform wearing school I attended in Guyana, a school ran by nuns. Although Eastside was still in the transformation stage when I got there, the personal attention was given to me by the Principal, Dr. Clark, Vice-Principal, Mr. Lighty and teachers such as Mr. Tyson, Mr. Korenda and Mr. Cocotus went a long way in establishing the foundation that enabled me to attend Rutgers University. I graduated in four years and moved on to a productive and fulfilling life. I could have easily been lost in a school that was alien to what I was used to, but instead, I excelled. I was in honor classes in my junior and senior years, played soccer, and was involved in numerous organization and school activities.

I lived directly across the street from Eastside High School, my sophomore, junior, and most of my senior year and can still vividly remember the sound of the Marching 100 band practicing in the parking lot as I watched from my bedroom window. From that window at 155 Park Avenue, Paterson, I saw the transformation of a school, but most importantly, the transformation of young people and the change it brought to their lives and community. My first wife, Sophia, was also an Eastside High School graduated, and we had two incredible sons, Nathaniel, and Christian who lives with me in Buford, Georgia. We watch the *Lean On Me* movie every time it is on television because it is a reminder that one man (or woman) can make a difference that can be far-reaching in the lives of many.

I salute Mr. Joe Clark and those who stood by him because I lived through the process and experienced it all on the most personal level.

52 – Ms. Lisa Webb-Carrington – Class of 1987

(Photos Courtesy of EHS & Lisa Webb-Carrington)

I have worked in the insurance industry since 1995. I am a licensed adjuster and agent. I am currently employed with the North Carolina Department of Insurance as a Communication Specialist. I have three children, ages 26 (Jada), 23 (Jessica), and 2 (Jeremiah).

I have since remarried Kenneth Carrington and now have a new addition to the family. My daughter Jada graduated from The University of Nevada, Las Vegas (UNLV), with her bachelor's degree. Jada is now married to Carl Reyes, and I am a "glam ma" for the first time, and his name is Carter. Jessica will graduate next year from Wake Tech Community college, and then she is going to North Carolina State University to pursue an additional degree in education.

My experiences at Eastside High School helped shape me to be the individual I am today.

Dr. Clark would tell us you can be whatever you wanted to be with hard work and perseverance. I used to love to hear him say, "if you cannot be a tree than be a branch, but be the best branch you could be." While I was in high school, I was in the Mock Trial Club, Glee club, and the Gospel Choir. I loved investigating court cases and arguing them until the conclusion. That allowed me to work for a prestigious Law Firm in Paterson by the name of Sternick, Flores & Anastos. At that time, they handled workman compensation files. Based on my past experiences from the Mock Trial Club and the law firm, I decided to pursue my career in insurance.

I have also been called to the ministry, and I am in training to become an evangelist. I always knew I was different from other people, and I could never get away with things that others would get away with. I can now talk about when I was pregnant in my senior year at Eastside. I was an A & B student and had influences over other people. I didn't want to leave school because I knew that I could handle my school work and being pregnant. However, due to school policy and also being threatened by other women, I had to finish my last semester at home.

I want to thank the best guidance counselor in the world, Mr. Heyer, who saw my potential and encouraged me to continue pursuing my dreams no matter what. I learned that no matter what happens in life, situations might slow you down, but they do not have to stop you. Your dreams may be delayed, but not denied.

Although I became pregnant in my senior year, I still was able to graduate with honors and go to William Paterson University to pursue a career in Sociology. At which time, I also became a mentor for other high school students with the help of Randy Lassiter (teacher). Telling other teenage girls about what I've been through so they don't give up or go down the same road I went down. I used to pray all the time that neither one of my daughters got pregnant while in high school. Thank you, Lord, for answering my prayers! It may have taken me longer, but with the grace of God, I was able to pull through; in spite of the many challenges I had to face, God has been good to my family and me. I can genuinely say that with the help of a caring, thoughtful, and concerned principal like Mr. Joe Clark, anything is possible. I would not trade my experiences at Eastside for anything in the world. I am proud of where I came from. I am currently pursuing the highest degree in insurance, a CPCU insurance designation.

53 - Mr. Keith Williams – Class of 1984

(Photos Courtesy of EHS & Keith Williams)

This Paterson, NJ native, is an alumnus of the Class of '84. Keith was a top graduate that year and was a full participant in the Eastside High School Experience. A junior when Principal Joe Clark first walked the halls with his bullhorn Keith was an advocate for the new changes. To this day, Keith is proud to say he is from Paterson and graduated from EHS.

Keith went on to Mason Gross School of the Arts at Rutgers University. There he majored in Graphic Design and Fine Arts. As the Delta Iota Chapter President of Alpha Phi Alpha Fraternity, Inc. Keith leads the way in producing the largest Greek Step show in the history of New Jersey. With that successful project came the opportunity to win State Chapter of the Year and to present eight $5,000k scholarships to young black HS seniors.

Keith started his career working in the print and design industries as an Art Director and then moved on to teach and manage technology in printing.

Now Keith is a National Technical and Business Analyst for a major retail company. As a creative person at heart, Keith is also a screenwriter who has written for motion pictures and is currently working on a few screenplays. For fun, he is a member of a comedy improv group in the Charlotte area and has performed regionally for a few years now.

For the last ten years, Keith has lived in the Charlotte NC area with his wife and three children.

54 – Mr. Mike Williams – Class of 1987

(Photos Courtesy of Mike Williams)

I attended Eastside High School from 1983-1987, and what I treasured most about the school was the pride that every student there shared. We were all proud of the Orange and Blue, and we still are today. Additionally, Dr. Clark was an immediate example of a leader. He led by doing the right thing even when others disagreed.

He remained true to his convictions when no one else was willing to stand with him. The fact is he was right most of the time. He also got it wrong sometimes; however, what I learned from him is that you can't lead by trying to be well-liked or popular, but you lead by doing what you feel is right and not to be afraid to fail. To me, that was leadership, and there are thousands of students who should be thanking him for that.

Mike A. Williams is the Senior Vice President and Division Executive for FIS, a Fortune 500 company, and a member of the S&P 500 index. Williams is also a member of FIS' Global senior management leadership team. Williams leads the Enterprise Technology Services (ETS) organization for FIS, where he is responsible for leading over 1300 global employees and is responsible for the overall management and strategic direction for various aspects of FIS enterprise technology assets.

Mr. Williams' teams are directly responsible for ensuring the availability of critical infrastructure platforms and applications that process more than $50B in monthly electronic, debit, and credit card payments for large financial institutions and community banks. Williams is considered a transformational change agent and has a track record of elevating service quality, building high-performing teams, developing aspiring talent, and enhancing and streamlining operational processes that align with the organizational top and bottom-line objectives.

Before joining FIS in 2008, Williams previous held executive IT leadership positions at ING, a global Fortune 20 banking, insurance, and financial services provider and held various roles of increasing responsibilities at UPS – A fortune 500 Supply Chain and Logistics company.

55 - Mr. Bernard Wilson – Class of 1984

(Photos Courtesy of EHS & Bernard Wilson)

Hello, my name is Bernard Wilson Jr., an EHS graduate class of 1984 under the leadership of Joe Clark. I grew up in Paterson, New Jersey, and attended public schools #28, #4, #24, and Eastside High School. Attending school during that time was a challenge for everyone. You can't imagine the hard times' families endured during that time. I grew up in a household with both parents and five brothers and one sister. I truly believe that to be a major part of my accomplishments.

Dr. Clark came to EHS in Sept. of 1982, and he was also a significant influence on my life as well as many teachers, administrators, and coaches. After graduating from EHS, I attended Michigan State University on a football scholarship. Being a student-athlete at a major university had its benefits. I was a member of many Bowl Teams but winning the Rose Bowl in 1988 was the ultimate! Upon my graduating from Michigan State University, I was afforded the opportunity to try out for several Canadian as well as NFL football teams. Due to an injury at one of the football training camps, I had to focus my educational accomplishment in other areas.

I worked as a counselor at a boy's home in Michigan and then as a Corrections Officer for the Michigan Department of Corrections for several years. At this present time, I reside in VA and teach and coach on the High School level. I want to thank Mr. Joe Clark, administrators, and coaches for attributing to the accomplishments. Special thanks to Dr. Pinky Miller for the opportunity to share my experiences.

(Mr. Pelosi, Dr. Clark, Bernard & Mom – Signing - Michigan State University)

REFERENCES

Amburn, E. (2012). Joe Louis Clark. *Senior Times, 13(9), 22-26.* Reprinted with permission from Tower Publications, SeniorTimesMagazine.com.

Bass, B. M. (1990). *Bass and Stogdill's handbook of leadership: A survey of theory and* research. New York: Free Press.

Beady, C., & Hansell, S. (1981) Teacher race and expectations for student achievement. *American educational research Journal 18,* 191-206.

Blockbuster.com Web. (2007). [Avildsen, DVD cover, 1989] Retrieved from Blockbuster.com Web site: http://www.blockbuster.com/catalog/movieDetails/20039.City of Paterson Silk City. (2009). *City of Paterson Silk City.* Retrieved from http://www.patersonnj.gov/

Clark's get-tough view airs nationwide Clark, J. (2009). Interview. Clark, J. (n.d.). Retrieved from http://www.joeclarkspeaker.com/biography.htm.

Clark, J. & Picard, J. (1989). *Laying down the law: Clark's strategy for saving our schools.* Washington, DC: Regnery Gateway.

Clark Speaks Website (1989). Retrieved from Clark Speaks Web site: http://www.joeclarkspeaker.com/past/htm. (1986, September 9).

Creswell, J. W. (2007). *Qualitative inquiry and research design: Choosing among five approaches.* Thousand Oaks: Sage Publications.

Drugs.com (2013). Retrieved from http://www.drugs.com/pcp.html

Eastside Yearbook, (1982). *Mirror (56).* Walsworth Publishing Company: Marceline, Missouri.

Eastside Yearbook, (1983). *Mirror (57).* Walsworth Publishing Company: Marceline, Missouri.

Eastside Yearbook, (1984). *Mirror (58).* Walsworth Publishing Company: Marceline, Missouri.

Eastside Yearbook, (1985). *Mirror (56)*. Walsworth Publishing Company: Marceline, Missouri.

Eastside Yearbook, (1986). *Mirror - The story behind the ghosts or the ghosts behind the story (60)*. Walsworth Publishing Company: Marceline, Missouri.

Eastside Yearbook, (1987). *Mirror (61)*. Walsworth Publishing Company: Marceline, Missouri.

Eastside Yearbook, (1988). *Mirror (62)*. Walsworth Publishing Company: Marceline, Missouri.

Eastside Yearbook, (1989). *Mirror (63)*. Walsworth Publishing Company: Marceline, Missouri.

Gang Center Bulletin. (2011). Retrieved from http://www.nationalgangcenter.gov/Content/Documents/Bulletin-5.pdf. National Gang Center Bulletin.

Glickman, C. D. (1990). *Supervision of instruction: A developmental approach*. Allyn and Bacon.

Grier, Roger – Gee's Photo - https://www.facebook.com/pages/Gees-Photo/213493368701067

Jost, D. (1997). *The American heritage college dictionary* (3ed ed.). Boston: Houghton Mifflin Company.

Lean, mean' Principal gets call from Reagan. (1983, September 16). Philadelphia Inquirer.

McGregor, D. (1985). *The human side of enterprise: 25th-anniversary printing*. New York: McGraw-Hill.

Moody, Jaycen - Jaycen Moody Photography https://www.facebook.com/jaycen.moodyphotography

Napier Academy (2013). Retrieved from: http://ps04-pps-nj.schoolloop.com/cms/page_view?d=x&piid=&vpid=1363595487663

National Youth Gang Center. (1997). *1995 National Youth Gang Survey*. [Program summary.] Washington, DC: U.S. Department of Justice, Office of Juvenile Justice, and Delinquency Prevention.

Noguera, P. (1999). Transforming urban schools through investments in social capital. *In Motion Magazine*. Retrieved from http://www.inmotionmagazine.com/pncap1.html.

Northouse, P. G. (2007). *Leadership theory and practice* (4th ed.). Thousand Oaks, CA: Sage Publications, Inc.

Principal Clark drops dukes, gets big gift for school. (1988, January 21). *The Washington Post.*

Principal in Paterson is directed to reinstate 50 expelled students. (1987, December 11). *The New York Times.*

Principal says he'll relock school doors if necessary. (1986, February 6). *Philadelphia Inquirer.*

Schools [2] with 2 remedies for drugs and violence: Discipline stressed in Paterson school. (1986, September). *The New York Times.*

Students (400) walk out, back Clark. (1989, March 14). *Press of Atlantic City*, New Jersey.

The Free Dictionary. (2013) Retrieved from http://www.thefreedictionary.com/molested

The Record, New Jersey. & York, R (1966). Equality of educational opportunity. [ED 012 275.] Arlington, VA. Conger, J. A. (1990). Accessed June *19*, 2011.

Tower Publications, Inc. Photo by T.J. Morrissey / Lotus Studios.

Tower Publications Reprinted with permission from, Senior Times Magazine.

U.S. Department of Health and Human Services (2011). Retrieved from http://aspe.hhs.gov/poverty/figures-fed-reg.shtml#dates. U.S. Department of Health and Human Services.

INDEX

Academic achievement,
173, 206

Achievement gap, 171

Advice to Parents, 319

African Americans,
182, 274

Agape, 374, 379,
380, 382, 470

Ainsworth Jackson,
12, 463

Alexander Hamilton,
175

Alfreda (Lawrence)
Paige, 12, 488

Allah, 181, 182

Alma Mater, 313,
357, 358, 423

Alonzo Moody, 269,
384, 387, 389

Amburn, 192, 319,
320, 321, 322,
442, 533

American education,
317

American Memory,

175, 176

Andre Ruff, 12, 499

Anjenett Ray, 360

Anthony, 260, 261,
262, 263, 343,
353, 426

Antoney Smith, 12,
508

Arsenio Hall Show,
413, 494

Ashon Curvy Moreno,
449

Ashon Curvy-Moreno,
12

assembly, 224, 226,
337, 369, 407

Atallah Shabazz, 241

baseball bat, 190, 263

Bass, 322, 323, 324,
533

Bass, B. M, 533

Beady, C, 533

Beady, C., & Hansell,
533

Beautiful, 260, 263,
264, 265, 352,
419, 422, 424,
426

Bernard Wilson, 12,
531

Blockbuster.com, 191,
533

Bookrags, 176, 533

Brent Keys, 298, 299

bullhorn, 190, 191,
196, 263, 264,
289, 304, 341,
350, 351, 421

bullied, 249, 335,
366, 369

Cheeks, 260, 265,
266, 331, 351,
354, 421, 424,
426

Chris Rock, 238

City of Paterson Silk
City, 176, 534

Clark & Picard, 174,
180, 182, 183,
184, 190, 191,
195, 198, 199,

200, 204, 206, 207

Clark Speaks, 197, 534

Clark, J. & Picard, 534

Clark, J. & Picard, J., 534

Clark's get-tough view, 534

Coach "O", 185, 211, 213, 214, 215, 216, 325, 335, 362, 364, 365, 366, 367, 369, 370, 372, 408

Coach Rosser, 211, 217, 218, 335, 362, 364, 365, 366, 367, 369, 370, 371, 372, 408

Controversies, 361, 364

Coretta Goodwin-Smith, 12, 460

Courtesy, 175, 176, 179, 189, 191, 193, 197, 198, 200, 238, 239, 240, 241, 242,

243, 244, 245, 309, 310, 311, 312, 313, 316, 318, 319, 320, 328, 331, 332, 335, 340, 350, 358, 360, 384, 388, 391, 392, 393, 394, 395, 396, 397, 399, 401, 403, 405, 406, 407, 409, 410,411, 412, 413, 415, 441, 443

Creswell, 327, 419, 534

Curtis Sliwa, 241

Darnell Van Rensalier, 522, 523, 524

Darren Napier, 12, 486

Daryl Miller, 474, 475

Deanna Michele De Vore, 12, 450

Demographic Information, 212

Denise Durnell, 11, 452, 453

Derrick McDuffie, 242

Diana "Dottie" Moore, 12

Diana Dottie Moore, 480, 481

Dilligaf, 260, 267, 268, 269, 270, 272, 273, 334, 343, 344, 356

disciplinarian, 233, 345, 366

discipline, 12, 186, 190, 195, 201, 213, 214, 221, 268, 288, 290, 295, 302, 303, 325, 327, 335, 340, 342, 345, 347, 349, 351, 352, 353, 354, 356, 359, 422, 425, 433, 436, 437

Dominicans, 182, 347

Donell Sellow, 396, 402

door locks, 183, 346

Dr. Frank Napier, 187, 188, 189, 243, 375, 387,

486

Dr. Napier, 188, 189, 222, 230

drug, 174, 176, 180, 183, 195, 198, 201, 202, 217, 232, 236, 249, 252, 262, 274, 287, 299, 302, 303, 306, 315, 327, 342, 346, 347, 349, 408, 434, 437, 440

Eastside High School, 11, 171, 172, 177, 179, 182, 184, 185, 186, 190, 191, 194, 198, 203, 206, 208, 209, 210, 213, 214, 216, 217, 218, 219, 222, 224, 230, 233, 237, 248, 255, 260, 261, 267, 269, 289, 290, 292, 309, 311, 324, 327, 336, 337, 342, 362, 364, 365, 406, 407, 408, 438,EHS

Ebony Magazine, 195

EHS Yearbook, 175,

177, 178, 179, 190, 197, 200, 238, 239, 240, 241, 242, 243, 244, 245, 309, 310, 311, 312, 313, 331, 332, 335, 340, 350, 358, 360, 388, 391, 392, 393, 394, 395, 396, 397, 398, 399, 403, 405, 406, 407, 409, 410, 411, 412, 413, 415

EHS Yearbook, 1983, 243

EHS yearbook, 1984, 193

EHS Yearbook, 1984, 198, 200

EHS Yearbook, 1985, 350

EHS Yearbook, 1986, 395

EHS Yearbook, 1987, 340

EHS Yearbook, 1988, 279, 330

EHS Yearbook, 1989, 190, 197,

309

Elena Payamps, 490

Elena Payumps, 12

Emerging Themes, 361

Eric Floyd, 413

Eric Gass, 12, 456

Eric McKenzie, 12, 381, 471

Eric Zimmerman, 401

Essence Magazine, 383

Essex County Youth Detention Center, 442

Evonne Seldon, 11, 298

Fabian, 277, 379, 380, 411

Fabian Theatre, 411

failure, 318

Fiedler, 324

Five-Percenters, 181, 182, 303, 333, 334

Flash, 260, 273, 274, 275, 326, 336,

345, 352, 356, 419, 421, 422, 423, 424, 426

Gala, 411

gang, 171, 172, 173, 176, 180, 181, 182, 183, 184, 195, 201, 249, 274, 303, 327, 334

Gang Center, 535

Gerard Booker, 11, 443, 444

ghetto, 180

Glickman, 322, 535

Governor Kean, 188

Governor Thomas Kean, 244

Greenleaf, 325

Gregory C. Scott, 12, 506

Guardian Angels, 241

Gwen Melvin, 242

Gwendolyn Goldsby Grant, 243

handcuffs, 252, 442

Harris, 11

heart surgery, 202

Helena Jones, 12, 467, 468

Hispanics, 182, 204, 274, 313, 347, 349

Identification Card, 183, ID Badge

Impact of African American Principals, 207

inner-city, 190, 228, 237, 317, 332, 427

Jamaican, 181, 210, 211, 212, 259, 260, 261

Jamie McDuffie, 12, 469

Janel D. Tinsley, 12, 519

Janice Robinson, 12, 494, 498

Jaycen Moody, 373, 469, 535

Jennifer (Carrion) McDowell, 469

Jermaine "Huggy" Hopkins, 413

Joe Clark website, 197, 238, 328

Joe Louis Clark, 12, 174, 190, 194, 309

John, 11, 172, 181, 182, 186, 225, 234, 260, 276, 277, 278, 279, 280, 281, 282, 284, 285, 286, 333, 343, 353, 387, 408, 409, 465, 497, 498

John Ring, 409

Jost, D., 535

Juanita Thomas-Boyd, 12, 515, 516

Karen Malina, 410, 413

Karen Malina White, 410

Karimah, 260, 287, 288, 289, 326, 341, 344, 348, 355, 422, 424, 427

Kawan Moore, 11

Keith Williams, 11, 416, 417, 528

Kenneth Eatman, 12, 454

Kid Fresh, 260, 289, 290, 328, 330, 333, 337, 340, 345, 419, 425, 427

Know Our Story, i, 476, 1

Korenda, 340, 525

Kwesi Moody, 388

Laron "Lateef" Moses, 12

Laron Lateef Moses, 485

Latino students, 438

Leadership and Power, 204

Leadership Theories, 203

Lean on Me, i, 2, 190, 191, 193, 201, 216, 218, 221, 226, 231, 233, 248, 254, 255, 267, 292, 361, 403, 405, 406, 407, 408, 432

Lean, mean' Principal gets call from

Reagan., 535

Leslie Etheridge, 12, 455

Leslie Gist-Etheridge, 11

Lisa Webb, 12, 526

Malik Moody, 388

Marc Stevens, 12, 511

Marvin Sykes, 12, 512, 513, 515

Mayor Frank Graves, 188, 196, 240, 243

McGregor, D, 535

Melanie Seldon, 298

Michael D. McDuffie, 11, 373, 470

Michael V. Jackson, 12, 465

Mike A. Williams, 12, 530

Mike Williams, 529

military, 275, 322, 339, 352, 419, 421, 422

Miss Paterson 1986, 299

Molestation, 297

Moody, 186, 260, 290, 291, 292, 295, 322, 324, 326, 342, 343, 345, 420, 422, 425

Morgan Freeman, 190, 216, 231, 233, 406

Mr. "B, 211, 221, 222, 223, 224, 225, 226, 227, 228, 229, 230, 335, 361, 366, 367, 369, 407, 408

Mr. 13, 184, 211, 218, 219, 220, 336, 363, 365, 368, 369, 370, 371, 372, 408

Mr. Clark's Leadership, 309

Mr. Nelson, 300, 391, 394, 395, 396, 400, 401, 518, 523

Mr. Will, 185, 211, 230, 231, 337, 363, 364, 366, 368, 369, 370, 371, 372, 408

Ms. Annette, 211, 231, 232, 233, 339, 362, 363, 364, 365, 366, 368, 369, 370, 371, 372, 408

Ms. De-Mo, 185, 211, 233, 235, 237, 245, 246, 247, 329, 339, 348, 351, 362, 363, 364, 365, 366, 368, 369, 370, 371, 372, 408

Ms. Florence Jones, 185, 211, 248, 335, 336, 337, 362, 363, 364, 365, 366, 368, 369, 370, 372

Ms. Smiley, 185, 211, 250, 251, 252, 253, 254, 257, 323, 324, 335, 342, 347, 362, 363, 365, 367, 368, 369, 371, 372, 409

Napier Academy, 188

Nathaniel Waithe, 12, 524, 525

Nation of Islam, 181, 303

New Jersey, 174, 175, 179, 187, 190, 191, 193, 194, 197, 207, 213, 215, 232, 234, 250, 251, 256, 261, 262, 263, 265, 266, 267, 276, 289, 290, 296, 299, 301, 304, 305, 348, 406, 439, 533, 536

Noguera, P., 535

Northouse, P. G., 535

of EHS Yearbook, 1986, 200

Participant Interviews, 361

Participants, 210

Participative leadership, 324

Paternalistic leadership, 325

Paterson Board of Education, 183, 196, 213, 219, 224, 254, 345, 348, 407, 409

Paterson, Falls, 176

Paterson, New Jersey, 175, 304

Paulette Steeves, 12, 510, 511

Peter Chin, 383

phenomenological, 361, 424, 426, 429

Philadelphia Inquirer, 195, 535, 536

Photo, 176, 192, 200, 242, 243, 244, 245, 309, 310, 311, 312, 313, 316, 318, 319, 320, 328, 330, 331, 332, 335, 340, 402, 443, 535, 536

Pinky, 1, 12, 208, 260, 296, 309, 347, 349, 354, 356, 359, 425, 427

poverty, 174, 179, 184, 185, 199, 200, 201, 266, 268, 299, 303, 306, 328, 363, 406, 438, 439, 536

President Reagan, 431

Principal Leadership and Effective Schools, 206

Profiles, 212, 213, 260, 261

public education, 317

racism, 171

Ralph Carter, 239

Rationale of the Study, 172

References, 533

Reggie, 260, 301, 302, 303, 333, 344, 346, 352, 420, 422, 425, 427

Researcher Role, 208

Richard H. Walter Collection, 176

Riff, 12, 411, 493, 494, 524

riots, 176, 182, 203, 274

Robert Guillaume, 406

Rodney De Vore, 12, 450, 451

Roger Grier, 383

Rory Sparrow, 242

Rosa Parks, 188, 242, 243

Run DMC, 238

Ruth, 11, 260, 304, 305, 324, 347, 349, 350, 359, 421, 422, 423, 425, 427

Salvatore Scarpinato, 179

Saul Cooperman, 245

Senior Times magazine, 319

Senior Times Magazine, 316, 536

Shanell "Red" Irving, 12

Shanell Irving, 462

Shwana Ruth, 501

Silk workers, 176

Sonji Barbour, 11, 332

Strategies, 327

strict, 12, 264, 302, 303, 339, 346,

420, 439

superintendent, 187, 198, 231, 234, 247, 329, 342, 372, 433, 438

suspension, 249, 264, 275, 345, 352

Table, *212, 260*

Tammy Barley, 12

Tammy Cockfield, 11, 448

T-Bird, 260, 305, 306, 307, 308, 334, 339, 349, 351, 358, 420, 421, 422, 423, 425, 428

Terrie Moore, 12, 482

The Board of Education, 345

The Free Dictionary, 298, 536

The New York Times, 535, 536

The Washington Post., 535

Timothy M. Tobias, 12, 520

TJ Morrissey, 318

TJ Morrissey / Lotus Studios, 319, 320, 441, 443

Tomacinia Carter, 11, 444, 445

Tomacinia Carter,, 11, 445

Tonya Ingram, 12, 461

Transformational leadership, 323, 324

Trophy Case, 331

Troy D. Gillispie, 458

Troy Gillispie, 11

U.S. Department of Health and Human Services, 184, 536

Unsung Heroes, 373

urban schools, 171, 535

US Sports Academy., 316

Vaughn McKoy, 11, 332, 472

Vera Ames, 375, 415

violence, 173, 174, 176, 187, 194, 195, 201, 218, 219, 231, 234, 235, 236, 249, 252, 264, 265, 266, 274, 287, 292, 297, 302, 303, 343, 363, 434, 437, 439, 536

Vivian Thorpe, 12, 517

Warner Bros., 279, 415

Warner Bros', 415

Westwood, 325

White House, 193, 199

William H. Cash, 12, 446, 447

William James "Bill" Pascrell, 389

William Paterson, 175

William Peter Nelson, 391, 394

Wilson Santos, 12, 503, 504

Winston Goode, 12, 459

Yolanda King, 241

Zatiti K. Moody, 476, 477

Zatiti Moody, 11, 388, 477, 479, 480

ABOUT THE AUTHOR

Dr. Pinky Miller, a native of Paterson, New Jersey, was educated through the public-school system, attending Public School #24 and the famed Paterson Eastside High School. Eastside was depicted in the 1989 movie *Lean on Me*, in which Morgan Freeman portrayed the controversial principal, Dr. Joe Clark. Dr. Miller received her Bachelor of Arts degree in Communication Studies and her Master of Arts degree in Counseling and School Guidance from Montclair State University. In 2011, she received her Doctor of Philosophy degree from Georgia State University.

Dr. Pinky Miller is an author and motivational speaker. She is also the Executive Producer of the forthcoming documentary *Know Our Story,* which chronicles the successes and failures of Mr. Joe Clark, his students, and the real-life legacy of the bullhorn and the baseball bat.

Dr. Miller has over eighteen years of experience working in higher education and has held positions as Hall Director/Academic Advisor, Area Coordinator, Assistant/Director of Residence Life & Housing, Assistant Dean of Students, and Vice President of Student Affairs. Dr. Miller loves working with college students, assisting them in times of crisis, and helping guide them toward becoming successful citizens. She has been recognized for her ability to organize and motivate people to achieve their goals. Dr. Miller is a proud member of Alpha Kappa Alpha Sorority Inc.

Dr. Miller has four beautiful, educated, loving daughters: Janay Boucan, Evonne Bazemore, Darylynn Miller, Olandha Miller, and one son Dominique Miller.

The *Life after Lean on Me* series can be found on Know-Our-Story.com as well as on Amazon.com.

Made in United States
Orlando, FL
30 June 2024

48469044R00367